Insurance Law in Japan

Insurance Law in Japan

Third Edition

Noboru Kobayashi
Yoshihiro Umekawa
Tamito Mikami
&
Shinichi Okuda

This book was originally published as a monograph in the International
Encyclopaedia of Laws/Insurance Law.

General Editors: Roger Blanpain, Frank Hendrickx
Volume Editor: Herman Cousy

Published by:
Kluwer Law International B.V.
PO Box 316
2400 AH Alphen aan den Rijn
The Netherlands
Website: www.wklawbusiness.com

Sold and distributed in North, Central and South America by:
Wolters Kluwer Legal & Regulatory U.S.
7201 McKinney Circle
Frederick, MD 21704
United States of America
Email: customer.service@wolterskluwer.com

Sold and distributed in all other countries by:
Turpin Distribution Services Ltd.
Stratton Business Park
Pegasus Drive, Biggleswade
Bedfordshire SG18 8TQ
United Kingdom
Email: kluwerlaw@turpin-distribution.com

DISCLAIMER: The material in this volume is in the nature of general comment only. It is not offered as advice on any particular matter and should not be taken as such. The editor and the contributing authors expressly disclaim all liability to any person with regard to anything done or omitted to be done, and with respect to the consequences of anything done or omitted to be done wholly or partly in reliance upon the whole or any part of the contents of this volume. No reader should act or refrain from acting on the basis of any matter contained in this volume without first obtaining professional advice regarding the particular facts and circumstances at issue. Any and all opinions expressed herein are those of the particular author and are not necessarily those of the editor or publisher of this volume.

Printed on acid-free paper

ISBN 978-90-411-8551-8

e-Book: ISBN 978-90-411-8565-5
web-PDF: ISBN 978-90-411-8579-2

This title is available on www.kluwerlawonline.com

Printed and Bound by CPI Group (UK) Ltd, Croydon, CR0 4YY.

The Authors

Prof. Noboru Kobayashi is Counsellor at Law, HIRATSUKA & Co. Tokyo and Professor Emeritus, Seikei University in Tokyo. He was Professor of Law, at the Faculty of Law, Seikei University. He studies and teaches commercial law, especially maritime law and insurance law. He taught Japanese commercial law at the Katholike Universiteit Leuven in 1992.

Mr Yoshihiro Umekawa is counsellor of NP Small Amount and Short-Term Insurance Provider. Formerly, he was Lecturer at the Faculty of Economics, Seikei University in Tokyo, and Director of Chiyoda Fire and Marine Insurance Co. Ltd and Auditor of Chiyoda Kasai 'EBISU' Life Insurance Co. Ltd.

The Authors

Mr Tamito Mikami is Surveyor of the General Insurance Rating Organization of Japan. He entered the former Chiyoda Fire and Marine Insurance Co. Ltd in 1965 and worked especially in the Automobile Underwriting Department and the Corporate Planning Department. He also worked in the Winthertur Ins. Co. (Japan) Inc.

Mr Shinichi Okuda is Manager of the Compliance Department of the Aioi Nissay Dowa Insurance Co. Ltd. He entered the former Chiyoda Fire & Marine Insurance Co. Ltd. in 1974 and worked in the Claims Department, Underwriting Department (Assistant Manager of the Casualty Insurance Section) and Legal Department (Manager).

Table of Contents

Table of Contents

6

Table of Contents

Table of Contents

Table of Contents

Table of Contents

14

Table of Contents

Table of Contents

Table of Contents

Table of Contents

List of Abbreviations

ADR	Alternative Dispute Resolution
AIRO	Automobile Insurance Rating Organization
ALSL	Automobile Liability Security Law
ARFI	Act Relating to Foreign Insurers
BAP	Basic Automobile Policy
BOJ	Bank of Japan
CAI	Comprehensive Automobile Insurance
CALI	Compulsory Automobile Liability Insurance
Civ. Code	Civil Code
Com. Code	Commercial Code
Comp. Act	Companies Act
EIL	Employment Insurance Law
FRC	Financial Reconstruction Committee
FSA	Financial Services Agency
GIROJ	General Insurance Rating Organization of Japan
IBL	Insurance Business Law
IBLCO	Insurance Business Law Cabinet Ordinance
IBLER	Insurance Business Law Enforcement Regulation
IBNR	Incurred But Not Reported
Ins. Law	Insurance Law
JHIU	The Japan Hull Insurers' Union
MITI	Ministry of International Trade and Industry
MOF	Ministry of Finance
NLIRO	Non-Life Insurance Rating Organization
NPA	National Pension Act
PAP	Private Automobile Policy
PCIRO	Property and Casualty Insurance Rating Organization

PDP	Paper Driver Policy
PPO	Policyholders' Protection Organization
PPO	Policyholders' Protection Organization
PPOS	Policyholders' Protection Organization System
SAP	Special Automobile Policy
SASTI	Small Amount and Short-Term Insurance
SASTIB	Small Amount and Short-Term Insurance Business
SASTIP	Small Amount and Short-Term Insurance Provider
US	United States of America

General Introduction

Chapter 1.   General Background Information

1. Japan is an island country situated beyond the eastern end of the Asian continent. The area of Japan extends to 378,000 km^2 with more than 127,110,000 inhabitants (in the year 2015). The largest city in Japan is Tokyo, its capital, and the cities of Yokohama, Osaka and Nagoya follow.

Japan is fundamentally a country of one-nation which speaks the language Japanese. But nowadays, especially after World War II, many people can speak and write English due to the educational system introduced by the United States of America (US).

§1.   POLITICAL AND LEGAL SYSTEM

2. The Constitution of Japan, which entered into force on 3 May 1947, stipulates the fundamental political system of Japan in addition to the principle of renunciation of war (Article 9).

3. The Emperor of Japan, unlike under the old Constitution, has become just a symbol of the state and of the unity of the people. Sovereign power is bestowed upon the people of Japan. Therefore, the Emperor of Japan can only perform the formal state acts provided for in the Constitution and does not have powers related to government (Articles 1, 4, 7).

4. The Diet of Japan is the highest organ of state power and is the sole law-making organ of the state (Article 41). It consists of two Houses, namely the House of Representatives and the House of Councillors (Article 42). Both Houses consist of elected members, representatives of all the people (Article 43).

5. Executive power is vested in the Cabinet (Article 65). The Cabinet, in the exercise of executive power, is collectively responsible to the Diet. The Cabinet consists of the Prime Minister, who is its head, and other ministers of state (Article 66). The Prime Minister is designated from among the members of the Diet (Article 67). The Prime Minister appoints the ministers of state. However, a majority of their number must be chosen from among the members of the Diet (Article 68).

6. Judicial power is vested in a Supreme Court and in such inferior courts as are established by law. No extraordinary tribunal can be established, and no organ or agency of the executive may be given final judicial power (Article 76). The Supreme

Court is the court of last resort with power to determine the constitutionality of any law, order, regulation or official Act (Article 81).

§2.   COMMERCE AND INDUSTRY

7.   Japan is a country with a free economy and the Japanese economy depends very largely on trade with the US, European Union (EU) and other Asian countries. Until recently, Japan enjoyed rapid economic development, but in the 1990s the Japanese economy was faced with many problems caused by the collapse of the bubble economy which has recovered at last from the year 2005. In the year 2014, the Japanese economy had a Gross Domestic Product (GDP) of Japanese Yen (JPY) 489,623 billion (nominal) and a national income of JPY 364,444 billion (nominal), and both figures are plus1.5% and plus 1.5% compared with those of the preceding year.

8.   In the year 2015, the amounts of exports from Japan and imports to Japan were JPY 75,613 billion and JPY 78,405 billion respectively. The major items of export consisted of machines, automobiles, steel and chemical products and imports consisted of machines, petroleum, clothes, meat and fishery products. Japan exports mainly high-technical products such as computers or precision machines while it imports machinery in addition to oil and food.

§3.   FINANCIAL INSTITUTIONS

9.   The Bank of Japan (BOJ), as the central bank of Japan, operates the functions of issuing banknotes and of controlling money and finance. The BOJ is required to maintain stability in the prices of commodities and to contribute to the sound development of the national economy.

The major operations of the BOJ are carried out in accordance with the decisions of its board committee consisting of nine members, which include the president and two vice-presidents. The functions of the BOJ are now regulated by the new BOJ Act (Law No. 89, 18 June 1997) which permits more independence of the BOJ from government than previously.

10.   Financial institutions comprise banks, security companies and insurance companies in addition to government financial institutions such as postal savings or annuity pensions. Those private financial institutions are all controlled by the Financial Services Agency (FSA) established in 2001 within the Cabinet Office (it formerly belonged to the Ministry of Finance).

In Japan, the demarcation of the business carried out by financial institutions was very rigorous and the Securities and Exchange Act (Law No. 25, 13 April 1948) prohibits banks, insurance companies, etc., from doing security business in principle (Article 65). However, today, in order to meet consumer needs, the demarcation is becoming less rigorous. In 2006, the Securities and Exchange Act was revised and renamed as the Financial Instrument and Exchange Act under which the former Article 65 is fundamentally maintained in Article 33. The security business which insurance companies are permitted to carry out as accompanying business will be discussed in Part I, Chapter 1.

§4. CURRENCY LEGISLATION AND MONETARY REGULATIONS

11. Foreign exchange control in Japan is now regulated by the Foreign Exchange and Foreign Trade Law (Law No. 59, 23 May 1997) which has largely revised the former Foreign Exchange and Foreign Trade Control Law (Law No. 228, 1 December 1949). The former law, as the word 'control' in its name indicates, had the main aim of putting almost all foreign investment and foreign trade under the control of government. However, following the development of the world economy after World War II, the law was revised in 1980 to liberalize foreign exchange trade largely. Foreign exchange trade has become free in principle by this revision and trade which requires the licence or approval of the minister concerned is mentioned individually.

The new law was also passed in order to secure harmonization with the movement of international globalization and electronic systems in foreign exchange and foreign trade. The former authorized bank and money exchange system was abolished and it has become possible for everyone to trade in foreign exchange, not just banks.

§5. INSURANCE BUSINESS, GENERAL ORGANIZATION AND SPECIAL FEATURES

12. In Japan there are no special restrictions on doing insurance business within the Japanese market. Therefore, those who wish to do insurance business in Japan, domestic or foreign, can do so if they obtain the authorization of Prime Minister or in case of Small Amount and Short-Term Insurance Providers (SASTIP) they may be registered in the register of Prime Minister in accordance with the Insurance Business Law (IBL), as mentioned in Part I, Chapter 1.

As of January 2016, forty-one life insurance companies (domestic thirty-eight and foreign three) and fifty-two non-life insurance companies (domestic thirty, foreign twenty-one and the Society of Lloyd's including eight professional reinsurance companies) were authorized and as of May 2016, eighty-four SASTIP were registered for insurance business in the Japanese market.[1]

13. As regards non-life insurance business, the Fire and Marine Insurance Rating Association of Japan was established in 1948, renamed as the Property and Casualty Insurance Rating Organization of Japan in 1996. It calculated the pure risk premium rates for fire and personal accident insurance as reference tariffs to which each company could add its own loading. It also calculated a standard premium rate for earthquake insurance on dwelling risks.

---

1. The SASTIP must deposit the amount prescribed in the Insurance Business Law Cabinet Ordinance (IBLCO) Art.38-4 for the protection of the contractors, etc., of insurance contract (IBL) Art. 272-5). This amount shall be JPY 10,000,000 for the first fiscal year and shall be increased according to the amount of premium earned each year afterwards.

In 1964, the Automobile Insurance Rating Organization (AIRO) of Japan was split off from the Fire and Marine Insurance Rating Association of Japan. It calculated pure risk premium rates for voluntary automobile insurance as reference tariffs and a standard premium rate for compulsory automobile liability insurance (CALI).

As from 1 July 2002, these two rating organizations merged and became the Non-Life Insurance Rating Organization of Japan (NLIRO), renamed afterwards as the General Insurance Rating Organization of Japan (GIROJ), taking over almost all the work of the former organizations.

14. The former Marine and Fire Insurance Association of Japan, Inc. was established in 1941 from the amalgamation of the Dai-Nippon Fire Insurance Association and several marine insurance organizations. In 1946, the present Marine and Fire Insurance Association of Japan, Inc. was re-established as their business association by almost all of the non-life insurance companies doing business in Japan (excluding the Earthquake Reinsurance Co.) and in 2003, it changed its name to the General Insurance Association of Japan, Inc. in accordance with the practice in foreign countries. It mainly expresses the opinion of non-life insurance companies, studies overseas non-life insurance markets and educates and trains solicitors in non-life insurance business.

The Life Insurance Association of Japan, Inc. was established in 1908 as their business association by almost all the life insurance companies doing business in Japan. It mainly represents the opinions of the life insurance industry, conducts surveys and research and prepares statistics and also offers education and examination systems for solicitors of life insurance business.

The Small Amount and Short-Term Insurance (SASTI) Association of Japan, Inc. was established in June 2008 as for the business association of the insurers of the small amount and short-term insurance.

15. Due to the recent reform of the financial system in Japan, the Non-life Insurance Policyholders Protection Corporation of Japan and the Life Insurance Policyholders Protection Corporation of Japan were established in 1998. Both corporations have been established to provide financial aid to an insurance company which relieves an insolvent insurance company by taking over its contracts or itself accepting the insurance contracts of insolvent company if no other company succeeds to them. They are thereby expected to play the role of ensuring the protection of policyholders' benefits and maintaining confidence in the insurance business.

Chapter 2.   Historical Background of Insurance

16. The modern style of insurance business started in Japan after the Meiji Restoration (1868) when Japan began to introduce many of the systems of European and Anglo-American countries. Of course, there was a kind of insurance system before the Meiji Restoration, especially in the field of marine business; however, insurance was not carried out in accordance with precise calculation based on modern statistics or the theory of probability.

The first non-life insurance company (the Tokio Marine Ins. Co.) started marine insurance business in 1879 and the first fire insurance company (the Tokyo Fire Ins. Co.) was established in 1887. The first life insurance company (the Meiji Life Insurance Co.) started life insurance business in 1881.

At the start of the twentieth century, many new types of insurance began to be sold in Japan, for example accident insurance (1911), automobile insurance (1914) and aviation insurance (1936) and this trend further continued after World War II, with liability insurance (1953), CALI (1955), earthquake insurance (1966), etc.

17. The Old Commercial Code (Com. Code) was enacted in 1890 and included laws of insurance contract and IBL. This was said to be the first modern law in Japan concerning insurance contract law and IBL but it did not come into effect until 1898 due to controversy on introducing the contents of foreign laws.

The New Com. Code was enacted and came into effect in 1899; this included the provisions for insurance contract law and the Law for the Enforcement of the Com. Code included provisions for IBL.

A special code for insurance business under the name of the IBL was enacted and came into effect in 1900. It succeeded most of the provisions for IBL in the Law for the Enforcement of the Commercial Code. This law was largely revised in 1939 and some minor changes have been made several times thereafter.

In 1900, the Imperial Order concerning Foreign Insurance Companies was enacted following the enactment of the IBL. This Order had the aim of controlling foreign insurance companies doing business in Japan, especially in financial aspects. After World War II, this Order was succeeded by the Law concerning Foreign Insurers (Law No. 184, 1949) which had the main aim of putting foreign insurers doing business in Japan on an equal footing with those of Japan.

As regards the solicitation of insurance, the regulation for the control of insurance solicitation was made in 1931. After World War II, this regulation was abolished in 1947 and the Law concerning the Control of Insurance Solicitation (Law No. 171, 1948) was newly made in order to protect policyholders of insurance.

As will be mentioned in detail below, these three laws, that is, the IBL, the Law concerning Foreign Insurers Law and the Law concerning the Control of Insurance Solicitation were integrated into one new Code in the IBL (Law No. 105) in 1995.

In 2008, the Insurance Law (Ins. Law) (Law No. 56, 6 June 2008) was promulgated in Japan. The Ins. Law replaces the article concerning the insurance contracts stipulated under Com. Code except marine insurance. The Com. Code was enacted in 1899 therefore we must admit that the economic and social situation has largely changed in Japan thereafter. The Ins. Law was enacted in order to make conformity with the present Japanese situation, which came into force as from 1 April 2010.

Chapter 3.   Sources of Insurance Law

§1.   LEGISLATION

I.   Supervisory Legislation

18. Insurance business in Japan is now supervised by the IBL 1995 (Law No. 105, 7 June 1995) which entered into force on 1 April 1996.

This new law was made in order to modernize the former law, that is, the IBL of 1939 (Law No. 41, 1939) and also to integrate two other insurance supervisory laws, that is, the Law concerning Foreign Insurers of 1949 (Law No. 184, 1949) and the Law concerning the Control of Insurance Solicitation of 1948 (Law No. 171, 1948). Insurers, domestic or foreign, and also insurance solicitors, agents or brokers who wish to do insurance business in Japan are controlled by this new law.

19. This law has been revised several times thereafter due to the recent policy of the government for the reconstruction of the Japanese economy. The following are the principal revisions that concern with this law:

–   1997; Law No. 55 (21 May 1997), Law No. 72 (6 June 1997), Law No. 102 (20 June 1997), Law No. 117 (10 December 1997), Law No. 120 (12 December 1997).
–   1998; Law No. 106 (15 June 1998), Law No. 107 (15 June 1998), Law No. 131 (16 October 1998).
–   1999; Law No. 125 (13 August 1999), Law Nos. 160, 225 (22 December 1999).
–   2000; Law No. 91 (31 May 2000), Law No. 92 (31 May 2000), Law No. 96 (31 May 2000), Law No. 126 (27 November 2000), Law No. 129 (29 November 2000).
–   2001; Law No. 7 (30 March 2001),Law No. 41 (8 June 2001), Law No. 50 (15 June 2001), Law No. 75 (27 June 2001), Law No. 80 (29 June 2001), LawNo.117(9 November 2001), Law No. 129 (28 November 2001), Law No. 150 (12 December 2001).
–   2002; Law Nos. 45, 47 (29 May 2002), Law No. 65 (12 June 2002), Law No.79 (3 July 2002), Law No.155 (13 December 2002).
–   2003; Law No. 39 (9 May 2003), Law No. 54 (30 May 2003), Law No. 129 (25 July 2003), Law No. 130 (30 July 2003), Law No. 134 (1 August 2003).
–   2004; Law No. 76 (2 June 2004), Law No. 87 (9 June 2004), Law No. 88 (9 June 2004), Law No. 97 (9 June 2004), Law No. 105 (11 June 2004), Law No. 124 (18 June 2004), Law No. 147 (1 December 2004),Law No. 154 (3 December 2004), Law No. 159 (8 December 2004).
–   2005; Law No. 38 (2 May 2005), Law No. 87 (26 July 2005).
–   2006; Law No. 10 (31 March 2006), Law No. 50 (2 June 2006), Law No. 65 (14 June 2006), Law No. 109 (15 December 2006).

- 2007; Law No. 74 (1 June 2007).
- 2008; Law No. 57 (6 June 2008), Law No. 65 (13 June 2008), Law No. 91 (16 December 2008).
- 2009; Law No. 58 (24 June 2009).
- 2010; Law No. 32 (19 May 2010), Law No. 51 (19 November 2010).
- 2012; Law No.23 (31 March 2012).
- 2014; Law No.45 (30 May 2014), Law No. 91 (27 June 2014).

The revision made by Law No.45 (30 May 2014) concerns mainly with reinforcement of the control on solicitation of insurance contract which has entered into force at the end of May 2016 (see paragraph 572.1).

II.   Insurance Contract Law

20. The Civil Code (Civ. Code) of 1896 (Law No. 89, 27 April 1896) has, in its Book III, Chapter 2, provisions concerning the civil contract in general, and these provisions are applied to insurance contracts. The Com. Code 1899 (Law No. 48, 9 March 1899) had, in its former Book III, Chapter 10, provisions concerning insurance contracts, non-life insurance (Articles 629–672), life insurance (Articles 673–683) which was now replaced by the new Ins. Law enacted in 2008 (Law No. 56, 6 June 2008). The Com. Code has, in its present Book III, Chapter 6, provisions concerning marine insurance (Articles 815–841*bis*) which are not yet replaced by the new Insurance Law. The Ins. Law classified the contracts of insurance under this law as non-life insurance contract (including accident and health damage insurance contract[2]), life insurance contract and fixed return accident and health insurance contract.[3] These provisions apply to insurance contracts prior to those of the Civil Code.

21. Formerly, in Japan, there was a controversy over whether insurance contract clauses should be regarded as a kind of law concerning insurance contracts. It was discussed how we could explain the effect that insurance contractors or assureds were bound by insurance contract clauses when they might not be well informed about them. Some scholars who wished to explain this by the idea that the insurance contract clauses were a kind of law. But today most scholars and judicial cases also admit that insurance contract clauses have binding force due to the general concept of usage. Therefore, insurance contract clauses are not to be regarded as law.[4]

---

2.   The accident and health damage insurance contract means the non-life insurance contract under which the insurer promises to pay for the personal damages caused by casualty or disease to the assured (Ins. Law Art. 2(7)).

3.   The fixed return accident and health insurance contract means the insurance contract under which the insurer promises to pay the fixed amount for the personal casualty or disease as insurance accident (Ins. Law Art. 2(9)).

4.   Supreme Court judgment, 24 Dec. 1915, *Minroku*, vol. 21, 2182.

III.   Compulsory Automobile Liability Insurance

22. In accordance with the rapid motorization in Japan after World War II, the Automobile Liability Security Law (ALSL) (Law No. 97, 27 July 1955) was passed in 1955. This law put persons who drive automobiles for their own benefit and cause death or bodily injury to other persons on a virtually no-fault liability basis. This law aims to protect the victims of traffic accidents and Article 5 of this law prescribes that every automobile should be driven with the CALI described in this law. The details of CALI will be discussed below in Part IV. Automobile Insurance.

§2.   GOVERNMENT REGULATIONS

23. The Insurance Business Law Cabinet Ordinance(IBLCO) (Cabinet Ordinance No. 425, 1995) was made to enforce the IBL (Law No. 105,1995) in 1995, which has been revised several times after entering into force.

The IBLCO prescribes such points as the following: The minimum amount of capital or the aggregate foundation fund of insurance companies is to be JPY 1,000,000,000(IBLCO Article 2-2, IBL Article 6(1), (2)). The minimum amount of capital for SASTIP is JPY 10,000,000 (IBLCO Article 38-3, IBL Article 272-4(1)). Insurance contracts which may be made with foreign insurers having no branch office in Japan shall be: (a) reinsurance contracts; (b) insurance contracts which cover Japanese vessels or aircraft which are used in international transport, their cargos or the liabilities arising therefrom; and (c) other insurance contracts as prescribed by the Insurance Business Law Enforcement Regulation (IBLER) (Article 19, Law Article 186). The deposit which has to be made by foreign insurance companies, etc., is JPY 200,000,000 (Article 24, Law Article 190(1)).

§3.   REGULATION BY GOVERNMENT AGENCIES

24. In 1995, when the new IBL was codified, the Ministerial Regulation on Insurance Business (Regulation MOF No. 5, 1996) was made to enforce both the IBL (Law No. 105, 1995) and the IBLCO (Cabinet Ordinance No. 425, 1995).

The IBLER prescribes such points as follows, that is, the use of premium income and assets as investments for the acquisition of securities, real property, loans, gold, deposits, savings or other similar (Article 47, Law Article 97(2)); the calculation of underwriting reserves of life insurance companies and non-life insurance companies and those for reinsurance contracts (Articles 69, 70, 71); the calculation of loss reserves to be established by insurance companies (Article 73); the amount of capital, foundation fund reserves and other items of insurance companies to be taken into the calculation of the solvency margin (Article 86, Law Article 130(1)).

25. Following the recent reorganization of ministries and governmental agencies in Japan, the FSA was set up as one of the governmental agencies of the Cabinet Office and started functioning from 2001. The FSA became the supervisory power on financial institutions including insurance companies, a role formerly exercised by the MOF. The MOF Regulations on insurance business are now replaced by the IBLER.

§4. Private International Law

I. Introduction

26. The private international law of Japan has been prescribed by the law concerning the application of laws (*Horei*, Law No. 10, 21 June 1898) which is now replaced by the new law under the name of the Act on General Rules for Application of Laws (Law No. 78, 21 June 2006).

According to Article 7 of this law, the formation and effect of a contract is governed by the law which has been chosen by the parties (paragraph 1). However, if the intention of the parties is not clear, the law of the place which has the most intimate contact will govern (Article 8 paragraph 1).

This Article 7 is construed to permit the autonomy of the concerned parties as regards the choice of law in respect of contract law, and in effect most contracts include a governing law clause which prescribes the law to be applied to the contract. Japanese judicial courts admit the validity of these governing law clauses within contracts in general as they consider that these clauses explicitly indicate the intention of the parties.

However, recently, there has been an argument in Japan about whether we should admit the principle of autonomy of the parties in full, especially in contracts of adhesion such as personal insurance contracts. Some scholars insist that the application of the principle of autonomy of the parties should be restricted when the balance of economic power of the parties is not equivalent as in contracts of adhesion. However, up till now there has been no judicial decision which has explicitly admitted such theories, at least as regards insurance contracts, in the Japanese courts. But in the new Act of 2006 on General Rules for Application of Laws, it is prescribed that when the parties of a consumer contract have not chosen the applicable law, the law of the habitual residence of the consumer will govern the contract (Article 11, paragraph 2), and that as regards the labour contracts when the labourer insists on the application of the compulsory provisions of the law with which the contract has the most intimate contact such provisions will be applied, while it is not the applicable law (Article 12 paragraph 1).

II. Non-life Insurance

27. Since we do not have a uniform law such as that based on the EC Directive concerning non-life insurance services (Second Council Directive 88/357, 22 June 1988), the applicable law of non-life insurance contracts is decided in accordance with the principle mentioned in paragraph 26 above.

28. Therefore, most Japanese non-life insurance companies usually include in their insurance contracts a governing law clause which indicates Japanese law as the applicable law of contracts. If no such explicit intention of the parties is indicated in the governing law clause in the contracts, it is suggested to search further for the implied intention of the parties considering all factors, for example, the type of contract, the contents of the contract, the language used in the contract, and so on. And, in fact, it is often agreed that the law of the principal place of business of the insurers should govern insurance contracts.

III. Life Insurance

29. We do not have either a uniform law such as that based on the EC Directive concerning life insurance services (Second Council Directive 90/619, 8 November 1990). Therefore, the applicable law for life insurance contracts is also decided in accordance with the principle mentioned in paragraph 26 above.

30. As life insurance contracts have fewer international factors than non-life insurance contracts, the governing law clauses are not so frequently included in the contracts. So it is necessary to search for the implied intention of the parties, taking into account that a life insurance contract contains more elements which require attention to consumer protection than that of non-life insurance contract. Therefore, not only the law of the principal place of the business of the insurers, but also the law of the domicile of those insured, will possibly be considered as the applicable law of the contract.

§5. JURISDICTION

I. Legislation

31. In Japan, the provisions on jurisdiction are contained in Article 4 to Article 22 of the Code of Civil Procedure 1996 (Law No. 109, 1996) which has modernized the old law, the Code of Civil Procedure 1890 (Law No. 29, 1890).

These articles stipulate as general jurisdictions, the domicile of the defendant (Article 4(2)) or the principal place of office or business of the defendant legal entity (Article 4(4)). In addition, as regards property claims, the place of the performance of obligations (Article 5(1)), the place of the payment of bills or cheques (Article 5(2)), the place of registry of a ship (Article 5(3)), the place where the act for the tort was committed (Article 5(9)), the place where real estate is located (Article 5(12)), etc., are to be selected as jurisdictions.

32. These articles on jurisdiction stipulate originally those within Japan, that is, domestic jurisdictions, and not international jurisdictions. However, according to the prevailing theory of judgments and scholars, international jurisdictions may be inferred from these articles of the Code of Civil Procedure. Consequently, the international jurisdiction of Japanese courts will be fundamentally admitted if the domestic jurisdiction prescribed by articles of the Code of Civil Procedure exists within Japan. However, in cases when the international jurisdiction of Japanese courts would be contrary to the properness of the judgment, the equality of the parties or the promptness of the judicial process, it might be denied.[5] In 2011, the articles concerning the international jurisdiction of Japanese courts were newly added in the Code of Civil Procedure (Article 3*bis*-Article 3-12, Law No.36, 2011) which mostly embody the above-mentioned prevailing theory of international jurisdictions.

II.   Jurisdiction Clause

33. The parties may choose and decide the jurisdiction of the court by contractual agreement so far as the Court of First Instance is concerned (Article 11(1)). The agreement is not valid unless it is made in writing and is made in respect of a suit concerning a particular legal relation (Article 11(2)).

Thus, Article 11 of the Code of Civil Procedure admits the validity of the jurisdiction clause and prescribes the necessary conditions for its validity. However, the courts may reject the validity of the jurisdiction clause for the reason of forum non conveniens or other reasons depending on the circumstances of individual cases even if they satisfy the conditions of Article 11.[6]

34. The validity of the international jurisdiction clause of insurance contracts, which in most cases stipulates the court of the place of principal office of the insurance companies as the exclusive jurisdiction, is also judged by the above-mentioned standard which is now stipulated by Article3-7 of the Code of Civil Procedure. But, unlike non-life insurance contracts which are often made between companies and have international elements in the contracts, life insurance contracts are usually made between individuals and insurance companies; therefore, the validity of the jurisdiction clauses in the life insurance contracts will be more severely checked than those in non-life insurance contract (Article 3-7(5)).

---

5.   Supreme Court judgment of 16 Oct. 1981, *Minshu*, vol. 35, No. 7, 1224. Tokyo District Court judgment of 20 Jun. 1986, *Hanji*, vol. 1196, 87.
6.   Supreme Court judgment of 28 Nov. 1975, *Minshu*, vol. 29, No. 10, 1554.

Chapter 4.   Dispute Settlement and Arbitration

35. Legal disputes about insurance contracts are ordinarily settled in the judicial courts.

According to the Judicial Code (Law No. 59, 16 April 1947), Japanese judicial courts are composed of the Supreme Court and inferior courts, which are the Appellate Courts, the District Courts, the Small Claims Courts and the Family Courts (Article 2). With the exception of the exclusive jurisdiction of the Small Claims Courts for those matters in which the claim's amount is less than JPY 1,400,000 (approximately US Dollars (USD) 12,500), disputes concerning insurance contracts are ordinarily brought to the District Courts as first instance (Article 24 and Article 33).

36. Japanese insurance policies do not usually have arbitration clauses, with the exception of marine insurance policies. Therefore, it is not so usual in Japan to settle legal disputes concerning insurance contracts by arbitration award. The reason for not using arbitration so much in insurance business may lie in the fact that Japan has no established courts of arbitration or arbitrators especially for insurance contracts.

However, in 2003, the Arbitration Act (Law No. 138, 1 August 2003) was codified in Japan and as this Act does not exclude disputes concerning insurance contracts, the number of the cases to be settled by arbitration will increase.

37. As preventive measures for avoiding legal disputes, both non-life and life insurance companies in Japan have their own sections to deal with the complaints of policyholders. There are also the counselling centres for Alternative Dispute Resolution (ADR) established by the Marine and Fire Insurance Association of Japan and the claims survey offices of the GIROJ, which fulfil this need for policyholders.

In addition, there is also a traffic accident consultation centre within the Japanese Bar Association which handles the complaints of the victims of traffic accidents and the National Consumers Affairs Centre under the Cabinet Office also hears various complaints of consumers, including those about insurance policies.

Chapter 5.   Consumer Protection

§1.   LEGISLATION

38. The Japanese Com. Code does not have any special provisions prescribing so-called consumer protection with respect to insurance contracts. The IBL, on the other hand, has several provisions which protect the interests of policyholders and those insured, especially in the field of solicitation of insurance contracts.

The IBL also prescribed for the first time the applicant's right of cooling-off in insurance contracts the duration of which is longer than one year. According to Article309 of this law, the applicant for insurance contracts or the policyholder can withdraw or cancel the application in writing on condition that eight days have not elapsed from the date of the receipt of the documents mentioning the withdrawal or cancelling of the application or the date of application, whichever is the later, and on condition that the applicant did not apply for the insurance contract in connection with his/her business, etc.

39. Recently, in order to further consumer protection, Japan has passed in 2000 two new codes which also concern insurance contracts. And in 2009, the Consumer Affairs Agency was set up as one of cabinet agencies for the purpose to strengthen consumer protection.

The first one is the Consumer Contract Act 2000 (Law No. 61, 12 May 2000) which entered into force as from 1 April 2001. This Act permits an applicant for a consumer contract to cancel it when it was made on the basis of a misunderstanding caused by the business enterprise's false notification about important items of the contract or confusion caused by refusal to leave the residence of the business enterprise, etc. (Article4). The Act prescribes that a contract clause which exempts the business enterprise from total liability for damages caused to the consumer due to breach of contract or wrongful act, etc., shall be null and void (Article 8). On the revision of this law in 2006, the system of injunction demand was introduced by which the qualified consumer organizations may demand injunction to stop or prevent the business operators' act which fall within Article 4 paragraph 1 to paragraph 3 of this Act.

The second code is the Financial Products Sales Act 2000 (Law No. 101, 31 May 2000) which also entered into force as from 1 April 2001. This Act prescribes the obligation of the sellers of financial products to explain to clients the interest, value of currency, risk of deficit in financial products, etc. (Article3). If sellers do not make such explanations, they must bear the loss caused to clients due to their failure to do so (Article 4). The amount of deficit in the financial products will be presumed to be the amount of damage caused to the client (Article 5).

40. Recently, anti-social forces (groups or individuals that pursue economic profits through the use of violence, threats and fraud), in particular, have become increasingly sophisticated in their efforts to obtain funds, disguising their dealings as legitimate economic transactions through the use of affiliated companies in order to develop business relations with ordinary companies. So, the FSA issued in June 2014

'Comprehensive Guideline for Supervision of Financial Instruments Business Operators, etc.' in which stated that Financial Business Operators have a public nature and play an important economic role, so that they need to exclude anti-social forces from financial instruments transactions in order to prevent damage from being inflicted not only on their officers and employees but also on their customers and other stakeholders.

In response to this Guideline, Insurance Companies have revised terms and conditions of their Insurance General Condition to be able to refuse the contract with anti-social forces, to be able to cancel the contract with anti-social forces after the counter party has been found to be an anti-social forces, and to be able to demand the return of the insurance money even after the insurance money had been paid, if the insured has been found to be anti-social forces.

41. The FSA, announced a stewardship code in February 2015 toward financial institutions, has requested to accept this code. Currently (as of March 2016), eighteen life insurance companies and four non-life insurance companies expressed their acceptance and announced basic policy of the company.

§2.   SELF-REGULATION BY THE INSURANCE INDUSTRY

42. The General Insurance Association of Japan Inc. and the Life Insurance Association of Japan Inc. are also very keen on the problem of consumer protection today. Therefore, they have drawn up several guidelines which must be observed by insurance companies with regard to consumer protection. For example, the General Insurance Association of Japan Inc. has drawn up guidelines for observing the provisions of anti-trust law, the Financial Products Sale Act, especially as regards the rating of premiums, claims services and sales of insurance contracts, etc.

They also have guidelines for the disclosure of insurance companies, standards for advertising insurance companies and guidelines for the protection of individual data.

The Life Insurance Association of Japan Inc. has also drawn up similar guidelines in order to force life insurance companies to observe the rules of consumer protection.

§3.   JUDICIAL CONTROL BY THE COURTS

43. The judicial courts in Japan also take the concept of consumer protection into consideration when they pass judgment on insurance cases. They often construe the meaning of the clauses of insurance contracts to the benefit of policyholders rather than the insurance companies who have drawn them up. This trend in general conforms with the so-called principle of *contra proferentem* and thereby the judicial courts in Japan try to ensure consumer protection in insurance contracts.

44. For example, the Supreme Court of Japan construed the obligation to notify a loss under an automobile insurance policy to the benefit of policyholders and those insured. According to this clause of automobile insurance, policyholders and insured persons are obliged to notify the insurance company of a loss within sixty days from the date of the accident and if they fail to observe this obligation, the insurance company is exempted from paying insurance money. The Supreme Court, however, construed this clause very narrowly and the insurance company may be exempted only when policyholders or insured persons did not keep this obligation fraudulently and otherwise the insurance company may only insist on deduction of insurance money according to the actual loss suffered from the delayed notification of loss.[7]

45. Another example of the construction of insurance clauses to the benefit of policyholders and those insured concerns personal accident insurance. According to a clause of accident insurance, policyholders or those insured for accident insurance have the obligation to disclose the existence of the same type of insurance contract already taken out and also have the obligation to notify the insurance company when they take the same type of insurance from another company afterwards. When they have failed to keep this obligation, the insurance company can cancel the contract and can be exempted from paying insurance money. The judicial courts of Japan have also construed this clause very narrowly and the insurance company can cancel the contract only when the policyholders or insured persons failed to observe this obligation intentionally or with gross negligence and the cancellation must be for a reason, for example the fact that the policyholder has the intention of receiving insurance money fraudulently.[8]

46. In order to cope with the problems of recent complicated society, Japan has enacted the Act on Promotion of Use of ADR (Law No. 151, 1 December 2004) which has gone into effect on 1 April 2007. This Act promotes to utilize the other means outside the judicial courts for the settlement of claims. Under this Act, the Minister of Justice admits and certifies the works of the civil persons or organizations, which intermediate reconciliation between parties when they satisfy the standard condition, set out in this Act. Now the General Insurance Association of Japan Inc., the Life Insurance Association of Japan Inc., the SASTIP Association of Japan, the Japanese Bankers Association, the Securities Dealers Association, etc., are the admitted organizations in the field of financial business. When one utilizes the admitted procedure of dispute resolution under this Act one can enjoy the special treatment as regards the interruption of prescription period.

---

7. Supreme Court judgment of 20 Feb. 1987, *Minshu*, vol. 41, No. 1, 159.
8. Tokyo District Court judgment, 25 Jul. 1991, *Hanji*, vol. 1403, 108.

Chapter 6. Compulsory Insurance

47. The ALSL (Law No. 97, 29 July 1955) prescribes that no one can drive a vehicle unless he/she takes out CALI (Article 5). The contents of CALI will be discussed in Part IV, Chapter 1 below. Those who violate this provision are punished by imprisonment for not more than one year or a fine of not more than JPY 500,000 (Article 86-3).

48. In Japan, there are some other insurances, which have also the nature of compulsory insurance.

The Law concerning Compensation for Nuclear Damage (Law No. 147, 17 June 1961) prescribes the no-fault liability of enterprises who handle nuclear reactors, etc., and requires them to take out liability insurance at a minimum JPY 60 billion per plant, etc. (Article 7).

The Law concerning Compensation for Oil Pollution by ship (Law No. 97, 27 December 1975) prescribes the strict liability of ship owners and requires them to take liability insurance or other security contract sufficient to cover the amount of liability (Article 14). This law was enacted to incorporate the International Convention on Civil Liability for Oil Pollution Damage, 1969 that is now replaced by the new Convention on Civil Liability for Oil Pollution Damage, 1992.

The Warehouse Business Law (Law No. 121, 1 June 1956) prescribes that licensed warehousemen should in principle take out fire insurance for property deposited when they issue a warehouse bill (Article 14).

49. Whether we can call it as compulsory insurance or not, several associations of professionals (e.g., medical doctors, lawyers) have so-called professional indemnity insurances with insurance companies and members are normally required to take out such insurance.

According to the IBL, the insurance brokers are required to deposit money before they start their business in order to cover their liabilities (Article 291), but they can be exempted from part of this obligation when they take out insurance brokers' liability insurance (Article 292).

50. In 2008, in Kobe City (Hyogo Prefecture), an elderly person was forced to spend bedridden life as a result of a collision accident with the bicycle of an elementary school boy while the boy was riding downhill in high-speed.

In relation with this incident, the Kobe District Court issued a ruling ordering the high compensation of approximately JPY 95 million to the boy's parents.

Hyogo prefectural assembly, as one of response to this incident, for the first time of the country, enacted an Ordinance of the Province relating to bicycles (Ordinance relating to the promotion of Safe and Proper Use of the Bicycle). By this Ordinance, bicycle-holders subscribe to liability insurance compulsorily. However, the provisions on penalties are not provided in this Ordinance.

Oosaka Fu (Prefecture) assembly also enacted a similar ordinance, and it has come up with similar movement in other prefectures.

Part I. The Insurance Company

Chapter 1.   The Insurance Company: Its Form

§1.   Legal Structure of Private Insurance Business

I.   Overview

51. Private insurance business in Japan is divided into life insurance business and non-life insurance business by law. Both life insurance business and non-life insurance business are businesses which need a licence, and Japanese insurance business consists of these licensed business persons.

In addition to these, mutual aid business such as 'JA mutual aid', 'agricultural mutual aid' carried out by a federation of agricultural cooperatives under the Agricultural Cooperatives Law (Law No. 132, 1947) and non-profit cooperatives' mutual aid business carried by a cooperative society,[9] for example, mutual aid business by the federation of labours' cooperative society (ZENROSAI) under the Consumers' Cooperative Society Law (Law No. 200, 1948) make up the broad spectrum of insurance business.[10]

In the broadest sense, the insurance industry also comprises the public insurance system in addition to the two types of insurance industry.

---

9.   According to the revision of the IBL in 2006, a cooperative society, with no legal basis, carrying non-profit cooperative mutual aid business had to acquire the licence for an insurance company or to be registered as a Small Amount and Short-Term Insurance Provider (see para. 57; seventy-eight companies, as of Jun. 2014, are registered as a Small Amount and Short-Term Insurance Provider).

10.   Non-profit governmental post office insurance business by the Postal Service Agency under the Postal Office Life Ins. Law (Law No. 68, 1949); Postal Service Agency was changed to be under private management in Oct. 2007 and divided into five enterprises such as Japan Post Holdings Co. Ltd., Japan Post Network Co. Ltd., Japan Post Service Co. Ltd., Japan Post Bank Co. Ltd. and Japan Post Insurance Co. Ltd., and on 1Oct. 2012 Japan Post Service Co. Ltd & Japan Post Network Co. Ltd were combined into Japan Post Co. Ltd. The stockholder of Japan Post Holdings Co. Ltd. is only the Minister of Finance, and Japan Post Holdings Co. Ltd. is the only stockholder of other group enterprises.

The public insurance system mentioned above comprises 'social insurance' which, for example, consists of health insurance, pension insurance, employment insurance, workmen's compensation insurance, nursing care insurance, etc.

II.   Legal Restriction on Private Insurance Business

A.   Limitation of the Form of Insurance Companies

52. The Com. Code stipulates, in Article 509, that the transaction of insurance is a commercial transaction, if effected as a business, and the Companies Act (Comp. Act) provides, in Article 2, that companies are of four kinds namely kabushiki-kaisya (joint stock company), *gomei-kaisha* (commercial partnership), *goshi-kaisha* (limited partnership) and *gohdo-kaisha* (limited liability company).

Although four kinds of companies are authorized in the Comp. Act, the IBL orders that insurance business should be transacted by a type of stock company. None of the other three kinds of companies, individuals or partnerships may transact insurance business. The IBL has authorized an original kind of company other than those mentioned above for the sole purpose of carrying out insurance business.

Therefore, there are two kinds of insurance companies: one is a stock insurance company and the other is a mutual insurance company.[11]

B.   Restriction on Minimum Amount of Capital or Sum of Foundation Funds

53. Although under the Old Commercial Code, the minimum amount of capital of a joint stock company shall not be less than JPY 10 million, there is no regulation for the minimum amount of capital under new Comp. Act (Law No. 86, 2005). As for an insurance company, IBL, however, requires its minimum amount[12] to be JPY 1 billion, in view of the expected stability and continuity of management of insurance companies (IBL Article 6).

A mutual insurance company has no 'capital', but instead a 'foundation fund'. The IBL requires its minimum amount to be the same as that for a stock company (IBL Article 6).

C.   Prohibition of Carrying on Both Life and Non-life Insurance Business by a Company

54. No person may carry on any insurance business unless authorized by the Prime Minister to do so (IBL Article 3(1)). The authorization is of two kinds, namely that for life insurance business and that for non-life insurance business (IBL Article

---

11.   In Japan, all non-life insurance companies are joint stock companies, and a few life insurance companies that have long history are mutual companies.
12.   Minimum amount for capital (or foundation fund) of SMSTIP shall be JPY 10 million (IBLCO Art. 38-3).

3(2)). No person shall be authorized for both life and non-life insurance businesses (IBL Article 3(3)[13]).

An insurance company must include in its trade name or appellation an indication that it is a life or non-life insurance company (IBL Article 7(1)), and at the same time, no person other than an insurance company may include in its trade name or appellation any characters which falsely represent it as an insurance company (IBL Article 7(2)).

D.   *Insurance Business Authorization*

55. The IBL defines that authorization for life insurance business shall be for the business of writing insurance mentioned in item (1) below or writing it and additionally any insurance mentioned in item (2) or (3) (IBL Article 3(4)):

(1)   insurance (other than that pertaining solely to death as mentioned in sub-item (c) of the following item) whereby, in consideration of an insurance premium, an undertaking is made to pay a specified sum of insurance claim in connection with survival or death (including a physical condition in respect of which a physician has diagnosed that the remainder of life is not likely to exceed a specified period; this inclusion applying in this and the following paragraph);
(2)   insurance whereby, in consideration of an insurance premium, an undertaking is made to pay a specified sum of insurance claim in connection with any of the events mentioned below or to indemnify any loss which may be sustained as a result of such events:

   (a) disease;
   (b) any condition arising from injury or disease;
   (c) death resulting directly from injury;
   (d) events (other than death) designated by a Cabinet Ordinance as being similar to those mentioned in sub-items (a) and (b);
   (e) medical treatments (including those designated by a Cabinet Ordinance as being similar to medical treatments) which may be carried out in connection with the events mentioned in sub-item (a), (b) or (d);

(3)   insurance mentioned in item (1) of the following paragraph which constitutes reinsurance and relates to any insurance mentioned in the preceding two items.

56. Authorization for non-life insurance business shall be for the business of writing insurance mentioned in item (1) below or writing it and additionally any insurance mentioned in item (2) or (3) (IBL Article 3(5)):

(1)   insurance (other than that mentioned in the following item) whereby, in consideration of an insurance premium, an undertaking is made to indemnify any loss which may arise from certain fortuitous accidents;
(2)   insurance mentioned in item (2) of the authorization for life insurance business;

---

13.   SASTIP may underwrite, on certain conditions, both life and non-life insurance (IBL Art. 2(7)).

(3) insurance mentioned in item (1) of the authorization for life insurance business which is connected with death occurring during the period between the departure from home for the purpose of travelling abroad and the return home ('overseas travel period') or with death directly resulting from any disease contracted during the overseas travel period;

(4) activities connected with surety bonds (which mean activities in making an undertaking, for a consideration, to guarantee the fulfilment of contractual or statutory obligations, which activities are carried on by determining the consideration therefore on the basis of insurance mathematics, establishing reserves, spreading risks through reinsurance and otherwise utilizing methods which are proper to insurance).

E.   *Special Provisions for Stock Companies Doing Insurance Business*

57. A stock company doing insurance business principally applies the Comp. Act, and at the same time, the IBL provides special provisions applying to stock companies doing insurance business as follows:

(a) Method of Public Notice (IBL Article 9)

(1) A stock company carrying on insurance business (hereinafter called 'Stock Company') shall specify any of the following methods as the Method of Public Notice in its articles of incorporation:

(a) publication in a daily newspaper that publishes matters on current events; or

(b) Electronic Public Notice (for a stock company and a foreign insurance company, etc., which is a foreign company, referring to the Electronic Public Notice provided for in Article 2 item 34 of the Companies Act (Comp. Act), and for a mutual company and a foreign insurance company, etc., (other than a foreign company), any of those Method of Public Notice meeting the definition provided in said item which allow many and unspecified persons to access the information to be published by electromagnetic means (referring to the electromagnetic means defined in said item); the same shall apply hereinafter).

(3) The provisions of Article 940(1) (excluding item 2) and Article 940(3) of Companies Act shall apply *mutatis mutandis* to the cases where a Stock Company gives public notice under this Act in the form of electronic public notice. In this case, any other necessary technical change in interpretation shall be specified by a Cabinet Ordinance.

(b) Offer for Shares for Subscription etc. (IBL Article 10)

A Stock Company shall, when it gives a notice pursuant to the provision of Article 59(1) (subscription for shares solicited at incorporation), Article 203(1) (application for shares for subscription) or Article 242(1) (application for share options for subscription) of the Companies Act, notify the matters listed in Article 59(1) item 1 to 5 inclusive, Article 203(1) item 1 to 4 inclusive or Article 242(1) item 1 to 4 inclusive, respectively, as well as any provision in its articles of incorporation mentioned in the second sentence of Article 113 (including the cases where it is applied *mutatis mutandis* pursuant to Article 272-18).

(c)   Reference Date (IBL Article 11)

For the purpose of applying to a Stock Company the provision of Article 124(2) (record date) of the Companies Act, the term 'three months' in said paragraph shall be read as 'three months (or four months for the right to exercise a voting right in an annual shareholder meeting and any other right specified by a Cabinet Ordinance)'.

(d)   Qualifications, etc., of Directors etc. (IBL Article 12)

(1) With regard to application of the provisions of Article 331(1) item 3 (Qualifications of Directors) of the Companies Act (including the cases where it is applied *mutatis mutandis* pursuant to Article 335(1) (qualifications of company auditors) and Article 402(4) (election of executive officers) of said Act) to a Stock Company, the term 'this act' in said item shall be deemed to be replaced with 'the insurance business law, this law'.

(2) The provisions of the proviso to Article 331(2) (including the cases where it is applied *mutatis mutandis* pursuant to Article 335(1) of the Companies Act), Article 332(2) (directors' terms of office) (including the cases where it is applied *mutatis mutandis* pursuant to Article 334(1) (accounting advisors' term of office), Article 336(2) (company auditors' terms of office), Article 389(1) (limitation of scope of audit by provisions of articles of incorporation) and the proviso to Article 402(5) of the Companies Act shall not apply to a Stock Company.

(e)   Reference Documents for Shareholders Meeting and Voting Forms etc. (IBL Article 13)

With regard to application of the provisions of Article 301(1) (giving of reference documents for shareholders meeting and voting forms), Article 432(1) (preparation and retention of account books), Article 435(1) and (2) (preparation and retention of financial statements, etc.), Article 436(1) and (2) (audit of financial statements, etc.), Article 439 (special provision on companies with accounting auditors) and Article 440(1) (public notice of financial statements) of the Companies Act to a Stock Company, the term 'Ordinance of the Ministry of Justice' in said provisions shall be deemed to be replaced with 'Cabinet Ordinance'.

(f)   Exclusion from Application of the Provision Regarding Request to Inspect Account Book (IBL Article 14)

(1) The provision of Article 433 (request to inspect account book) of the Companies Act shall not apply to account books of a Stock Company and materials relating thereto.

(2) With regard to application of the provision of Article 442(3) (keeping and inspection of financial statements, etc.) of the Companies Act to a Stock Company, the term 'and creditors' in said paragraph shall be deemed to be replaced with 'policyholders, beneficiaries of the insurance claims, and other creditor and insurers'.

(g) Reserves (IBL Article 15)

Notwithstanding the provision of Article 445(4) (Amounts of stated capital and amounts of reserves) of the Companies Act, in the case where a Stock Company pays dividends of surplus, it shall record the amount equivalent to one-fifth of the amount of the deduction from surplus as a result of the payments of such dividends of surplus as capital reserves or retained earnings reserves (hereinafter referred to as 'reserves'), pursuant to the provisions of an enforcement regulation.

(h) Keeping and Inspection of Documents Pertaining to Reduction of Stated Capital etc., (IBL Article 16)

(1) A stock company shall keep at each of its business offices a document or electromagnetic record that describes or records any proposal regarding the reduction of the stated capital as well as any other matter specified by an enforcement regulation, for a period ranging from two weeks before the date of the shareholders meeting pertaining to the resolution on the reduction (excluding the cases where the whole of the amount by which the reserves are reduced is appropriated to the stated capital) of the stated capital or reserves (hereinafter referred to as 'stated capital, etc.' in this section) (or, the date of the board of directors meeting where Article 447(3) (Reductions in Amount of Stated Capital) or Article 448(3) (Reductions in Amount of Reserves) of the Companies Act applies) to six months from the Effective Date of the reduction of the stated capital, etc.; provided, however, that this shall not apply to the cases where only the amount of the reserves is reduced and all of the following apply:

(a) An annual shareholder meeting has decided on the matters listed in Article 448(1) item 1 to item 3 inclusive of the Companies Act.

(b) The amounts mentioned in Article 448(1) item 1 of the Companies Act does not exceed the amount calculated in the manner specified by an enforcement regulation as the amount of the deficit as at the date of the annual shareholders meeting referred to in the preceding item (or, in the cases provided for in the first sentence of Article 439 (Special Provision on Companies with Accounting Auditors) of said Act, the date of authorization under Article 436(3) (Audit of Financial Statements, etc.).

(3) Shareholders, policyholders and other creditors of a Stock Company may make the following requests at any time during the operating hours of the company; provided, however, that they pay the fees determined by the Stock Company when making a request falling under item 1 or 4:

(a) a request to inspect the document set forth in the preceding paragraph;
(b) a request for a transcript or extract of the document set forth in the preceding paragraph;
(c) a request to inspect anything that displays the matter recorded on the electromagnetic record set forth in the preceding paragraph in a manner specified by an enforcement regulation; or
(d) a request that the matters recorded on the electromagnetic record set forth in the preceding paragraph be provided by electromagnetic means (referring to any of the methods using an electronic data processing system or any other information and communication technology and specified by an enforcement regulation; the same shall apply hereinafter) designated by the Stock Company or request for any document that contains such matters.

(5) For the purpose of applying the provision of paragraph (1) item 1 to the cases where the articles of incorporation include a provision mentioned in Article 459(1) (Provisions of Articles of Incorporation that Broad of Directors Determines Dividends of Surplus) of the Companies Act, the term 'annual shareholders meeting' in said item shall be read as 'annual shareholders meeting or the board of directors under Article 436(3) of the Companies Act.'

(i) Objection of Creditors (IBL Article 17)

(1) Where a Stock Company reduces the amount of its stated capital, etc., (excluding the cases where the whole of the amount by which the reserves are reduced is appropriated to the stated capital), policyholders or other creditors of such Stock Company may file their objections to the reduction in the amount of the stated capital, etc., to the Stock Company; provided, however, that this shall not apply to the cases where only the amount of the reserves is reduced and each item of paragraph (1) of the preceding Article apply.

(2) Where policyholders or other creditors of a Stock Company may state their objections pursuant to the provision of the preceding paragraph, said Stock Company shall give public notice of the following matters below in the official gazette and by the method of public notice stipulated in the company's articles of incorporation; provided, however, that the period under item (iii) may not be less than one month:

(a) the details of such reduction in the amount of the stated capital etc.;
(b) the matters specified by an enforcement regulation regarding the financial statements of such stock company;
(c) that policyholders or other creditors may file their objections within certain period of time;

(d) in addition to what is listed in the preceding three items, any matter specified by an enforcement regulation.

(5) Where policyholders or other creditors do not raise any objections within the period under item (iii) of the preceding paragraph, such policyholders or other creditors shall be deemed to have approved such reduction in the amount of the stated capital, etc.

(6) Where policyholders or other creditors raise objections within the period under paragraph (2)(iii), the Stock Company mentioned in paragraph (1) shall make payment or provide equivalent security to such policyholders or other creditors, or entrust equivalent property to a trust company, etc., (referring to a trust company as defined in Article 2(2) (Definitions) of the Trust Business Act (Act No. 154, 2004); the same shall apply hereinafter) or financial institution carrying on trust business (referring to a financial institution approved under Article 1(1) (Authorization of Trust Business) of the Act on provision, etc., of Trust Business by Financial Institutions (Act No. 43, 1943); the same shall apply hereinafter) for the purpose of ensuring that such policyholders or other creditors receive the payment; provided, however, that this shall not apply to the cases where the reduction of the stated capital, etc., poses no risk of harming the interest of such policyholders or other creditors.

(7) The provision of the preceding paragraph shall not apply to the rights of policyholders or other persons who hold any right pertaining to insurance contracts (excluding insurance claims that have already arisen at the time of public notice under paragraph (2) due to the occurrence of insured events or for other reasons, and any other right specified by the cabinet ordinance (referring to as 'Insurance Claims, etc.' hereinafter in this section, as well as in section 3 and Chapter VIII, sections 2 and 3)).

(8) Any resolution pertaining to the reduction of the stated capital, etc., under Article 447(1) (Reductions in Amount of Stated Capital) or 448(1) (Reductions in Amount of Reserves) of the Companies Act shall be null and void if the number of policyholders who have stated their objections within the period mentioned in paragraph (2)(iii) (excluding the holders of policies under which insurance claims, etc., had already arisen at the time of public notice under said paragraph (but limited to those policies that would be terminated with the payment of the insurance claims, etc.); hereinafter the same shall apply in this paragraph, as well as in paragraph (4) of the following Article) exceeds one-fifth of the total number of policyholders, and the amount specified by an enforcement regulation as the credits (excluding insurance claims, etc.) belonging to the insurance contracts of the policyholders who have stated such objections exceeds one-fifth of the total amount of credits belonging to the policyholders.

(9) In addition to what is provided for in the preceding paragraphs, any necessary matter for the application of those provisions shall be specified by the Cabinet Ordinance.

(j)   Effectuation (IBL Article 17-2)

(1) The reduction of the amounts listed in the following items takes effect on the dates specified by each items, respectively; provided, however, that this shall not apply to the cases where the procedure under the preceding Article has not been completed, or when and if a resolution pertaining to the reduction of the stated capital, etc., under Article 447(1) (Reductions in Amount of Stated Capital) or 448(1) (Reductions in Amount of Reserves) of the Companies Act becomes null and void pursuant to the provision of Article 17(6):

- Reduction of the stated capital: the date specified in Article 447(1)(iii) of the Companies Act.
- Reduction of reserves: the date specified in Article 448(1)(iii) of the Companies Act.

(2) A stock company may change the dates specified in items (i) and (ii) of the preceding paragraph at any time before the relevant dates.
(3) Notwithstanding the provision of paragraph (1), any reduction of the stated capital of a stock company shall not be effective unless it is approved by the Prime Minister.
(4) Any reduction of the stated capital, etc., pursuant to the provision of the preceding article (or, pursuant to the provisions of said article and the preceding paragraph for any reduction of the stated capital) shall also be effective against the policyholders who have stated their objections under said article, paragraph (6) and other persons who hold any right (other than insurance claims, etc.) pertaining to insurance contracts involving the policyholders.

(k) Special Provision for Registration (IBL Article 17-3)

(1) The following documents shall be attached to a written application for registration of change due to a reduction of the stated capital of a Stock Company, in addition to the documents specified in Article 18, Article 19 (Documents attached to written application) and Article 46 (General Rules on Attached Documents) of the Commercial Registration Act (Act No. 125, 1963). A document certifying that the public notice under Article 17(2) has been given:

- Where any policyholder or other creditor has stated objection under Article 17(4), a document certifying that the company has made payment or provided equivalent security to such policyholder or other creditor, or has entrusted equivalent property to a trust company, etc., for the purpose of ensuring that such policyholder or other creditor receive the payment, or that the reduction of the stated capital poses no risk of harming the interest of such policyholder or other creditor; and
- A document certifying that the number of policyholders who stated their objections under Article 17(6) has not exceeded one-fifth of the total number of policyholders as specified in said paragraph, or a document certifying that the amount specified by an enforcement regulation as

belonging to such policyholders as specified in said paragraph has not exceeded one-fifth of the total amount as specified in that paragraph.

(2) The provision of Article 70 (Registration of Change Due to Reduction of Stated Capital) of the Commercial Registration Act shall not apply to a registration of change due to a reduction of the stated capital of a Stock Company.

(l) Keeping and Inspection of Documents Concerning Reduction of Stated Capital, etc. (IBL Article 17-4)

(1) A Stock Company shall keep at each of its business offices a document or electromagnetic record that describes or records the progress of the procedure provided for in Article 17 as well as any other matter specified be an enforcement regulation as a matter pertaining to the reduction of the stated capital, etc., for six months from the effective date of the reduction of the stated capital, etc.

(2) Shareholders, policyholders and other creditors of a stock company may make the following requests at any time during the operating hours of the company; provided, however, that they pay the fees determined by the Stock company when making a request falling under item (ii) or (iv):

  – A request to inspect the document set forth in the preceding paragraph.
  – A request for a transcript or extract of the document set forth in the preceding paragraph.
  – A request to inspect anything that displays the matter recorded on the electromagnetic record set forth in the preceding paragraph.
  – A request that the matters recorded on the electromagnetic record set forth in the preceding paragraph be provided by electromagnetic means designated by the stock company, or a request for any document that contains such matters.

(m) Exclusion from Application, etc. (IBL Article 17-5)

(1) The provision of Article 449 (Objection of Creditors) of the Companies Act shall not apply to the reduction of the stated capital, etc., of a Stock Company.

(2) For the purpose of applying to a Stock Company the provision of Article 740(1) (Special Provisions on Objection Procedures for Creditors) of the Companies Act, the following text shall be inserted after the term 'Article 819' in said paragraph, or 'Article 17, Article 70, Article 165-7 (including the cases where it is applied *mutatis mutandis* pursuant to Article 165-12 of the Insurance Business Law), Article 165-24 or Article 173-4 of the Insurance Business Law'.

(n) Restriction on Dividends of Surplus to Shareholders Etc., (IBL Article 17-6)

(1) Where any amount is credited to assets in the balance sheet pursuant to the provision of the first sentence of Article 113 (including the cases where it is applied *mutatis mutandis* pursuant to Article 272-18), a Stock Company shall not carry out any of the following activities unless such amount has been fully amortized:

- Purchase of any share of the Stock Company at a request made under Article 138(i)(c) or (ii)(c) (Method for Requests for Authorization of Transfer) of the Companies Act.
- Acquisition of any share of the Stock Company based on a decision under Article 156(1) (Determination of Matters Regarding Acquisition of Shares) of the Companies Act (but limited to acquisition of any share of the Stock Company where Article 163 (Acquisition of Shares from Subsidiaries) or Article 165(1) (Acquisition of Shares by Market Transactions) of said Act applies).
- Acquisition of any share of the Stock Company based on a decision under Article 157(1) (Determination of Acquisition Price) of the Companies Act.
- Acquisition of any share of the Stock Company under Article 173(1) (Effectuation) of the Companies Act (excluding the cases where no money or other property is delivered).
- Purchase of any share of the stock company at a request made under Article 176(1) (Demand for Sale) of the Companies Act.
- Purchase of any share of the stock company under Article 197(3) (Auction of Shares) of the Companies Act.
- Purchase of any share of the stock company under Article 234(4) (Treatment of Fractions) of the Companies Act (including the cases where it is applied *mutatis mutandis* pursuant to Article 235(2) (Treatment of Fractions) of said Act).
- Dividend of surplus.

(2) The provision of Article 463(2) (Restriction on Remedy over against Shareholders) of the Companies Act shall apply *mutatis mutandis* to the cases where a stock company, in violation of the provision of the preceding paragraph, has carried out any of the activities listed in each item of said Article. In this case, any other necessary technical change in interpretation shall be specified by the Cabinet Ordinance.

(3) For the purpose of applying to a stock company the provision of Article 446(vii) (Amounts of Surplus) of the Companies Act, the term 'Enforcement Regulation of the Ministry of Justice' in said item shall be read as 'Cabinet Office Ordinance'.

(4) For the purpose of applying to a stock company the provision of Article 461(2) (vi) (Restriction on Dividends) of the Companies Act, 'the sum of the amounts recorded in each account title specified by an Ordinance of the Ministry of Justice' shall be read as 'the amount of entity conversion surplus under Article 91(1) of the Insurance Business Law, the amount of merger surplus under Article 91(1) of said Law, as applied *mutatis mutandis* with relevant change

in interpretation pursuant to Article 164(4) and Article 165(6) of said Law, or the sum of the amounts recorded in each account title specified by a Cabinet Office Ordinance'.

(o) Matters to be Recorded in Registering Incorporation (IBL Article 17-7)

(1) In registering the incorporation of a stock company, the matters listed in each items of Article 911(3) (Registering the Incorporation of a Stock Company) of the Companies Act shall be recorded, along with any provision in its articles of incorporation in the second sentence of Article 113 (including the cases where it is applied *mutatis mutandis* pursuant to Article 272-18).

(2) Where any change has occurred in the matters prescribed in the preceding paragraph, the stock company shall complete registration of such change within two weeks at the location of its head office.

III. Mutual Company

58. The mutual company is the specially permitted form of the company under the IBL (Article 18). Company members are the policyholders, and the company organ is the 'assembly of members' or 'assembly members' representatives'. Here, the 'assembly members' representatives' is an organ permitted under the IBL.

Article 42 of the law says as follows:

Subject to the provisions of the articles of incorporation, a mutual company may, as an organ to substitute for the assembly of members, set up an organ composed of representatives elected from among the members.

A mutual insurance company is not a company incorporated under the Comp. Act, so that is outside the registration of the Comp. Act as it is. Therefore, the IBL gives the original rule applicable to the mutual company, additional to the many *mutatis mutandis* regulations of the Comp. Act applying to the mutual company.[14]

A.   Small Amount and Short-Term Insurance Provider

59. There were two types of mutual aid business in Japan. One is the business carried under certain governing law, such as JA mutual aid or Zenrosai, etc., (see paragraph 49) and the other is the business having no such law.

On April 2006, FSA revised IBL to inspect such mutual aid businesses carried under no governing law.

According to the revision of IBL, cooperatives, carrying on mutual aid business under no governing law, had been forced to obtain a licence for Insurance Company or SASTIP.[15] From the other point of view, persons who intended to enter into insurance business may have a new way to set up insurance company.

---

14.   Recently, mutual companies have considered that their legal form is a hindrance in the case of financing and/or reconstruction of the company.

15.   SASTIP may underwrite both life insurance and non-life insurance (IBL Art. 2(17)).

SASTI Business means the Insurance Business of underwriting insurance limited to that whose insurance period is within the period specified by the Cabinet Ordinance within the limit of two years, and whose insurance amount is not more than the amount specified by the Cabinet Ordinance within an amount not exceeding JPY 10 million (except those specified by a Cabinet Ordinance[16]) (IBL Article 2(17)).

SASTIP means a person who has obtained the registration set forth in Article 272(1) and carried on Small Amount and Short-Term Insurance Business (SASTIB) (IBL Article 2(18)).

The following documents shall be attached to the written application for registration:

(1)   Articles of Incorporation.
(2)   Statement of business procedures.
(3)   General policy conditions.
(4)   Statement of calculation procedures for insurance premium and policy reserves.

Insurance amount per an insured: death insurance (except death by accident); JPY 3 million, death insurance (death by accident); JPY 6 million, medical insurance, etc., JPY 800 thousand, serious permanent disability insurance (except those by accident); JPY 3 million, serious permanent disability insurance (those by accident); JPY 6 million, non-life insurance JPY 10 million. Total insured amount of insurance contracts underwritten for one insured by one SASTIP shall be set up within the limit of JPY 10 million but personal liability insurance can be underwritten up to JPY 10 million separated from other insurance contracts.

SASTIP, having underwriting-restriction in insurance term and amount of insurance, is not able to underwrite following insurance further (IBLCO Article 1-7):

(1)   Insurance to pay a fixed amount of insurance claims in condition with the survival of individuals (e.g., personal pension insurance and saving insurance).
(2)   Insurance with refund upon its expiration.
(3)   Reinsurance (except reinsurance ceded).
(4)   Insurance where the premium shall be invested in securities (e.g., stock, bond, etc.) and the amount of insurance may be fluctuated with the result of investment.
(5)   Insurance where the premium, the amount of insurance claims are set up in foreign money.
(6)   Insurance where all or a part of the amount of insurance claims shall be paid regularly or by instalment for over one year.

As to a SASTIP, IBL is prescribing its scale of business that a SASTIP shall be a small scale entrepreneur (referring to an entrepreneur receiving insurance premium in an amount not exceeding the relevant threshold to be prescribed by an IBLER (IBL Article 27(2)), and the IBLER provides in Article 38 that its relevant threshold shall be under JPY 5 billion in net premium basis.

IBL also prescribes that a SASTIP may carry out the SASTIB and any other business incidental thereto (IBL Article 272-11(1)), and SASTIP may not carry on any

---

16.   Insurance Period: one year for life insurance, two years for non-life insurance.

other business than that carried on pursuant to the provision of the preceding paragraph; provided, however, that this shall not apply when the SASTIP has received the approval of the Prime Minister pursuant to the provisions of the applicable IBLER for any of those businesses to be prescribed by an IBLER as related to the SASTIB which are found to pose no risk to the insurer in carrying on its SASTIB in an appropriate and secure manner (IB Article 272-11(2)). And the IBLER provides, in its Article 211-24, that SASTIP may execute only to represent the businesses or to carry out services (limited to those specified by IBLER) on behalf of other SASTIP or insurance companies (including foreign insurers).

A SASTIP may not become a membership of a Policyholders' Protection Organization (IBL Article 262).

A SASTIP, however, shall deposit the amount of money[17] to be prescribed by a Cabinet Ordinance as necessary and appropriate for the protection of policyholders, etc., (IBL Article 272-5).

A SASTIP shall, in general, invest money received as insurance premiums and other assets by deposit with any of the banks or acquisition of national government bonds.

IV. Other Legal Forms

A. Foreign Insurance Company

60. One of the objects of the IBL is to regulate foreign insurers in Japan on an equitable basis with domestic insurance companies, such as stock insurance companies or mutual insurance companies. Therefore, foreign insurers who wish to carry on insurance business in Japan are required to be licensed and supervised by the FSA.

A 'foreign insurer' means any person (other than an insurance company) doing insurance business outside Japan under the laws and ordinances of another country (IBL Article 2(6)).

Otherwise, 'foreign insurance company, etc.' means a 'foreign insurer' authorized by the Prime Minister, licensed to carry on insurance business in Japan (IBL Article 2(7)).

A 'foreign insurer, etc.' needs to set up a branch office in Japan to be licensed as a 'foreign insurance company, etc.' This licence is divided into a licence for life insurance business and for non-life insurance business, and the same 'foreign insurance company' cannot hold both, as for domestic insurance companies. Except where otherwise provided by a Cabinet Ordinance, a foreign insurance company may effect insurance contracts in Japan only if such insurance contracts relate to persons having their address or place of abode in Japan or to property situated there or to vessels or aircraft of Japanese nationality.

61. Foreign insurers without a branch office in Japan are not allowed to underwrite risks pertaining to:

---

17.   The beginning of the business: JPY 10 million After 2nd business year: JPY 10 million + (5% of net premium appropriated previous account year).

- persons having their address or place of abode in Japan;
- property situated in Japan; and
- vessels or aircraft of Japanese nationality.

Any person wishing to take out a policy concerning the above-mentioned risks from a foreign insurer with no branch office in Japan must apply to the Prime Minister for permission. In such a case, the Prime Minister will not grant permission if it is found that:

- the insurance contract proposed contravenes laws or ordinances or is unfair;
- it is easy to effect an alternative insurance contract or equivalent on more favourable terms with an insurance company or with a foreign insurance company;
- the terms of the insurance contract are considerably out of balance with those ordinarily offered for insurance contracts of the same kind effected with an insurance company or with a foreign insurance company;
- the effecting of the insurance contract is likely to unduly prejudice the interests of the insured or other persons concerned;
- the effecting of the insurance contract is likely to adversely affect the sound development of the insurance industry in Japan or injure the public interest (IBL Article 186).

62. However, no approval of the Prime Minister is necessary, if the proposed insurance with an unlicensed foreign insurer is:

(a) reinsurance contracts;
(b) insurance contracts which cover vessels having Japanese nationality used for international marine transportation and cargos being transported by such vessels and the liabilities arising therefrom, or any of them;
(c) insurance contracts which cover aircraft having Japanese nationality used for commercial airline business and cargos being transported by such aircraft and the liabilities arising therefrom, or any of them;
(d) insurance contracts which cover launches into cosmic space, cargos relating to such launches (including satellites) and means of transportation of such cargos and the liabilities arising therefrom, or any of them;
(e) insurance contracts (excluding both b and c mentioned above) which cover cargos that are located in Japan and are being internationally transported; and
(f) insurance contracts which cover injury and sickness suffered by overseas travellers during the period of overseas travel provided for in Article 3, paragraph 5, item (3) of the IBL, and the death directly resulting therefrom and the baggage carried by the overseas travellers, or any of them (Cabinet Ordinance Article 19, IBLER Article 116).

63. The regulations of the IBL for 'foreign insurance companies, etc.' are almost as same as those for domestic insurance companies, but there are some specific regulations on 'foreign insurance companies'. Those are as follows:

(1)   Deposit (IBL Article 190)

A foreign insurance company, etc., must deposit with the deposit office nearest to its principal office an amount (in Japanese money)designated by the Cabinet Ordinance as being necessary and proper for the protection of policyholders in Japan. The amount to be prescribed by the Cabinet Ordinance shall be JPY 200,000,000 in the case of a foreign insurance company, or JPY 10,000,000 in the case of a conditionally licensed foreign life insurance company (Cabinet Ordinance of IBL Article 24). When the Prime Minister deems it necessary for the protection of policyholders in Japan, he/she may order a foreign insurance company to deposit money to an amount which the Prime Minister considers reasonable, in addition to the amount designated by the Cabinet Ordinance under the preceding paragraph, before the foreign insurance company commences its insurance business in Japan (Article 190(2)). If a foreign insurance company, in accordance with a Cabinet Ordinance, enters into a contract whereby an underwriting is made to make a necessary money deposit on behalf of the foreign insurance company in compliance with any order issued by the Prime Minister, and has notified the Prime Minister of this contract, then the foreign insurance company may, during the effective period of the contract, omit to deposit the whole or part of the amount referred to in the preceding two paragraphs up to the sum offered for deposit under the contract (hereinafter called 'the contract sum') (Article 190(3)). The other party to the contract which substitutes all or portion of the deposit, as entered into by a foreign insurance company, must be a non-life insurance company (including a foreign non-life insurance company and underwriting member(s) (meaning the underwriting member(s) provided for in Article 219, paragraph 1 of the IBL) of the party which was granted the license referred to in paragraph 5 of the said Article) and such other financial institution as prescribed by IBLER, and the contents thereof must comply with the following requirements (Cabinet Ordinance Article 25):

- – that when an order is issued by the Secretary of FSA, the amount specified in the order shall be deposited on the account of the foreign insurance company without delay;
- – that the contract shall remain effective for a period of not less than one year; and
- – that, except where the approval of the Secretary of FSA is obtained, the contract may not be cancelled or any content thereof be amended.

Also, in this case, the Prime Minister, when he/she deems it necessary for the protection of policyholders in Japan, may order either that the person who has entered into the contract with a foreign insurance company shall deposit the whole or part of the amount equal to the contract sum, or that the foreign insurance company shall do so (Article 190(4)). No foreign insurance company may commence authorized insurance business until after it has made (including having entered into a contract) the monetary deposit and has submitted notice to the Prime Minister (Article 190(5)). Policyholders, those insured and beneficiaries under insurance contracts in Japan are entitled to payment in preference to any other creditors from the money deposit relating to the foreign insurance company in respect of any claims under insurance contracts (Article 190(6)).

In substitution for money to be deposited, a foreign insurance company may deposit government bonds or other securities specified by IBLER (Article 190(9)).

(2)   Obligation to Localized Assets (IBL Article 197)

A foreign insurance company must, in accordance with IBLER, hold in Japan assets equivalent to the total sum of the amount calculated in accordance with the ordinance on the basis of the underwriting reserves and payment reserves established in Japan on the one hand, and on the other the amount equal to the deposit of money and to other net assets.

B.   Specified Juristic Person (Lloyd's) (IBL Article 219)

64. The IBL has a provision that a juristic person to which descriptions in both items below apply (hereinafter referred to as 'specified juristic person') may obtain authorization from the Prime Minister for an insurance-writing member of it (hereinafter referred to as 'underwriting member') to do insurance business in Japan, the specified juristic person having appointed a person to act as agent for the underwriting member in writing insurance in connection with his/her insurance business in Japan, and to represent the specified juristic person and the underwriting member in their activities there (hereinafter referred to as 'general agent') provided:

–   the juristic person is incorporated under the special laws and ordinances of another country; and
–   its members are entitled by special provisions of laws and ordinances of its country to do insurance business without obtaining authorization (or permission, registration or other administrative disposition similar to authorization) for insurance business in that country.

The only juristic person fulfilling these two requirements is the Cooperative of Lloyd's, so this regulation is a special provision for Lloyd's to carry on direct insurance business in Japan.

The authorization mentioned above is of two kinds, namely that for specified life insurance business and that for specified non-life insurance business. And no specified juristic person may be authorized for both specified life and non-life insurance business.

Authorization for specified life insurance business enables an underwriting member to write insurance mentioned in item (1) of paragraph 4 of Article 3 of the IBL or to write it and, additionally, any insurance mentioned in item (2) or (3) of that paragraph as business in Japan.

Authorization for specified non-life insurance business will enable an underwriting member to write the insurance mentioned in item (1) of paragraph 5 of Article 3 of IBL or to write it and, additionally, any insurance mentioned in item (2) or (3) of that paragraph as business in Japan.

When a specified juristic person has obtained authorization under paragraph 1, the underwriting member may do insurance business in Japan at the office of a general agent in accordance with the kinds of authorization under paragraph 2 notwithstanding the provisions of paragraph 1 of Article 3 and paragraph 1 of Article 185.

C.   Professional Reinsurance Company

65. According to the definition of the insurance contract in the Insurance Law, a reinsurance contract has the nature of non-life insurance contract (Article 2, Insurance Law). And also in the IBL, one of the factors of authorization for non-life insurance business is for the business of writing insurance whereby, in consideration of an insurance premium, an undertaking is made to indemnify any loss which may arise from certain fortuitous accidents; consequently, reinsurance business is considered as including authorization for non-life insurance business.

In a general, both a life insurance company and a non-life insurance company underwriting direct insurance contracts are authorized for reinsurance business according to their insurance business licence, but there are two professional reinsurance companies as domestic insurance companies carrying on reinsurance business only.

Under the legislation of the law, there is no specified authorization for reinsurance business. A professional reinsurance company means an insurance company whose licence is only to underwrite reinsurance contracts.

D.   Insurance Holding Company

66. After World War II, in Japan, the Law relating to Prohibition of Private Monopoly and Methods of Preserving Fair Trade (hereinafter, the 'Anti-monopoly Act') prohibited the establishing of holding company for a long time. In December 1997, however, the Anti-monopoly Act was revised, to progress diversification of management of enterprises in order to make them internationally competitive, and holding companies could be established without general restriction.

In accordance with this revision of the Anti-monopoly Act, a holding company[18] owning an insurance company as its subsidiary may be established. The IBL was revised logically to include provisions for such an insurance holding company (from Articles 271-18 to 271-31) in October 1998.

To become a holding company having an insurance company as its subsidiary or a person who intends to establish a holding company having an insurance company as its subsidiary an enterprise must be authorized in advance by the Prime Minister (IBL Article 271-18).

An insurance holding company may manage its main business and its subordinated business of a non-life insurance company and/or a life insurance company established as its subsidiary; such companies must be accepted by the law and authorized as subsidiaries by the Prime Minister. An insurance holding company must not manage any other business than that mentioned above.

The IBL stipulates the duty of an insurance holding company to submit its business report to the Prime Minister, the right to enter an insurance company's place of business for the inspection, etc.

---

18.   A holding company having a SASTIP as its subsidiary may be established (IBL Arts 275-35–43).

E.   *Large Insurance Stockholder and Major Insurance Stockholder*

67. A person having more than 5% of total right of voting in insurance company or an insurance holding company must submit a report containing the matters such as proportion of voting rights held, funds for the acquisition, the purpose of holding the voting rights, etc., (items to be contained are stipulated in IBL Article 271-3, IBLER Article 205) to the Prime Minister (IBL Article 271-3).

If there is any false description of important items or any misrepresentation as to important items in the report, the Prime Minister may order his/her office staff to enter the person's office for inspection (IBL Article 271-9).

A person who intends to hold more than 20% of the total stock of an insurance company (15% in the case of a person stipulated by IBLER) must be authorized in advance by the Prime Minister (IBL Article 271-10).

The Prime Minister has power over major insurance stockholder as follows:

(a) to secure the sound and proper operation of activities of an insurance company, and to protect policyholders and other persons; when the Prime Minister finds it necessary, he/she may require the major insurance stockholder to submit a report or materials relating to the state of the insurance company's operational activities and/or assets, or cause his/her office staff to enter the major insurance stockholder's office for inspection (IBL Articles 271-12, 13);

(b) if the major insurance stockholder has come to be in situation not appropriate to the criteria for authorization, the Prime Minister may order the major insurance stockholder to take appropriate action to conform with the criteria (IBL Article 271-14);

(c) to secure the sound and proper operation of activities of an insurance company, when the Prime Minister finds it necessary, he/she may, insofar as necessary, require the major insurance stockholder to submit a reform plan for securing the soundness of the insurance company (IBL Article 271-15);

(d) if the major insurance stockholder contravenes any law or order, etc., or acts to damage the public interest, the Prime Minister may act to revoke the authorization (IBL Article 271-16).

§2.   Public Nature of Private Insurance Business

I.   Public Nature of Insurance Business

68. The IBL, considering the public nature of insurance business, stipulates in its Article 1 that the purpose of the law is to secure, in view of the significance of insurance business to the public, the sound and proper operation of activities by persons doing insurance business as well as equity in insurance solicitation in order to protect policyholders and other persons and thereby contribute to stability in the life of the people and to the sound development of the national economy.

The IBL may regulate persons doing insurance business in various ways, and the scope and content of the regulations may reflect the economic, social, political and international background prevailing.

Under the old IBL, regulations on insurance business, with the historical background of too many small insurance companies and too many disappearances thereof in the early days of Japanese insurance business, had reflected political protection for the insurance industry. This had appeared not only in the law but also in the control of the competent authority and the self-regulation by the insurance industry.

The contents and scope of regulation under the new IBL, coming at the time of deregulation, self-governance and internationalization, are limited insofar as possible, and the criteria and procedures for control by the competent authority are also clear in the law.

II.   Securing of Safety Management of Insurance Business

A.   *Supervision*

1. Submission of Report and Materials

69. Insurance companies must, for each business year, submit a business report containing information regarding the state of their activities and assets to the FSA (IBL Article 110), and the Prime Minister may require insurance companies to submit a report or materials relating to the state of their activities and assets when he/she deems it necessary for the purpose of securing the sound and proper operation of the activities of the insurance company and for the protection of insurance policyholders (IBL Article 128). And an insurance company shall, for each business year, prepare explanatory documents describing the matters specified by a Cabinet Office Ordinance as pertaining to the status of its business and property, and keep them for public inspection at its head office or principal offices and branch offices or secondary offices, or any other equivalent place specified by a Cabinet Office Ordinance (IBL Article 111 Item 1).

2. Examination at the Insurance Company's Office

70. When the Prime Minister deems it necessary for the purpose of securing the sound and proper operation of activities of the insurance company and for the protection of insurance policyholders he/she may order staff of the Cabinet Office to enter the place of business of an insurance company and make inquiries as to the state of its activities and assets or to examine its books and other property (IBL Article 129).

This inspection is not compulsory for an insurance company but a person who refuses, hinders or evades the examination will be liable to a fine (IBL Article 329(4)).

B.   *Measures of Early Correction*

71. In accordance with the results of the report, materials and the examinations mentioned above, the Prime Minister may order the insurance company, insofar as necessary, to submit a reform plan for the purpose of securing the soundness of management, to alter statements of methods of operation, to suspend, for a period prescribed by the FSA, all or some of its activities, to deposit assets, to displace its directors or statutory auditors from the office, or may withdraw the authorization of business (IBL Articles 131–133).

III. Relationship Between Insurance Company and Policyholder

A. Registration of Insurance Solicitors and Agents

72. A person who makes an insurance solicitation is restricted to a certain extent, and moreover a person who makes an insurance solicitation, life insurance solicitors, non-life insurance agents and insurance brokers, are registered by the Prime Minister (IBL Article 275).

'Registration' is, indeed, a comparatively minor restriction for a person intending to make insurance solicitation. The restriction is limited to the minimum and to allow a person to start insurance solicitation business as easily as possible.

On the other hand, the IBL, for the protection of policyholders, and to establish the fairness of insurance solicitation, stipulates authorizations of supervision such as conditions for refusal of registration, withdrawal of registration and prohibitions relating to the effecting of insurance contracts or insurance solicitations.

B. Policyholders' Protection Organization System

73. At the revision of the IBL (1996), the Policyholders' Protection Funds System was introduced to provide financial assistance in the case of bankruptcy of an insurance company, to rescue an insurance company for the purpose of smoothly carrying out an insurance portfolio transfer or a business merger, etc. This fund system, however, did not

74. work well when no rescue insurance company appeared to accept an insurance portfolio transfer.

For this reason, the IBL was revised, in July 1998, and introduced the Policyholders' Protection Organization System (PPOS). Both the life and non-life insurance industry in Japan have a PPOS. This may provide financial assistance to a rescue insurance company for the transfer of an insurance portfolio, receive the transfer of an insurance portfolio in the absence of any rescue insurance company, instigate its subsidiary company to receive the transfer of an insurance portfolio, accommodate an insurance company in difficulties which is ordered to stop payment of insurance money, supply a certain policyholder with money corresponding to insurance money, etc.

Before 1998, the fund of the Policyholders' Protection Organization (PPO) to provide financial assistance to rescue an insurance company for the purpose of smoothly carrying out an insurance portfolio or a business merger was collected, at each bankruptcy of an insurance company, from members of PPO.

After 1998, the member of PPO shall pay an assessment to the PPO pursuant to the provisions of the articles of incorporation, during each of the Organization's business year, to be allocated for covering expenses incurred in implementing the business of financial assistance, etc. (IBL 265-33(1)).

In case that the fund necessary to rescue an insurance company, etc., exceeds an accumulated reserve, the PPO may borrow money (up to JPY 460 billion for life insurance industry, up to JPY 50 billion for non-life insurance industry) from banks.

The Organization may, in the case that the specified insurance company has suspended all of its payments pertaining to the insurance contract, make a ruling to purchase right to insurance claims; provided, however, the purchase may be multiplied by the rate specified by the applicable IBLER and Ordinance of the Ministry of Finance (MOF) (IBL Article 270-6-8).

C. Withdrawal of Application for Insurance Contract (Cooling-Off Period)

75. Home selling, by an insurance agent or solicitor, is the main method of insurance sale in Japan. A customer is ordinarily in a passive situation in buying an insurance product, so he/she may conclude an insurance contract with an indefinite intention and may get into difficulties with an insurance agent, etc.

At the revision of the IBL (1996), a cooling-off period during which an insurance applicant may effect the withdrawal[19] of application for the insurance contract or cancellation of the insurance contract without reasons for cancellation or withdrawal but with a certain limitation was introduced to avoid trouble and to protect policyholders.

These following insurance contracts may not be revoked or cancelled:

(1) An insurance contract over eight days, in general, has lapsed counting from the issue date of a document describing the matters concerning the revocation of application.
(2) An insurance contract with one year or less insurance period.
(3) An insurance contract being required to take it out by a law or regulation.
(4) An insurance contract for the purpose of, or on behalf of, operation or business and so on.

IV. Accumulation of Insurance Funds and Investment of Assets

76. The insurance company must accumulate:

–   underwriting reserves to provide for the fulfilment of future obligations under insurance contracts (IBL Article 116);
–   loss reserves for any insurance claims (including Incurred But Not Reported (IBNR) payable under insurance contracts but not having been in the book as payment of claims at the end of each accounting period (IBL Article 117);

---

19.   The IBL, in its Art. 309(4), stipulates that the revocation of application, etc. for an insurance contract shall take effect when the document pertaining to the revocation of application, etc. is issued, while the Civ. Code provides in Art. 97(1) that a declaration of intention made inter absents shall be effective as from the time when notice thereof has reached the other party.

– price fluctuation reserves which must be maintained for losses due to fluctuation of prices in shares, etc., (assets more fluctuating in price), to the amount calculated in accordance with Enforcement Regulation (IBL Article 115);
– reserves for policyholders' dividends (IBL Article 114 Enforcement Regulation Article 62).

An insurance company may use such reserves mentioned above, as its proper business, for investment and there is a certain restriction, in the interest of safe and good investment, on the methods of and amount for investment (IBL Article 97(2)).

V.   National Participation in Insurance Products

A.   *Earthquake Insurance*

77. Japan is known as an earthquake-prone country, and there are 5,232 imperceptible earthquakes, 1,339 perceptible earthquakes and 0.8 earthquakes that cause damage to a building or injury to persons on average each year.

There was popular demand, whenever a big earthquake occurred, to develop earthquake insurance for residential property (an earthquake insurance for industry had been underwritten with some limitations) but, according to the frequency of earthquakes, the assumed scale of the loss, earthquake insurance for residential property was not developed (only short-term, from 25 April 1944 to 28 December 1945 did the government develop, based on the Wartime Special Non-Life Insurance Law, a system to compensate loss or damage from an earthquake).

After the experience of the Niigata earthquake (which occurred in the Niigata Prefecture, in the north-west part of Japan on 16 June 1964), however, earthquake insurance for houses and household goods started with the support of the government's excess cover reinsurance scheme.

At the start of this earthquake insurance, the aggregate limit of indemnity payable by all insurers to all claimants in one earthquake was JPY 300 billion, but the amount has been continuously increased to JPY 11,300 billion (as of April 2016).

The government covers loss or damage of 50% of over JPY 115.3billion up to JPY 437.9 billion and approximately 99.7% of over JPY 437.9 billion up to JPY 11,300 billion. Private insurers cover loss or damage of JPY 115.3 billion (1st layer) and 50% of over JPY 115.3 billion up to JPY 437.9 billion (2nd layer) and JPY 4.3 billion of over JPY 437.9 billion up to JPY 1,844.7 billion and JPY 28.9 billion of over JPY 1,844.7 billion up to JPY 11,300 billion (3rd layer).

JPY 115.3 billion	JPY 161.3 billion		JPY 10,828.9 billion	
	JPY 35.5 billion	JPY 125.8 billion		
			JPY 4.3 billion	JPY 28.9 billion

1st Layer □□2nd Layer   3rd Layer
– 1st Layer shall be covered by Japan Earthquake Reinsurance Co. Ltd. (JER).

– JPY 35.5 billion of 2nd Layer shall be covered by direct-writing insurance companies and JPY 125.8 billion of 2nd Layer shall be covered by JER.

– JPY 4.3 billion of 3rd Layer shall be covered by direct-writing insurance companies and JPY 28.9 billion of 3rd Layer shall be covered by JER.

– JPY 161.3 billion of 2nd Layer and JPY 10,828.9 billion of 3rd Layer shall be covered by the government.

The government covered loss or damage of 50% of over JPY 10 billion up to JPY 50 billion and 100% of over JPY 50 billion up to JPY 300 billion at the start of this scheme.

At the time, the Great East Japan Earthquake happened, the aggregate limit of indemnity payable by all insurers (including the government) in one earthquake was JPY 5,500 billion and the indemnity of private insurers was first JPY 115 billion loss or damage and loss or damage of 50% of over JPY 115 billion up to JPY 1,925 billion and 5% of over JPY 1,925 billion up to JPY 5,500 billion. Against loss or damage of the Great East Japan Earthquake, however, JPY 1,234,593 million has been paid as insurance money (as of 31 May 1912).

After the Great East Japan Earthquake, the government, in view of the social responsibility that comes along with its having promoted a nuclear energy policy, built up in September 2011 based on Nuclear Damage Compensation Facilitation Corporation Act.

Function of this corporation is to help and to ensure a nuclear operators' prompt and appropriate implement of compensation for nuclear damage, the smooth management of a stable supply of electricity and other business connected with reactor operation, etc., in the event that nuclear damage has occurred and amount of compensation for which the nuclear operator is liable pursuant to the provision of Article 3 of the Act on Compensation for Nuclear Damage exceeds the amount of Financial Security set forth in Article 7(1) of the Act on Compensation for Nuclear Damage, by granting the necessary funds for the relevant nuclear operator to compensate for damage and by conducting other such business, thereby stabilizing and improving the lives of the citizenry and contributing to the sound development of the national economy (Article 1).

B.   *Compulsory Automobile Liability Insurance*

78. In Japan, the number of retained automobiles exceeded 1 million at the end of 1953 fiscal year and in line with this growth in motorization, the number of accidents increased, and so the ALSL was enacted on 29 July 1955 (in force from 1 December 1955) to protect victims of traffic accidents. CALI took effect on 1 December 1955.

At the start of this insurance, the government had accepted, as reinsurance, 60% of liability of this insurance for the reason that an insurance company might not select the insured or the automobile to be insured, and that premium rates were calculated on inadequate statistical data. And as to another 40%, a reinsurance pool was established to spread risks among insurers.

Since the reinsurance to the government was originally executed to hedge insurance risks, the ALSL was revised in June 2001 and the reinsurance to the government was abolished from April 2002 because of the increased solvency of insurance companies and the increased accuracy of statistical data.

§3. BUSINESS DATA

I. Life Insurance

79. Forty-one life insurance companies were licensed under the IBL as of January 2016 (thirty- eight domestic insurers, three foreign insurers). Five of domestic insurers are mutual companies and fifteen of them were so-called foreign-affiliated companies. The business in force (individual life, individual annuities, group life and group annuities) of the life insurance companies in the 2015 fiscal year was 164,359,773 policies for individual, 84,813 groups and a value of JPY1,365,361 billion.

II. Non-life Insurance

80. As of January 2016, thirty domestic non-life insurance companies (having their main office in Japan, including two reinsurance companies) and twenty-two foreign non-life insurance companies (having branch offices in Japan, including six reinsurance companies and Lloyd's) are licensed under the IBL. The business in force of the non-life insurance companies in the 2013 fiscal year was JPY 8,875,157 million (including JPY 460,765 million saving premiums), and reinsurance net premiums received were JPY 1,518,474 million (including JPY 394,933 million of professional reinsurance companies), reinsurance premiums ceded were JPY 2,081,462 million (including JPY 155,263 million of professional reinsurance companies).

III. Small Amount and Short-Term Insurance

81. Eighty-seven SASTIPs are registered under the IBL as of May 2016, and nineteen of them are underwriting life insurance and fifty-three are doing non-life insurance (including nine companies which are underwriting only animal insurance), three are doing both of life insurance and non-life insurance and twelve of them are underwriting only insurance mentioned in the IBL Article 3(4) item 2 (medical expense insurance, etc.).

Chapter 2. Access to Business

§1. REQUIREMENT FOR AUTHORIZATION

I. Domestic Insurance Companies

A. Procedure for Applying for Authorization (IBL Article 4)

82. A person[20] seeking authorization must submit to the Prime Minister an application for authorization stating therein:

- the trade name or appellation;
- the amount of capital or the total amount of foundation funds;
- the names of directors and statutory auditors;
- the kind of authorization desired; and
- the address of the head or principal office.

The application for authorization shall be accompanied by the following and such other documents specified by IBLER:

(1) the articles of incorporation;
(2) statements of the methods of operation;
(3) general conditions of insurance;
(4) statements of the methods of calculating insurance premiums and underwriting reserves.

The documents mentioned in (2), (3) and (4) must contain matters specified by IBLER.

B. Criteria for Authorization (IBL Article 5)

83. When the authorization has been applied for, the Prime Minister will determine whether or not the following criteria are fulfilled, namely that:

(1) the person making the application ('the applicant') maintains an adequate financial base for a sound and efficient operation of the activities of an insurance company, and has good forecasts for income and expenses in respect of such activities;
(2) taking into consideration the human resources available to it and other circumstances, the applicant commands sufficient knowledge and experience to carry on the activities of an insurance company justly, fairly and efficiently, and has a sufficient social reliability;

---

20. In case of SASTIP, application and documents mentioned above shall submit to the Local Finance Bureau of FSA.

(3) the matters stated in the documents of 'statements of the methods of operation' and 'general conditions of insurance' fulfil the following criteria:

    (a) that the insurance contracts are not likely to operate without regard to the protection of policyholders, those insured, persons entitled to insurance claims or any other persons concerned (hereinafter referred to as 'policyholders');
    (b) that the terms of the insurance contracts are not unfairly discriminatory against any specific persons;
    (c) that the terms of the insurance contracts are not likely to promote or induce behaviour detrimental to the public order or good morals;
    (d) that the rights and obligations of the policyholders and other matters under the insurance contracts are clearly and plainly stated; and
    (e) any other criteria established by IBLER; and

(4) the matters stated in the documents of 'statements of the methods of calculating insurance premiums and underwriting reserves' fulfil the following criteria:

    (a) that the methods of calculating premiums and underwriting reserves are reasonable and valid on the basis of insurance mathematics;
    (b) that the insurance premiums are not unfairly discriminatory against any specific persons; and
    (c) any other criteria established by IBLER.

When, in light of the criteria for examination specified in the preceding paragraph, the Prime Minister finds it necessary in the public interest, insofar as necessary, attach conditions to the authorization for insurance business or alter such conditions.

II. Foreign Insurance Companies

A.   Application Procedure for Authorization (IBL Article 187)

    84. A foreign insurer seeking authorization as a foreign insurance company must submit to the Prime Minister an application for authorization stating therein:

(1) the name of its country (which means the country which has enacted the laws and ordinances under which that foreign insurer commenced doing insurance business or, if a juristic person, was incorporated), its name, trade name or appellation and address, or the location of its head or principal office, and the day and year of commencement of insurance business or of incorporation;
(2) the name and address of the representative in Japan;
(3) the kind of authorization desired; and
(4) the principal office in Japan (which means the branch offices, etc., as has been determined by the foreign insurer-to-be the base and centre of its insurance business in Japan).

The application for authorization for a foreign insurance company must be accompanied by certificates by authorized agencies of the country of the foreign insurer verifying:

(1) that its insurance business was lawfully commenced, or that it was lawfully incorporated; and
(2) that it is lawfully doing in its country the insurance business of the same kind as it desires to be authorized to do in Japan.

The application for authorization for a foreign insurance company must, in addition to the documents referred to in the preceding paragraph, be accompanied by the following and other documents specified by IBLER:

(1) the articles of incorporation or a document for similar purposes;
(2) statements of the methods of operation in Japan;
(3) general conditions of insurance for insurance contracts to be effected in Japan;
(4) statements of the methods of calculating premiums and underwriting reserves for insurance contracts to be effected in Japan.

And the documents of 'statements of the methods of operation in Japan', 'general conditions of insurance for insurance contracts to be effected in Japan' and 'statements of the methods of calculating premiums and underwriting reserves for insurance contracts to be effected in Japan' must contain matters specified by IBLER.

B.   Criteria for Authorization

85. Criteria for authorization for the domestic insurance company (Article 5) will apply *mutatis mutandis* when authorization has been applied for by a foreign insurer.
If the insurance business in Japan which the foreign insurer applying for authorization for foreign life insurance business proposes to do relates only to the writing of insurance contracts for which the insured amounts are nominated in a foreign currency and which are effected with persons specified by a Cabinet Ordinance, the Prime Minister may give his/her authorization on the condition that only the activities of writing such insurance contracts may be carried out (IBL, Article 188).

III.   Specified Juristic Person

86. The old Act Relating to Foreign Insurers (ARFI) stipulated that a foreign insurer had to obtain the authorization of the Minister of Finance when a foreign insurer intended to have a branch office in Japan to do insurance business in Japan (ARFI Article 3(1)), and 'foreign insurer' meant the juristic person or the individual who was doing the insurance business, being based on a foreign country's law (ARFI Article 2(1)).

Owing to these stipulations, Lloyd's, as itself, was not able to do insurance business in Japan and each 'name' had to obtain the authorization of the Minister of Finance.

Therefore, the new IBL provides specific stipulations to authorize Lloyd's to be able to obtain a licence to do insurance business in Japan as the sole agent for its underwriting members.

A.   Authorization for a Specified Juristic Person

87. The specified juristic person, having appointed a person to act as the sole agent for the underwriting members, may obtain authorization from the Prime Minister for its underwriting members who are intending to conduct insurance business in Japan (IBL Article 219(1)).

The specified juristic person must satisfy both of the following criteria:

(1)   be a juristic person incorporated under special laws of foreign country; and
(2)   be a member or members of the juristic person that is or are entitled by the special law of that country to do insurance business without obtaining an insurance business license (including any license similar to, registration or any other administrative action) in that foreign country.

The sole agent must satisfy both of the following:

(1)   the sole agent must act as an underwriting agent with respect to the insurance business to be conducted in Japan by members of the said specified juristic person; and
(2)   the sole agent must represent the specified juristic person and the underwriting members in their activities in Japan.

These provisions mentioned above are provided keeping Lloyd's in mind, but are not limited to Lloyd's.

B.   Kind of Licence

88. The kind of licence shall be either a licence for specific life insurance business or a licence for specific non-life insurance business. Neither the licence for specified life insurance business nor the licence for specified non-life insurance business must be obtained by the same specified juristic person (IBL Article 219(2), (3)).

§2.   SCOPE OF BUSINESS OF AN INSURANCE COMPANY AND RESTRICTION ON
      OTHER ACTIVITIES

I.   Restriction on Other Activities

89. An insurance company[21] shall not engage in any other business than its proper businesses, subordinated business, other businesses permitted by the IBL and other business pursuant to other laws (IBL Article 100).

A.   Proper Business

90. An insurance company may conduct, as its proper business, the writing of insurance in accordance with the type of authorization, and use for investment moneys received as insurance premiums or any other assets (IBL Article 97).

B.   Subordinated Business

91. An insurance company may carry on, as its subordinated businesses, the following activities (IBL Article 98):

(1)   acting as agent or providing of services (restricted to those specified by IBLER) for other insurance companies (including foreign insurance companies) in their activities connected with insurance businesses on condition of the permission of Prime Minister;
(2)   guarantying debts;
(3)   underwriting government bonds, local government bonds or government-guaranteed bonds (excluding underwriting for the purpose of secondary sales) or handling of public offerings of such bonds;
(4)   acquisition or transfer (excluding such activities to be done as investment of assets) of monetary claims (including those represented by negotiable certificates of deposit and any other instrument regulated by IBLER);
(5)   handling of private placement of securities (excluding monetary claims mentioned above in (4)), etc.;
(6)   derivative transaction (excluding those which are carried out for the investment of assets and those which fall under the category of transaction securities-related derivatives) that are specified by IBLCO.

II.   Other Business Permitted by the IBL

92. An insurance company may carry on, as other business permitted by the IBL, the following activities to the extent that the pursuit of such business will not disrupt the conduct of its proper business (IBL Article 99):

---

21.   Restrictions for SASTIP (see para. 57).

(1) 'dealing' in public bonds, etc., (i.e., selling or buying public bonds, acting as intermediary in selling or buying public bonds, acting as an agent for selling or buying public bonds, underwriting of public bonds for the purpose of secondary sales, sales of public bonds and handling of public offering or selling of public bonds);

(2) public offering or administering local government bonds, corporation bonds or other bonds, or becoming a trustee with regard to the management of secured corporation bonds;

(3) activities of insurance money trusts (only for life insurance companies and a few life insurance companies are doing this business) etc.

93. An insurance company may have such a Subsidiary as only specified in Article 106 of IBL as followings:

(1) insurance company (including SASTIP);
(2) bank;
(3) financial instruments business operators;
(4) financial instruments intermediary service providers;
(5) companies specialized in trust business;
(6) companies which conduct specialized banking-related business, specialized securities-related business and a specialized trust-related business;
(7) companies exploring new business field, etc.

94. In case that an insurance company intends to merge and amalgamate other foreign insurer, the foreign insurer may have subsidiary doing such business as not permitted in the IBL of Japan. By the amendment of IBL 2015, in above case, it is supposed to be not to apply restrictions on the scope of work of the subsidiary of the IBL. However, the insurance company, as a general rule, shall take necessary measures for making the company, which become its subsidiary in a manner as described as above, cease to be its subsidiary by the day on which five years has elapsed from the date on which that event arose.

III.   Other Business Pursuant to Other Laws

95. An insurance company may carry on activities with regard to the Government Compensation Plan (based on the ALSL, Article 77) for the victims of 'hit and run' accidents, etc.

§3.   CONTINUING SUPERVISION

96. At the time of making the application for authorization, the statements of the methods of operation (endorsements of insurance must be stipulated in these statements), general conditions of insurance and the statements of the methods of calculation of premium rates and reserves must be submitted to the FSA for examination.

After obtaining the authorization, insurance products and premium rates can be said to be still continually supervised by the FSA through authorization in alternation of those matters stated in the documents mentioned above.[22, 23]

§4.   OTHERS

I.   Acting as Agent or Providing Administrative Services for Other Insurance Companies

97. To act as agent or provide administrative services for other insurance companies is one of the subordinated business of an insurance company (IBL Article 98).

Although the old IBL only stipulated that non-life insurance companies were able to act as agents or providers of services for other non-life insurance companies, the new IBL allows both non-life insurance companies and life insurance companies to act as agents or providers of administrative services for other insurance companies unless such acts are against the intention of prohibiting insurance company from doing both life and non-life insurance business (IBL Article 3(3)) and allow an insurance company to do life or non-life insurance business by way of subsidiary company.[24]

---

22. When an insurance company wishes to change matters stated in the documents stated above relating to matters designated by IBLER as not being likely to operate in such a way as to be detrimental to the protection of policyholders, an insurance company is able to submit prior notice to the SFA instead of applying for authorization (the so-called file and use system). The system may be applicable, for instance, to insurance where the insured is a big industry or person who has technical knowledge of his/her business (such as medical doctors, accountants, etc.), and as relating to international businesses.

23. As for SASTIP, the statements of the methods of operation and other documents shall be submitted to the Local Financial Bureau of FSA, and in case to change matters stated in the above documents a SASTIP shall also submit new documents to the said Local Financial Bureau.

24. When an insurance company acts as agent or providing of administrative services for other insurance companies (including foreign insurers), the insurance company must acquire the prior approval of the Prime Minister. The enforcement regulation (Art. 51) stipulates agency services and administrative services as follows:

(1) preparation, delivery and receipt, etc., of documents etc., relating to underwriting of insurance and any other business;

(2) collection and receipt of premiums and payment of claims payable, etc.;

(3) investigation of insured's accidents and any other matters relating to insurance contracts;

(4) education and management of person engaged in insurance solicitation; and

(5) agency services for loss adjustment and any other activities relating to insurance business that are deemed reasonable to be operated by an insurance company in view of increasing the convenience for policyholders, etc.

II. Restriction on Acquisition of Shares

98. See Chapter 4, Technical reserves, §2, Restriction on financial investment.

III. Relationship Between the Parent Corporation and Its Subsidiary, and Restriction on Related Companies

99. The IBL formerly allowed a non-life insurance company to have life insurance companies as subsidiary companies, and a life insurance company to have non-life insurance companies as subsidiary companies. A non-life insurance company could hold a non-life insurance company as a subsidiary company, or a life insurance company holds a life insurance company as a subsidiary company only to secure bankrupted insurance companies and the like.

The IBL had been revised several times thereafter, and the subsidiaries and related companies permitted to an insurance company to hold were increased in kind. Today, an insurance company may hold, as its subsidiaries, non-life insurance companies, life insurance companies, banks, security corporations, etc., (IBL Article 106) and as its related companies (more than seventy type of business in kinds), investment consulting corporations, computer system designing/program designing/system and program selling companies, advertising/publishing agencies, etc., (IBL Enforcement Regulation Article 56, 56–2).

IV. Restriction on Cross-Border Business

100. A foreign insurer that has no branch office in Japan must not deal, in general, in insurance contracts with respect to a person who has an address or is resident in Japan, or a property located in Japan or a vessel or aircraft of Japanese nationality (IBL Article 186(1)). A person who violates this restriction is liable to imprisonment with hard labour for a term not exceeding two years or to a fine not exceeding JPY 3 million, or to both (IBL Article 316(1)). If, however, the policyholder obtained the prior approval of the Prime Minister, such application of an insurance contract to a foreign insurer is legal (IBL Article 186(2)). A person who makes an insurance contract without approval with a non-authorized foreign insurer is liable to a non-penal fine not exceeding JPY 500,000 (IBL Article 337(1)).

101. There are some exceptions to restrictions on cross-border business, so that insurance contracts relating to the cross-border business under the exceptions can be legally contracted, without prior approval, with a foreign insurer that has no branch office in Japan.[25]

---

25.   Insurance contracts to be able to be contracted with a foreign insurer that has no branch office in Japan without prior approval are the following:

(1)   reinsurance contracts (Cabinet Ordinance Art. 19, item 1);
(2)   insurance contracts which cover vessels with Japanese nationality used for international marine transportation and cargos in the process of international marine transportation by such vessels and liabilities arising therefrom, or any of them (Cabinet Ordinance Art. 19, item 2);
(3)   insurance contracts which cover aircraft with Japanese nationality used for commercial airline business and cargos in the process of international transportation by such aircrafts and liabilities arising therefrom, or any of them (Cabinet Ordinance Art. 19, item 3);
(4)   insurance contracts which cover launches in cosmic space, transported cargos relating to such launches (including satellites) and means of transportation of such cargos and liabilities arising therefrom, or any of them (Enforcement Regulation Art. 116, item 1);
(5)   insurance contracts which cover cargos located in Japan and being in the process of international transportation (excluding those mentioned above in (2) (3)) (Enforcement Regulation Art. 116, item 2); and
(6)   insurance contracts which cover personal injury and disease suffered by overseas travellers during the period of overseas travel and the death directly resulting therefrom and the baggage carried by the overseas travellers, or any of them (Enforcement Regulation Art. 116, item 3).

Chapter 3.   Supervision

§1.   SOLVENCY MARGIN STANDARDS INNOVATED AS A METHOD OF SUPERVISION

102. To protect policyholders from the increasing management risks facing insurance companies the authorities have created a new method of early checks on whether an insurer's business is sound or not.

The solvency margin standard[26] has been newly introduced by the IBL, as well as reports or data submitted from insurance companies concerning the condition of their business or assets, and the authority's inspection, as methods of supervision to check how solvent an insurance company is against risks which may occur in excess. The IBL stipulates in Article 130 that the Prime Minister may prescribe such a solvency standard to estimate the soundness of the financial conditions of insurance companies, by using figures concerning the conduct of insurance companies (the total amount of the insurance company's capital, foundation fund, reserves and other amounts as prescribed by the Enforcement Regulation, and the amount of risk which, calculated in accordance with the methods as prescribed by the Enforcement Regulation, exceeds the amount normally expected to result from the occurrence of an insured accident covered by the underwritten insurance or for any other cause).

103. The total amount of the insurance company's capital, foundation fund, reserves and other amounts as prescribed by the Cabinet Ordinance means the aggregate amount of these following amounts (IBLER Article 86):

(1)   the amount of reduced profit or surplus appropriated from 'total stockholder's equity' on the balance sheet;
(2)   the amount of reserve for price fluctuations;
(3)   the amount of catastrophe reserve and the amount of allowance for doubtful accounts, etc.

104. The amount of risk which, calculated in accordance with the methods as prescribed by the Enforcement Regulation, exceeds the amount normally expected to result from the occurrence of an insured accident covered by the underwritten insurance or any other cause means these following amounts (IBLER Article 87):

(1)   the amount corresponding to underwriting risk (a risk which may arise when the actual rate of occurrence of insured events, etc., exceeds normal expectations);
(2)   the amount corresponding to the assumed interest rate risk (a risk of not securing the assumed interest rate);
(3)   the amount corresponding to asset management risk (a risk which may arise due to fluctuation of prices of securities and any other assets held beyond normal expectation, or any other reasons); and

---

26.   Solvency margin standard may also be applied to a SASTIP (IBL Art. 272-28).

(4)   the amount corresponding to management risk (a risk which may arise beyond
      normal expectation in business operations and which is not any of the risks
      mentioned in the preceding three items).[27]

§2.   Insurance Conditions and Rates

105. General conditions, special clauses (which have to be described in the
statements of methods of operation) and premium rates (which have to be described
in the statements of methods of calculating insurance premiums and underwriting
reserves) must be submitted to the Prime Minister for authorization when a person
seeks authorization for insurance business.

Moreover, even after obtaining business authorization, general conditions, special
clauses and premium rates for new products must also be submitted to the Prime
Minister for authorization.[28]

106. Concerning the premium rate of non-life insurance, there is a specific
organization, the GIROJ. This is an insurance rating organization established in
accordance with the Law Concerning General Insurance Rating Organization (called
'Rating Organization Law' 29 July 1948, Law No. 193, recent revision: 22 December
1999, Law No. 160).[29]

---

27.   The specific calculation methods for the above are instructed by bulletin.
28.   Insurance companies must obtain the approval from the Prime Minister when they introduce
      new special clauses and change any matters set forth in the general conditions, special clauses
      and premium rates (IBL Art. 123). Concerning insurance for a big industry or person who has
      technical knowledge of his business (medical doctors, accountants, etc.), insurance companies
      must submit a prior notification to the Prime Minister when they change any matters set out in
      the general conditions, special clauses and premium rates (IBL Art. 123 Proviso).
29.   GIROJ, established on 1 Nov. 1948 as the Fire and Marine Insurance Rating Association it
      afterwards changed its name to the Property and Casualty Insurance Rating Organization (called
      hereinafter PCIRO), had started to calculate fire insurance rates. In the beginning, PCIRO,
      however, had not been admitted to obtain the approval of the Ministry of Finance (competent
      authority in those days) for fire insurance rates calculated. Therefore, members (non-life insurance
      companies) had no obligation to use the rates calculated by PCIRO but used them as reference
      rates. In 1951, the Rating Organization Law was revised so that PCIRO was able to obtain
      approval from the MOF for insurance rates calculated thereby, and members of PCIRO were
      obliged to use such rates.
  In 1964, with the development of motorization, the Automobile Insurance Rating Organization (AIRO)
      was established as an independent organization for calculating automobile insurance rates.
      Then, fire insurance, personal accident insurance and automobile insurance, the main insurances
      in the Japanese non-life insurance market, became those insurances for which the Rating
      Organization might calculate the premium rates and these rates had to be used by members of
      the Rating Organization.
  In 1995, with progressive innovation of the financial system, the IBL was revised throughout (afterwards
      being revised continuously) and the Rating Organization Law was also revised several times.
      Through these revisions the observance by insurance companies of the rate calculated by the
      Rating Organization was abolished. In 2002, the merger of AIRO and PCIRO resulted in the
      formation of NLIRO, and, from 1 Apr. 2013, NILIRO changed her name to GIROJ.

107. The GIROJ (two or more non-life insurance companies may, upon receiving the approval of the Prime Minister, establish GIROJ (Rating Organization Law Article 3(1))) makes standard conditions of fire insurance, personal accident insurance, automobile insurance, medical expenses insurance and nursing care expenses insurance and calculating reference pure rates thereof (Regulation Article 3), and also makes standard conditions of CALI and earthquake insurance for houses and calculates the standard full rates thereof (Rating Organization Law Article 3(5)).

A life insurance company may be deemed as a non-life insurance company insofar as to underwrite so-called third-party insurances (personal accident insurance, medical expenses insurance and nursing care expenses insurance, etc.) and can use reference pure rates thereof (Rating Organization Law Article 2(2)).[30]

108. Reference pure rates and standard full rates must be reasonable and adequate, and not be unfairly discriminatory (Rating Organization Law Article 8). These elements are called the 'Three principles in the calculation of insurance premiums', and these elements must be considered in the calculation of insurance premium rates which are not matters for which the Rating Organization calculates insurance premium rates (including reference pure rates).

109. There is no rating organization, standard conditions and standard rates for life insurance. However, all life insurance companies must use the mortality table drawn up by the Institute of Actuaries of Japan (legal corporation), in calculation of their underwriting reserves, and the IBL sets up a standard underwriting reserve system (the Prime Minister, concerning life insurance, may lay down the method of establishment of underwriting reserves, expected mortality rate, expected interest used for calculation of reserves and other coefficients as a basis for calculation of reserves – IBL Article 116(2)), and plans to maintain the soundness of financial condition and solvency of a life insurance company.

§3. THE COMPETENT AUTHORITY

110. Until June 1998, the competent authority for an insurance company had been the MOF (Insurance Department of the Banking Bureau), and then, with innovation to the financial system in Japan, the MOF had jurisdiction over the planning and framing of the financial system, and the Financial Reconstruction Committee (FRC) (Prime Minister's Office) and the Financial Supervisory Agency, the lower organization of the FRC, had the jurisdiction over the inspection and supervision of financial institutions.

---

30.   Reference pure rates mean a proportion of the part of premium rate expected to be allocated to the payment of insurance money in future in relation to the amount insured (Rating Organization Law Art. 2(1), item 2) and if such reference pure rates computed by the Rating Organization have been approved by the FSA, insurance companies (members of the Rating Organization) may use them as the basis for computation of premium rates (Rating Organization Law Art. 2(1), item 5). Standard full rates mean a premium rate computed by the Rating Organization, and if such standard full rates have been approved by the FSA, their use by insurance companies (members of the Rating Organization) shall be deemed to have been approved or filed under the stipulation of the IBL (Rating Organization Law Art. 2(1), item 6).

From July 2000, jurisdiction over the planning and framework of financial systems, and the inspection and supervision for financial institutions, was unified to the Financial Service Agency (the name of the Financial Supervisory Agency was changed).

From 5 January 2001, the Cabinet Office was established to assist and strengthen the Cabinet function, and under the Cabinet Office, the FSA restarted as an agency having jurisdiction over the transaction of bankruptcy of financial institutions and the authority to approve the organization of holding companies of financial institution, together with jurisdiction over the existing authorities.

The authority with the inspection and supervision, etc., for insurance companies is invested with the Prime Minister as the FSA belonging to the Cabinet Office, but in practice such authority (except authorization for insurance business, etc.) is generally delegated to the Director of the FSA[31] according to IBL Article 313.

---

31.   Regarding to a SASTIP, such authority is generally delegated to the Director of the Local Financial Bureau (IBLCO 47-2).

Chapter 4.   Technical Reserves and Investment

§1.   PRICE FLUCTUATION RESERVE, UNDERWRITING RESERVES, PAYMENT RESERVES

I.   Price Fluctuation Reserve (Article 115)

A.   Price Fluctuation Reserve

111. With regard to shares and other assets designated by IBLER as liable to incur losses due to fluctuation of prices, an insurance company must establish and maintain a fluctuation reserve to the amount calculated in accordance with IBLER; provided, however, that the foregoing will not apply to the extent that any approval may have been given by the Prime Minister totally or partially exempting the insurance company from the reserving obligation.

112. The reserve mentioned in the preceding paragraph may not be appropriated for any other purpose than to make up for a deficit when the amount of loss incurred from sale, purchase, etc., (which means any loss due to sale, purchase, reappraisal, and fluctuations in foreign exchange rates, and redemption loss of shares, etc.,) exceeds the amount of gain accruing from sale, purchase, etc., (which means any gain due to sale, purchase, and fluctuations in foreign exchange rates, and redemption gain) of shares; provided, however, that the foregoing shall not apply if the approval of the Prime Minister has been obtained.

B.   Assets Subject to Reserve for Price Fluctuation (IBLER Article 65)

113. Assets subject to reserve for price fluctuation are the following assets, provided that the assets belonging to the special account, the assets relating to the business listed in Article 99, paragraph 1 of the law or the assets belonging to the specified trading account are not included:

(1) shares issued by a domestic corporation and any other assets provided by the Secretary of the FSA;
(2) shares issued by a foreign corporation and any other assets provided by the Secretary of the FSA;
(3) debentures denominated in Japanese currency and any other assets provided by the Secretary of the FSA; provided, however, that those assets stipulated in Article 8, paragraph 20 of the Regulation concerning Terminology, Forms and Method of Preparation of Consolidated Financial Statements, etc., are excluded;
(4) debentures, deposits and loans denominated in a foreign currency which may incur a loss arising from foreign exchange fluctuation and any other assets provided by the Secretary of the FSA; and

(5)   gold bullion.

C.   *Calculation of Reserve for Price Fluctuation (IBLER Article 66)*

    114. An insurance company must credit an amount not less than the total of the amount obtained by multiplying book value of each category of assets as listed in the left column of the following table 1 by the relevant rate listed in the column of 'Standard Credit Rate' of the following table 1 to the reserve for price fluctuation.

    In this case, the maximum amount of the price fluctuation reserve shall be the total of the amounts obtained by multiplying each year-end book value of each category of assets as listed in the left column of the following table 1 by the relevant rate listed in the column of 'Maximum Credit Rate' of the following table.

Table 1 Subject Asset and Credit Rate Subject Asset

	Standard Credit Rate	*Maximum Credit Rate*
Asset listed in Article 65, item (1)	1.5/1,000	50/1,000
Asset listed in Article 65, item (2)	1.5/1,000	50/1,000
Asset listed in Article 65, item (3)	0.2/1,000	5/1,000
Asset listed in Article 65, item (4)	1/1,000	25/1,000
Asset listed in Article 65, item (5)	3/1,000	100/1,000

D.   *Exemption from the Obligation of Reserve for Price Fluctuation*

    115. The obligation of reserve for price fluctuation, however, shall not apply to the extent that any approval may have been given by the Prime Minister totally or partially to exempt the insurance company from the reserving obligation.

E.   *Appropriation of Reserve for Price Fluctuation (Article 115(2))*

    116. The reserve for price fluctuation may not be appropriated for any other purpose than to make up for a deficit when the amount of loss incurred from sale, purchase, etc., (which means any loss due to sale, purchase, reappraisal, and fluctuations in foreign exchange rates, and redemption loss of shares, etc.,) exceeds the amount of gain accruing from sale, purchase, etc., (which means any gain (except any gain through the reappraisal stipulated in Article 112, paragraph 1) due to sale, purchase, reappraisal and fluctuations in foreign exchange rates, and redemption gain) of shares, etc.;

provided, however, that the foregoing shall not apply when the approval of the Prime Minister has been obtained.

II. Underwriting Reserves (Article 116)

117. At the end of each accounting period, an insurance company must establish underwriting reserves to provide for the fulfilment of future obligations under insurance contracts.

A. *Standard Underwriting Reserve (Article 116(2))*

118. With regard to long-term insurance contracts specified by IBLER, the Prime Minister may lay down necessary rules for the establishing of underwriting reserves as well as for the levels of expected mortality ratios and other factors on which the calculation of underwriting reserves should be based.[32]

1. Standard Underwriting Reserve of Life Insurance Companies (IBLER Article 68)

119. The insurance contracts to be covered by the standard underwriting reserve of life insurance companies will be insurance contracts which are concluded by a life insurance company on or after the date of implementation of the law and which do not fall under any of the following items:

(1) insurance contracts in relation to which the relevant underwriting reserves fluctuate according to the value of the assets belonging to the special account;
(2) insurance contracts for which the premium reserve referred to in item (1) of paragraph 1 of the Article 69 of IBLER is not established;
(3) insurance contracts whose policy conditions stipulate that the insurance company may change the coefficient which serves as the basis of calculation of the underwriting reserves and premiums; or
(4) any other insurance contracts (these are notified by the Secretary of the FSA) for the purpose of which it is not appropriate to make necessary stipulation as to the level of the coefficient which serves as the basis of calculation of the underwriting reserves provided for in Article 116, paragraph 2 of the IBL.

2. Standard Underwriting Reserve of Non-life Insurance Companies

120. There is no regulation for the standard underwriting reserve applied to a non-life insurance company.

---

32. A Cabinet Ordinance provides the method of establishing underwriting reserves for any insurance contracts that may have been reinsured, and for other matters related to the establishing of underwriting reserves.

B.   Underwriting Reserves of Life Insurance Companies (IBLER Article 69)

121. A life insurance company must calculate the amounts referred to in the following items pursuant to the methods described in the document 'statements of the methods of calculating insurance premiums and underwriting reserves (Article 4, paragraph 2, item (4) of the law)', in accordance with the classifications set forth in each of the following items, and credit such amount to the underwriting reserves at each settlement of accounts:

(1)   premium reserve – the amount calculated on an actuarial basis against required performance of future obligations under insurance contracts;
(2)   unearned premiums – the amount calculated as the amount equivalent to the liabilities corresponding to the unexpired period (which means any period not elapsed at the settlement of accounts out of the insurance period set forth in the relevant insurance contract; the same in the Article 70 (IBLER)) based on the premiums received prior to the settlement of accounts;
(3)   reserve for refund – the amount appropriated for refund in connection with insurance contracts stipulated, in the insurance conditions, for refund to policyholders of the whole or part of the insurance premiums and earnings from investment of money received as insurance premium; and
(4)   reserve for future risk – the amount calculated against any risk likely to occur in the future in order to secure due performance of future obligations under the relevant insurance contracts.

C.   Underwriting Reserves of Non-life Insurance Companies (IBLER Article 70, Paragraph 1)

122. A non-life insurance company must, at each settlement of accounts, credit the amount listed in the following items according to the category listed therein to the underwriting reserves; provided, however, that such provisions shall not apply to the underwriting reserves relating to the contract of automobile liability insurance as referred to in Article 5 (compulsory execution of contracts of liability insurance) of the ALSL and the earthquake insurance contract as provided for in Article 2, paragraph 2 (definition) of the Law Concerning Earthquake Insurance:

(1)   ordinary underwriting reserve – total amount of the following amounts, but not less than the amount of the premium received for the relevant fiscal year, deducting the claims paid for the insurance contracts for which premiums are received during the fiscal year, refund and loss reserve (including IBNR) and business expenses for the fiscal year:

(1) insurance due reserve – the amount calculated pursuant to actuarial science in order to secure due performance of future obligations under the relevant insurance contract (exclude refund reserve);

(2) reserve for future risk – the amount calculated against any risk likely to occur in the future in order to secure, without fail, due performance of future obligations under the relevant insurance contracts;

(c) unearned premium – the amount equal to the liability which corresponds to the unexpired period, based on the premiums received.

(2) catastrophe reserve – the amount calculated based on the premiums received, which is to be appropriated for indemnification of losses arising from a catastrophe:

(a) reserve for future risk – the amount calculated against any risk likely to occur in the future in order to secure, without fail, due performance of future obligation under the relevant insurance contract.

(3) refund reserve – the amount to be appropriated to the refund of all or part of the amount of revenues earned from investment of premiums or any money received as premiums under the insurance contract which stipulates such refund; and

(4) reserve for policyholders' dividends – the amount of the reserve for policyholders' dividends referred to in Article 64 (IBLER) or any other amount similar thereto.

A non-life insurance company must calculate the amount mentioned above, and the amount of the underwriting reserves relating to CALI contract and those of earthquake insurance in the manner described in 'the statements of the methods of calculating premiums and underwriting reserves'.

D.   Underwriting Reserves for Reinsurance Contracts (IBL Article 71, paragraph 1)

123. An insurance company may, when it reinsures an insurance contract, refrain from crediting an amount to the underwriting reserves corresponding to the portion of reinsurance against any of the following parties:

(1) insurance company;

(2) foreign insurance company etc.;

(3) the underwriting member provided for in Article 219 (specified juristic person), paragraph 1 of the Law in respect of which the notification referred to in Article 224, paragraph 1 of the Law has been made; and

(4) a foreign insurer which is other than the parties listed in the immediately preceding two items and which, in the light of its condition of business or assets, is not threatening to undermine the sound operation of the insurance company which has made such reinsurance.

III. Reserves for Outstanding Claims (Article 117)

124. At the end of each accounting period, an insurance company must establish reserves for outstanding claims if any insurance claims, returns or other benefits (hereinafter called 'claims, etc.') are payable under insurance contracts but have not been in the book as payment of claims, etc.

IV. IBNR

125. At the end of each accounting period, an insurance company must establish payment reserves if any insurance claims, returns or other benefits (referred to as 'claims, etc.', hereinafter) are in a state designated by IBLER as similar to being payable (IBL Article 117).

§2. RESTRICTION ON FINANCIAL INVESTMENT

126. The insurance company is able to invest, as its proper business, money received as insurance premiums, and other assets but methods of investment and amounts of assets to be managed are restricted in a certain way. Financial investment has to be managed, as restrictions on the methods of investment, in accordance with the methods (e.g., acquisition of securities, acquisition of real estate, lending of money, etc.,) prescribed by IBLER (IBL Article 97).

As to restrictions on amount of assets to be managed, the assets to be prescribed by the IBLER shall not be managed in an amount exceeding the amount calculated in accordance with IBLER (IBL Article 97(2) (1)).[33]

127. The investments concentrated with the same party may bring about big risks to an insurance company, and so the amount of assets, invested in the same party, to be prescribed by IBLER must not be managed to an amount exceeding the amount calculated in accordance with IBLER (IBL Article 97-2(2)).

The IBL stipulates to ensure observation of those restrictions that the amounts of investigation managed by subsidiaries, etc., of the insurance company must be included in the amounts of those invested by the insurance company (IBL Article 485), and the insurance company may not be exempted from the restrictions by way of a trust of money, monetary claims, securities, real estate, etc. (IBL Article 49).

---

33. Shares: the amount calculated by multiplying the amount of total assets by 30%; real estate: the amount calculated by multiplying the amount of total assets by 20%; loans: the amount calculated by multiplying the amount of total assets by 10%.

Chapter 5.   Accountancy

§1.   INTRODUCTION

128. As to rules for accounts of company, the Comp. Act stipulates them in its Book II (stock company), Chapter V (Accounts, etc).

These rules of the Comp. Act are applied to the accounts of stock insurance companies, but may not be applied naturally to those of mutual insurance companies.

Therefore, the IBL, in its Article 59, stipulates the accounting for a mutual insurance company shall be subject to generally accepted business accounting practices. However, comparing a general enterprise with an insurance company, a heterogeneous process of accounting is necessary for an insurance company. For instance, the gross profits of a general enterprise in each fiscal year can be calculated by subtracting the gross cost of sales of the fiscal year from the gross sales, but insurance premiums (corresponding to gross profits of a general enterprise) may be paid in advance and the payment of claims (corresponding to gross cost of sales) may not be closed in the fiscal year. And, moreover, a mutual insurance company necessitates a heterogeneous process of accounting compared with stock insurance companies, according to their characteristics. Hence, the IBL stipulates special rules of the accounts for mutual insurance companies, in its Book II (insurance company etc.) Chapter II (stock company and mutual company) section 2 (mutual company) subsection 5 (accounts), and also stipulates in its Chapter V (accounting) in the same Book II, special common rules of the accounts for both stock companies[34] and mutual companies.[35]

§2.   AUDIT

129. The Comp. Act, in its Book II, Chapter IV, section 3 (organs of the company) section 7 (corporation auditor) and 8 (board of corporation auditor), stipulates power of a corporation auditor, relation with a director, duties of board of corporation auditor, and so on. The Comp. Act, in Article 328, stipulates that a large corporation[36] shall have a board of corporation auditors and an accounting auditor.

---

34.   Special common rules for stock insurance companies and mutual insurance companies: business year, business report, etc. (to submit to the FSA), valuation of shares, reserve for valuation profits, amortization of founding costs and business expenses, policyholders' dividends, price fluctuation reserves, underwriting reserves, loss reserves, special account, actuary.

35.   Special rules for mutual insurance companies: reserves for loss payment, limitation on payment of interest on foundation funds, reserve for amortization of the foundation fund, distribution of surplus.

36.   A Large Corporation means any stock company which satisfies any of following requirements (Comp.Act Art. 2, item 6).

An insurance company comes into a large corporation for reason that the IBL, in Article 5-2, an insurance company shall have set up such the organs: board of directors, board of corporation auditors or committee and accounting auditor:

(1)   company with the capital in the balance sheet as of the end of most recent business year, JPY 500 million or more (Comp.Act Article 328, item 6-a);
(2)   company with total sum of amount in the liabilities section of the balance sheet as of the end of most recent business year, JPY 200 billion or more (Comp. Act Article 328, item 6-b);
(3)   company with a board of corporation auditors and an accounting auditor (Comp. Act Article 328).

130. The number of corporate auditors of a large corporation must be a minimum of three and more than half of them must be Outside Corporation auditors (Comp.Act Article 335-(3)). Outside corporation auditor means an auditor of any stock company who has neither ever served in the past as a director, accounting adviser or executive officer, nor as an employee, including manager, of such stock company or any of its subsidiaries (Comp.Act Article 2, item 16).

131. In large corporations, the corporate auditors must constitute a board of corporation auditors. The board of corporation auditors has powers to give its consent to a directors' proposal concerning the appointment of the corporate auditors (Comp. Act Article 343). The corporate auditors must be appointed at a general meeting of shareholders (Comp.Act Article 329) and the term of office of a corporate auditor shall be four years (Comp.Act Article 336). The corporate auditor may state his/her opinion, in a general meeting of shareholders, with respect to the appointment or dismissal (including resignation) of corporate auditors (Comp.Act Article 345(1)) and a corporate auditor who has resigned may state his/ her opinion in the first general meeting of the shareholders after his/her resignation, with respect to the reason for his/her resignation (Comp.Act Article 345(2)).

132. A stock company shall prepare Financial Statements (meaning balance sheet, profit and loss statements and other statement prescribed by the applicable ordinance of the Ministry of Justice as necessary and appropriate in order to indicate the status of the assets and profits and losses of a stock company) and business reports for each business year and supplementary schedules of thereof pursuant to the applicable ordinance of Ministry of Justice (Comp.Act Article 435(2)).

At companies with auditors, the Financial Statements and business reports and supplementary schedules thereof shall be audited by corporation auditors (Comp.Act Article 436(1)). An accounting auditor shall audit the Financial Statement and supplementary schedules thereof (Comp.Act Article 436(2)).

133. The directors must, for making a proposal concerning the appointment of accounting auditor to a general shareholders' meeting (in case of a mutual company, a membership general meeting or assembly of members' representatives), obtain the consent of the board of corporate auditors (Comp.Act Article 344), and the accounting auditor must be appointed at a general shareholders' meeting (a membership general meeting or assembly of members' representatives).

The accounting auditor must either be a certified public accountant (including a foreign certified public accountant) or an auditing corporation (Comp.Act Article 337(1)). The accounting auditor, when he/she has completed the audit, has to submit the audit report and other auditing matters to the board of corporate auditors (Corporate Accounting Rules Article 155).

134. The basic role of the corporate auditor is to monitor, from the standpoint of protecting stockholders' profits, and legality, the entire scope of corporate management and directors' operation, and he/she is obliged to report to each general shareholders' meeting (general membership meeting or assembly of members' representatives) whether or not the corporate business is being carried on properly and whether or not the agenda proposed by the directors is appropriate.

135. The corporate auditor, in order to perform his/her duties, may be present in the meeting of directors, and may state opinions (Comp.Act Article 383), and may request the director to cease an act if where a director has committed an act not within the scope of the object of the company or any other act in violation of laws, ordinances or articles of incorporation, and there exist fears of serious damage to the company thereby (Comp.Act Article 385), and he/she may have powers to investigate the affairs of the company, the state of its property and its subsidiaries (Comp.Act Article 381), etc.

The corporate auditor also may receive, every period of account, from the directors a balance sheet, a profit and loss account, a business report, proposals relating to the disposition of profits or the disposition of loss, and the annexed specifications thereof, and may audit them as to whether or not they are proper and appropriate, and submit the auditing report to the directors (Comp.Act Article 436, Corporate Accounting Rules Article 50, 152). These auditing reports (both reports of the corporation auditor and the account auditor) must be submitted to the stockholders at the general stockholders' meeting.

136. The company adopted, in the articles of incorporation, the committee system that was introduced, with reference to the system in the US, as special provisions for large stock companies, in the 2002 amendment of the Commercial Code. Committees may constitute the nomination committee, the compensation committee and the audit committee.

In such a company, the role of the meeting of the board of directors is mainly to decide the basic management policies of the company and to select the members of the committees and executive officers. Hence, the committees come to hold a key position in the corporate governance. Corporate management shall be done by executive officers and the audit committee may monitor the corporate management and operations instead of the corporate auditors.

§3. SPECIAL COMMON RULES FOR A STOCK INSURANCE COMPANY AND A
      MUTUAL INSURANCE COMPANY

I.   Business Year

137. The business year for an insurance company is one year, which commences on the 1 April and ends on the 31 March of the following year (IBL Article 109).

II.   Business Report

138. An insurance company shall, for each business year, prepare an interim business report and business report describing the status of its business and property for submission to the Prime Minister (IBL Article 110(1)). Where an insurance company has any subsidiary or any other company specified by a Cabinet Ordinance as having a special relationship with the insurance company (subsidiary, etc.) the insurance company shall, for each business year, prepare in addition to the report set forth in the preceding paragraph an interim business report and business report describing the status of the business and property of the insurance company and subsidiary company, etc., in a consolidated manner for submission to the Prime Minister (IBL Article 110(2)). The matters to be described on the report – interim business report and business report – their submission dates and other necessary matters regarding those reports shall be specified by a Cabinet Ordinance (IBL Article 110(3)).

An Insurance company shall, for each business year, prepare explanatory documents describing the matters specified by a Cabinet Ordinance as pertaining to the status of its business and property, and keep them for public inspection at its head office or principal office and branch offices or secondary offices, or any other equivalent place prescribed by a Cabinet Ordinance (IBL Article 111(1)).

In the case where an insurance company has a subsidiary company, etc., the insurance company shall, for each year, prepare in addition to the explanatory documents set forth with regard to the insurance company and the subsidiary, etc., the matters specified by a Cabinet Ordinance as pertaining to the status of the business and property of the insurance company and subsidiary, etc., in a consolidated manner, and keep them for public inspection at the insurance company's head office, etc. (IBL Article 111(2)).

III.   Special Rules for Valuation of Shares and Reserve of Profit on Revaluation of Shares

139. Notwithstanding the provisions of Article 432 of the Companies Law, an insurance company may value, subject to the approval[37] of the Prime Minister, shares owned (excluding those credited to the special account) at the amount in excess of

---

37.   To obtain the approval, an insurance company submits the written application with following documents to the commissioner of the FSA.

acquisition cost but not in excess of the market value (IBL Article 112(1)). To obtain such approval, the insurance company must submit the application to the Commissioner of the FSA (IBLER Article 60).

Any profits from the revaluation of shares must be kept in the reserve fund[38] for policyholders (IBL Article 112(2)) and where an insurance company fails to credit the required amount to reserve or use the reserve, the company will be liable to a non-penal fine not exceeding JPY 1 million, except where the acts in question are subject to a criminal penalty (IBL Article 333(1), item 12):

(1)   document describing the issue, number/volume, acquisition price, market price and appraised value of the shares to be revalued;
(2)   document describing the amount of profit to be recognized as a result of the revaluation;
(3)   document describing the name of, and the amount to be credit to the *reserve* provided for in the immediately following Article to which the profit to be recognized as a result of the revaluation will be credited; and
(4)   document(s) describing any other referential matters.

The *reserve* mentioned above:
    Life insurance company (stock company) – underwriting reserves or the reserve for policyholder's
    Non-life insurance company (stock company) – underwriting reserves Insurance company (mutual company) – underwriting reserves or the reserve for dividends to members.

IV.   Amortization of Founding Costs and Business Expenses

140. The Companies Law has no stipulation for amortization of founding costs and business expenses, a corporation, however, according to the accounting practices, is treating that the amounts expensed for incorporation and preparing commencement of business may be accounted on the asset side of the balance sheet and the said amount shall, within five years after the coming into existence of the company (or after commencement of business), be amortized by the average or more amount in each period for the settlement of accounts. The IBL, however, has relaxed this accounting practices that an insurance company may credit to the assets on the balance sheet an amount pertaining to its business expenditures for the first five years following the establishment of the insurance company as well as any other amount specified by a IBLER (IBLER Article 61-2). In this case, the insurance company shall, pursuant to the provisions of its articles of incorporation, amortized the amount thus credited within ten years from the establishment of the insurance company (IBL Article 113).

---

38.   Reserve fund for policyholders means: for life insurance stock companies: underwriting reserves of IBL Art. 116 or reserve for dividends to policyholders of Regulation Art. 64(1); for non-life insurance stock companies; underwriting reserves of IBL Art. 116; for insurance mutual companies, underwriting reserves of IBL Art. 116 or reserves for dividends to members of Regulation Art.30-5(1).

V.   Dividends to Policyholders

141. While a mutual insurance company may make distribution of a surplus to its members, a stock insurance company may also make distribution of policyholders' dividends where the insurance policy conditions provide for the distribution to policyholders of the whole or part of the insurance premium and earnings from investments of money received as insurance premiums other than those appropriated for payments of insurance claims or other profits, returns or other profits, for defrayal of business expenses or for other expenditures (IBL Article 114). That is to say, dividends to policyholders made by a stock insurance company are not the distribution of profits but the liabilities based on the insurance contracts.

VI.   Price Fluctuation Reserves

142. With regard to shares and other assets that may incur losses due to fluctuation of prices, an insurance company must reserve a certain amount of money or more (except when an insurance company has obtained the approval of the Prime Minister not to reserve them) for potential losses in future, at the end of every account year and maintain them as price fluctuation reserves, and an insurance company may not appropriate such reserves for another purpose than to make up a deficit when the amount of loss incurred from sales, purchase of shares, etc., exceeds the amount of gain accruing from sales, purchase of shares (IBL Article 115). Provided, however, that when an insurance company fails to establish reserves or uses reserves it will be liable to a non-penal fine not exceeding JPY 1 million (IBL Article 333(1), item 12).

VII.   Underwriting Reserves

143. Underwriting reserves are the reserve that an insurance company must establish at the end of every fiscal year to provide for the performance of future obligations of the insurance contract (IBL Article 116(1)), but there are some differences in the structure of underwriting reserves between life insurance and non-life insurance.

A life insurance company must maintain, as underwriting reserves,[39] insurance due reserves, reserves for refunds, unearned premium and reserves for future risk

---

39.   The insurance due reserve of a life insurance company is the amount calculated against required performance of future obligations under the insurance contracts (called 'Premiums for saving element'). Premiums for saving element is the amount equivalent to reduce the amount applying for claims of the fiscal year concerned from pure premiums (the amount equivalent to reduce the loading part from the premium income of the fiscal year concerned). The IBL chooses, as the standard underwriting reserve system, the reserve on net premium method between the reserve on net premium method and Zillmer's method (newly established insurance company and specific insurance contracts like variable life insurance are excluded from the standard underwriting reserve system – Regulation Art. 68). The interest rate to be used for calculating the standard underwriting reserve must be ordered by the FSA, and is generally lower than the assumed interest rate of each insurance product.

(IBLER Article 69), and a non-insurance company must maintain, as underwriting reserves, ordinary underwriting reserves (unearned premiums and insurance due reserves),[40] catastrophe reserves,[41] reserves for refund,[42] reserves for policyholders' dividends, etc. (IBLER Article 70).

VIII. Reserve for Outstanding Claim

144. An insurance company must reserve, at the end of each fiscal year, as loss reserves the amounts equivalent to insurance claims, returns and other benefits being payable, which have not been in the book as payment of claims, etc., and IBNR (IBL Article 117(1), IBLER Articles 72, 73).

IX. Special Accounts

145. With regard to specific insurance contracts (variable life insurance etc.), it is necessary to create a separate account and to invest separately those assets which correspond to the amount of the underwriting reserve for the particular insurance contracts which may be reasonable for policyholders' profit, so that an insurance company may establish a special account in order to treat such assets separately from other assets (IBL Article 118).

X. Actuary

146. Under the old IBL, only a life insurance company had to appoint an actuary but the new IBL (Article 120) requires both life insurance companies and non-life insurance companies except which underwrite only CALI and/or earthquake insurance for dwelling houses (IBLER Article 76). An insurance company[43] must appoint an actuary at the meeting of board of directors (Article 120(1)) and an actuary must have the necessary knowledge of actuarial mathematics (an actuary, in principle, has to be a member of the Institute of Actuaries of Japan) and also have engaged in the business relating to actuarial mathematics for not less than a certain number of years (specific years are stipulated in Article 78 of IBLER).

---

40.   The concept of the insurance due reserve of a non-life insurance company is the same as for a life insurance company, but the stipulations of premium reserve are applied only to insurance products with a long insurance term, classified in the third insurance field (medical expenses insurance, nursing care expenses insurance, etc.).

41.   Catastrophe reserve is calculated based on the premiums received, which is to be appropriated for covering losses arising from a catastrophe.

42.   Reserves for refund is the amount to be appropriated to the refund of whole or part of the amount of profits earned by management of insurance premium and earnings from investments of money received as insurance premium under the insurance contract which stipulates such refund.

43.   The provisions regarding Actuary shall generally apply *mutatis mutandis* to a SASTIP (IBL Art. 272-18).

When an insurance company appoints an actuary or the actuary retires, the insurance company must, without delay, submit to the Secretary of the FSA the notification, together with the personal history of the actuary and the documents evidencing that the actuary satisfies the requirements (in case of appointment of an actuary) or together with the statement of reason of retirement (IBLER Article 79(1) (2)).

The insurance company may retain two or more actuaries, and in this case, the insurance company must, in addition to the personal history and documents mentioned above, submit to the FSA the documents describing the matters for which each of those actuaries is responsible (IBLER Article 79(3)).

An actuary must confirm the matters mentioned below (IBL Article 121(1)) and submit his/her written opinion concerning the results thereof to the meeting of the Board of Directors and the Prime Minister (IBL Article 121(2)):

(1) whether or not the underwriting reserves are established and maintained in accordance with actuarial soundness;
(2) whether or not policyholders' dividends are distributed to policyholders and surpluses are distributed to members in a fair and equitable manner;
(3) other matters prescribed by IBLER.

The Prime Minister may, on application, designate a general incorporated association that he/she considers to meet the requirement regarding actuarial science as a person to carry on such businesses as actuarial matters (IBL Article 122-2).

§4.   SPECIAL RULE FOR A MUTUAL INSURANCE COMPANY

I.   Reserves for Loss Payment

147. This reserve of a mutual company corresponds to the legal earned reserve of a stock company. The IBL stipulates, in Article 54, the maximum amount of reserves for loss payment and the minimum amount credited to reserves for loss payment at the end of each fiscal year. The maximum amount of reserves for loss payment is the total amount of the foundation fund (including the reserve for amortization of the foundation fund) or, if the articles of incorporation provide for the higher amount, such an amount.

II.   Limitation of Payment of Interest on the Foundation Fund Etc.

148. Payment of interest on the foundation fund may generally be made within the limit of the value of net assets on the balance sheet after deducting the aggregate amount of the foundation fund, the amount of the reserve for loss payment and the amount of the reserve for amortization of the foundation fund therefrom (IBL Article 55).

III.   Reserve for Amortization of the Foundation Fund

149. Amortization of the foundation fund may reduce the solvency of the insurance company, so that, if the foundation fund is to be amortized, the amount equivalent to the amount of this amortization must be credited to the reserve for amortization of the foundation fund (IBL Article 56).

IV.   Distribution of Surplus

150. The old IBL left the manner of the distribution of surplus to the self-government of the members, but the new IBL stipulates that distribution of surplus must be effected in accordance with the standard prescribed by IBLER as a standard for just and fair distribution (IBL Article 55, IBLER Article 30-2).

As for a non-life insurance mutual company, it may establish an account to manage all or part of the assets equivalent to the amount of the underwriting reserves for the saving-type insurance contracts by segregating the same from other assets in order to make fair and equitable distributions (IBLER Article 30-3).

Chapter 6.   Others

§1.   ACT CONCERNING PROHIBITION OF PRIVATE MONOPOLIZATION AND
MAINTENANCE OF FAIR TRADE ('ANTI-MONOPOLY ACT')

I.   Introduction

151. The subject matter of the Anti-monopoly Act is 'to prohibit private monopolization', 'to prohibit unreasonable restriction of trade', 'to prohibit unfair business practices' and 'to prevent the excessive concentration of power over enterprises'.

The Japanese Anti-monopoly Act (Act Concerning Prohibition of Private Monopolization and Maintenance Fair Trade: Law No. 54, 14 April 1947) was introduced in 1947 with reference to the Anti-Trust Law of US, as a part of the policies of the Occupation Troops. At the beginning, the Anti-monopoly Act prohibited any domestic company from establishing a holding company (Article 9(1)), prohibited a company engaged in a business other than financial business from obtaining the stocks of a domestic company (Article 10) and prohibited a financial company from obtaining the stocks of other financial companies (Article 11).

Afterwards, through three significant amendments in 1949 (relaxation of the regulation), 1953 (relaxation of the regulation), 1977 (strengthening of the regulation), a company engaged in a business other than financial business came, in general, to hold stocks of other domestic companies freely, and a financial company came to obtain up to 5% of the total outstanding stock of other domestic companies (for a company engaged in insurance business, 10%). According to those amendments, a company (excluding a financial company) came to be able to act as an operating holding company, but a financial company was still limited to holding the stocks of other companies, and establishment of a pure holding company remained prohibited.

152. In 1990s, in a long depression, the urge to remove the prohibition on a holding company to promote flexibility of business activities was strengthened more and more.

In 1993, under the reform of financial institutions, a financial company came to be permitted to enter into other financial industry (for insurance companies, by the amendment of the IBL, 1995) by way of establishing a subsidiary in each financial industry, and in June 1997 the Anti-monopoly Act was amended so that a pure holding company, in general, was permitted to be established. In December 1997, the New Act (Act relating to reform laws etc., regarding the finance system accompanying a removal of the ban on a holding company: Law No. 120, 12 December 1997) was enforced and according to this Act, many laws supervising a financial company were amended.

The Anti-monopoly Act, as mentioned above, had not accepted the pure holding company (of which the principal business is to control the business activities of a company or companies in Japan by means of stockholding) for a long time but, by the amendment of the Anti-monopoly Act in 1997, the pure holding company was finally enabled to be established. By the amendment, in 2002, of Article 9 of the Anti-monopoly Act (which article prohibited establishing a holding company with excessive concentration of economic power), any company is prohibited from being a company with excessive concentration of economic power, and if the gross assets of a company (including those of subsidiaries) exceed the standard amount set forth for: (1) a holding company; (2) a bank, insurance company or security company; and (3) other company, the company must submit the case to the Fair Trade Commission. By the amendment of 2002, a financial company (excluding banks and insurance companies) is permitted to obtain and hold more than 5% of stocks of other domestic companies.

II.   Exemption from Application of the Anti-monopoly Act Regarding Concerted Acts among Non-insurance Companies

153.   Under the old IBL, non-life insurance companies were permitted, for fixing insurance premium rates, determination of insurance policy conditions, determination of parties to reinsurance and of the volume of the transactions of reinsurance, etc., to do concerted acts with another non-insurance company or companies as regarding such insurances having the high possibility of a huge loss such as marine insurance, cargo insurance, aviation insurance, etc., and as to other insurances concerted activities for determination of insurance policy conditions (excluding matters for fixing insurance premium rates), determination of parties to reinsurance and of the volume of the transactions of reinsurance were also permitted.

The concerted acts of the NLIRO, established based on the Law concerning NLIRO (Law No. 193, 1948), were exempted from application of the Anti-monopoly Act through the Exemption Act.[44]

154.   The Rating Organization calculated insurance premium rates for fire insurance, automobile insurance, personal accident insurance, etc., and member insurance companies had to abide by the insurance premium rates.

Therefore, under the old IBL, applications of the Anti-monopoly Act to the non-life insurance industry can be said to have been rather moderate.

Under the new IBL, as to concerted activities of non-life insurance companies, exemption from application of the Anti-monopoly Act still remains to a certain extent. When a non-life insurance company proposes to engage in any concerted acts or modify any concerted acts, an insurance company must obtain approval from the Prime Minister (IBL Article 102(1)). The Prime Minister must obtain the consent of the Fair Trade Commission in advance when he/she proposes to give his/her approval, and the Fair Trade Commission may request the Prime Minister to alter concerted acts or withdraw their approval (IBL Article 105).

As for the concerted acts of the Rating Organization, exemption from application of the Anti-monopoly Act still remains but the Rating Organization is limited to

---

44.   The Exemption Act gives exemption from applying the Act concerning Prohibition of Private Monopolization and Maintenance of Fair Trade.

calculating pure premium rates, and member insurance companies have no obligation to use these premium rates.[45]

III.   Restriction on the Total Amount of Stockholding by a Bank and Insurance Company

155. The Anti-monopoly Act used to stipulate that no company engaged in financial business should acquire or own stock of another company or companies in Japan if it owned stock of a company or companies exceeding 5% (for a company engaged in insurance business, 10%) of the total outstanding stock thereof. By the amendment in 2002, only banks and insurance companies are prohibited from holding more than 5% (10% in the case of insurance companies) of voting rights of Japanese non-financial companies (however, they can hold more than 5%–10% for insurance companies – if the authorization of the Fair Trade Commission has been obtained). This regulation may not apply if they hold stocks in other banks or insurance companies.

§2.   INSURANCE HOLDING COMPANY

156. The IBL provides, subject to Article 4 of the Act relating to Reform laws, etc., regarding the Finance System accompanying Removal of the Ban on a Holding Company, stipulations for an insurance holding company in its section 3 of Chapter 10-2. These stipulations are composed of items such as General Provisions (from Article 271-18 to Article 271-20), Activities and Subsidiaries (from Article 271-21 to Article 271-22), Accounting (from Article 271-23 to Article 271-26), Supervision (from Article 271-27 to Article 271-30) and Others (Article 271-31).

157. An insurance holding company is a company established, with advance approval from the Prime Minister, as a holding company with an insurance company, etc., as its subsidiary or a holding company approved by the Prime Minister as such a holding company (Article 271-18). An insurance holding company may not engage

---

45.   Concerted acts between a non-life insurance company or companies and another non-life insurance company or companies with regard to aviation insurance business (including rocket insurance business), nuclear energy insurance business, automobile liability insurance business as provided for in the ALSL or earthquake insurance business as provided for in the Earthquake Ins. Law are exempted, in general, from application of the Anti-monopoly Act. In reference to the business of insurance other than those specified above, concerted acts, specified below, between a non-life insurance company or companies and another non-life insurance company or companies relating to contracts of reinsurance or to insurance contracts thereby reinsured are exempted, in general, from application of the Anti-monopoly Act:

(a)   determination of insurance policy conditions (excluding those regarding insurance premium rates);
(b)   determination of the methods of settling claims;
(c)   determination of parties to reinsurance and of the volume of the transaction of reinsurance;
(d)   fixing of reinsurance premium rates and reinsurance commissions.

in any activities other than the business management, including activities incidental thereto, of such a subsidiary insurance company (Article 271-21).

'Subsidiary' means a company of which voting rights exceeding 50% of the voting rights held by all the shareholders, etc., are held by another company. In this case, a company of which voting rights exceeding 50% of the voting rights held by all shareholders, etc., are held jointly by the company and one or more of its subsidiary companies or by one or more of the subsidiary companies of the company shall be deemed to be the subsidiary company of the company (Article 2(12)).

158. An insurance holding company must be a stock company, so that a mutual company is not permitted to become a holding company, but a company established basing on the regulations of foreign country is not required to be a stock company (Article 271-19(2)).

159. The scope of subsidiaries of an insurance holding company is stipulated in Article 271-22 (those are, in general, an insurance company, bank, long-term credit bank, securities company and their business activities incidental thereto which are stipulated, in detail, in Enforcement Regulation Article 210-7). Supervision or restrictions, by the IBL, on an insurance holding company itself are basically the same as those for an insurance company.

Chapter 7.   Taxation of the Company

§1.   TAXATION OF COMPANIES IN GENERAL

160. The Japanese taxation system, from the standpoint of the taxation authority, can be classified into the national taxation system and local taxation system, and the local taxation system consists of the TO (metropolis), DO (circuit), FU (prefecture) and KEN (prefecture) taxation system (hereinafter called 'prefecture tax') and the city–town–village taxation system (hereinafter called 'municipal tax').

Income tax, corporation tax, securities exchange tax, general consumption tax, automobile-weight tax, stamp duty, registration licence tax and custom duties are the main national taxes. The prefecture taxes are represented by prefecture-inhabitant tax, corporate enterprise tax, automobile tax, local consumption tax, real estate acquisition tax, automobile acquisition tax and the main municipal taxes are the municipal inhabitant tax, property tax, corporate office tax.[46]

161. Income tax, levied on interest and dividends, for domestic companies shall be paid as withholding tax by undertakings which are paying interest or dividends thereof; income tax, levied on interest and dividends received by financial corporations (including insurance companies) shall be paid by financial corporations themselves.

162. Corporation tax is levied at a fixed rate corresponding to the type of the juristic person (such as ordinary corporation, middle or small corporation, public corporation, specific association), and corporation tax is levied on all types of a juristic person (stock company, limited corporation, limited partnership, unlimited partnership, limited liability company, mutual company).

Taxable income is calculated according to the following formula:

(1)   Profits from the standpoint of accounting + (ii) Loss to be excluded (loss from the standpoint of accounting and unacceptable as loss under Corporation tax law) – (iii) Profit to be excluded (profit from the standpoint of accounting and unacceptable as profit under corporation tax law).[47]

---

46.   In the case of Tokyo (TO) it has the right to impose, as prefecture taxes, the municipal inhabitant tax (for judicial persons), property tax and corporate office tax notwithstanding that those taxes are typical municipal taxes.

47.   The amount of profit to be excluded relating to dividends, etc. = (1) + (2) + (3) + (4):

(1)   the amount of dividends, relating to stocks of consolidated corporations;

(2)   'The amount of dividends, relating to stocks of affiliated companies' – 'The amount of dividends relating to stocks of affiliated companies acquired with borrowed funds';

(3)   ('The amount of dividends, etc., relating to other stocks' – 'The amount of dividends, etc., relating to stocks acquired with borrowed funds') 50% (in case of ordinary corporations; it was 80% before 2002);

(4)   The amount of dividends, etc. received from a foreign subsidiary (owned 25% or more of outstanding shares).

(2) Profit to be excluded relating to dividends received: if a corporation receives dividends, etc., from other domestic corporations, the corporation may deal them as profits from the standpoint of accounting but under the Corporation Tax Law,[48] such dividends, in full or part, may be excluded from profits according to the category of stocks according to the principles for receiving dividends. However, if a corporation pays interest for the debt which is used to acquire stocks, such dividend corresponding to stocks acquired with debts may be exempted from the total amount of divided received.

(3) Profit or loss from valuation on securities: securities held by a corporation may be categorized into securities for sales, held-to-maturity securities and other securities. If securities for sales are held at the end of accounting year, appraised profits or losses on the securities must be included either in the profit or in the loss for the purpose of calculating the income of the accounting year. In the next account year, profits or losses on securities appraised in previous business year must be included in loss or profit for the purpose of calculating the income of the accounting year. Securities not for sale must be assessed on the cost basis (the amount added or subtracted by an amount to be allocated to each accounting year out of the difference between the book value and redemption prices).

(4) Carryover and carryback of losses (in the case of a corporation consecutively filing a blue return): a corporation may deduct carry forward losses arose within the last seven years from its income of the current year, and losses arose in the current year may not be carried back to its income tax relating to the previous business year (middle and small corporation may carry back it thereof).

(5) Consolidated tax payment system: this system presumes that a corporation and its subsidiaries (only such subsidiaries all stocks issued are held either directly or indirectly by the parent corporation) are one taxpayer. A corporation may select this system voluntarily, and new group tax payment system, according to the tax reform 2010, shall be enforced.

   163. Corporation inhabitants tax (prefecture tax and municipal tax) is levied on a corporation having its office in a prefecture or a municipality on a per capita basis, as well as on a tax amount of the national corporation tax. A tax amount on the national corporation tax may be calculated by the following formula:
   (the amount of corporation tax) × set tax-rate (standard prefecture tax; 5%, standard municipal tax; 12.3%).
   The tax on a per capita basis may be set by the amount of the capital of the corporation (prefecture tax) and by the amount of the capital of the corporation and the number of workers in the municipality (municipal tax).
   164. Corporate enterprise tax, in general, is levied on income (for a corporation with JPY 100 million or more capital; income, capital and added value); however, electric supply industries, gas supply industries and insurance companies are levied on their gross receipts (tax on business activities). If a corporation has its offices in plural prefectures, corporate enterprise tax is levied on the income (or gross receipts)

---

48.   The tax rate of Corporation Tax is for an ordinary corporation (capital stock or subscription; JPY 100 million or more) 30%, middle or small corporation 22% for a part under JPY 8 million of income and 30% for over JPY 8 million of income, public corporations 22%.

divided into each prefecture with the number of offices or number of workers. After April 2004, the tax base of corporate enterprise tax for a corporation with capital of JPY 100 million or more may be changed from income to business activities.

165. Corporate office tax is levied on a corporation having its offices in cities with population of not less than 30,000, to be designated by the Cabinet Ordinance, on a per capita basis as well as on workers. Tax on a per capita basis is calculated with floor space, and tax on workers is calculated according to the amount of their wages.[49]

166. Consumption tax or local consumption tax, if a corporation or a self-employed person transacts business domestically, is levied on the amount of sales at the 8% (national tax 6.3%, local tax 1.7%) tax rate. The payment of insurance premiums, however, is exempted from consumption tax.

§2.   NON-LIFE INSURANCE COMPANY TAXATION

167. The main differences in the taxation system between non-life insurance companies and general companies are as follows:

(a)   Corporation Tax

  (1) Reserve for outstanding claims; the full amount of outstanding claims and a portion of IBNR may be allowed as losses.
  (2) Underwriting reserves:

    (a) normal underwriting reserve is the total amount of premium reserve and unearned premium that may be allowed as losses. As for hull insurance, cargo insurance, transport insurance and ship's passengers accident liability insurance, either the total amount of premium reserve and unearned premium or the account balance of those insurances whichever is the largest may be allowed as a loss;
    (b) reserves for refund, reserves for dividends to policyholders – additional provisions for these may be allowed as losses;[50]
    (c) catastrophe loss reserves: reserves for group 1 insurances (hull and aviation), group 2 insurances (fire, cargo, transit, windstorm and flood, movable all risks, contractor's all risks and liability) and nuclear energy insurance may be allowed, up to a certain limits, as losses. Reserves for other insurances may not be allowed as losses;
    (d) compulsory automobile liability insurance: the obligatory reserve may be allowed as a loss, but other reserves such as the adjustable reserve, the reserve of investment gains and the reserve of loading charge may not be allowed as losses;
    (e) earthquake risk reserve: among earthquake risk reserves, the amount of the account balance may be allowed in full as a loss, but the amount of investment gain may be allowed up to a certain limit as a loss.

---

49.   Corporate office tax on newly constructed or used offices was abolished in Apr. 2002.
50.   Reserves for dividend not yet allotted to a policyholder shall not be allowed as losses.

(6) Profit to be excluded relating to dividends received: dividends received are basically excluded from revenue like those of a general corporation. However, interest coming from accounts of the savings-type insurance maturity fund reserve in which the funds are not allowed to invest in shares may be excluded, until the 2003 business year, from interest from the debt-borrowed fund.
(7) Price fluctuation reserve: additional provisions for the price fluctuation reserve are excluded from a loss.

(b) Corporate Enterprise Tax

Corporate enterprise tax (standard tax rate: 1.3%) is levied on the total amount of a certain percentage of domestic net premiums classified by line of insurance. The percentages:

–   hull insurance – 25% of domestic net premiums;
–   transit, cargo insurance – 45% of domestic net premiums;
–   compulsory automobile liability insurance – 10% of domestic net premiums;
–   earthquake insurance (for dwelling risks) – 20% of domestic net premiums;
–   other insurances – 40% of domestic net premiums.
(c) Consumption Tax

The payment of insurance premiums is exempted from consumption tax therefore very few items among loading may be dealt with as objects of consumption tax.

§3.   LIFE INSURANCE COMPANY TAXATION

168. The main differences in the taxation system between a life insurance company and a general corporation are as follows.

I.   Application of Minimum Taxation System

169. This system was introduced in 1967. If the taxable income for corporation tax calculated by the normal method does not exceed 7% of the surplus (total amount of profit and additional provisions for policyholders' dividends reserves, but additional provisions concerned with group term insurance is the amount equivalent to 50% of them) of the concerned business year, the authority, by reducing the amount of additional provisions for policyholders' dividends which is allowed as a loss, may deem the amount equivalent to 7% of surplus as the taxable income and corporation tax is levied on that amount.

II. Exclusion from the Application of the Rule 'Dividends Received to Be Excluded from Revenue' May Not Be Applied to an Account of a Life Insurance Company

170. If a life insurance company excluded dividends received from revenue, no taxable income may be increased, because dividends to policyholders arising through investment of dividends received is allowed as a loss.[51]

III. Reserves

171. Premium fund and unearned premium are allowed as losses. The premium fund is allowed as a loss up to the amount calculated by the net level premium method (the method of setting aside the funds against future performance of the obligations under insurance contracts by equalizing the same over the entire period for premium payment), but as for insurance contracts subject to the standard reserve, the premium fund is allowed as a loss up to the amount calculated by the net level premium method specified for such insurance contracts (if the amounts calculated fall below the policyholders' value, the amount equivalent to the policyholders' value is allowed as a loss).

Reserve for future risk is generally not allowed as a loss. However, if a company calculates the amounts for the reserves by another method than the net level premium method, and if the amount of such additional provisions to the reserves is less than the amount calculated by the net level premium method, the amount of the reserve for future risk equivalent to the amount being short may be allowed as a loss.[52]

IV. Reserve for Policyholders' Dividends

172. The amount of the additional provisions to the reserve for policyholders' dividends (in the case of a mutual company, the amount of the additional provisions to the reserve for appropriating a surplus to the members) may be allowed as a loss up to the amount that shall be scheduled to be paid to the policyholders as dividends. However, the amount to be allowed as a loss may be adjusted to reduce in some cases mentioned above in II and III.

V. Reserve for Outstanding Claims

173. There is no specific stipulation for life insurance as to reserve for outstanding claims under corporation tax law, but the amounts accepted as fixed obligations may

---

51.   Even if a life insurance company selects the rule 'Dividends received to be excluded from revenue', the amount of additional provisions for policyholders' dividends received which is excluded from revenue must be subtracted from the amount of loss.
52.   Reserve for future risk – the amount calculated against any risk likely to occur in the future in order to secure due performance of future obligations under the relevant insurance contracts.

be allowed as losses. As for group term insurance and consumer group credit life insurance, IBNR may be allowed as a loss up to a certain amount.

VI.   Securities Corresponding to Reserves

174.   Under corporation tax law, securities held by a corporation are categorized into securities for sales, held-to-maturity securities and other securities, but for a life insurance company, there is another category of securities corresponding to reserves. If the accounting standard for financial products (market value accounting for the asset side) is applied, securities on the asset side may be estimated at market value while reserves on the liabilities side should not be estimated at market value. Hence, securities with necessary conditions as the securities corresponding reserve may be exempted from applying the market value estimation, and under corporation tax law, taking this accounting transaction into consideration, the securities corresponding reserve may be assessed at the cost basis as well as held maturity securities.

VII.   Valuation Profits from Shares Based on IBL Article 112

175.   Under corporation tax law, shares belonging to the category of securities for sales must be assessed at the market value, and valuation profits may be calculated into revenue, while the valuation profits from shares belonging to the category of other securities may be excluded from revenue.

As a special rule for the above, valuation profits from shares calculated based on IBL Article 112 may be included in revenue.[53]

VIII. Corporate Enterprise Tax

176.   Corporate enterprise tax for a life insurance company is levied on net premiums alike the case of a non-life insurance company. The standard tax rate is also 1.3%.

Percentage for each line of insurance:

–   individual policies (except some savings policies) – 24% (some savings policies 7%);

---

53.   Article 112 (IBL):

(1)   In the event that the market value of the shares owned by an insurance company, and which shares have a price quoted by a stock exchange, exceeds the acquisition cost for the said shares, such shares may be valued at an amount in excess of such acquisition cost, but not in excess of the market value, with the authorization of the approval of the Prime Minister, pursuant to the provisions of IBLER.

(2)   The profit accrued from the revaluation carried out as provided for in the immediately preceding paragraph shall be credited to the reserve prescribed by IBLER.

–   group policies – 16%;
–   group pension insurance – 5%.

IX.   Consumption Tax

177.   The same as for a non-life insurance company.

Part II. The Insurance Contract (General)

Chapter 1. Overview

178. The Com. Code (Law No. 48, 1957) provides that the transaction of insurance, if effected as a business, is a commercial transaction (Article 502); the Commercial Code, however, has no provision for an insurance contract. An insurance contract is entrusted to the Ins. Law (Law No. 56, 2008).

This Ins. Law is composed of five chapters that is, general provisions, non-life insurance, life insurance, fixed return accident and health insurance and miscellaneous provisions.

179. In the Ins. Law, some enforceable clauses are provided indeed, but basically, these provisions of the Ins. Law provide only the basic and simple structure of insurance contract, so that the actual insurance contract must be completed with general and/or special conditions of insurance contracts formed between the insurer and insured.

Chapter 2.   Subject Matter of a Contract of Insurance

180. The Insurance Law, in its Article 2, makes provisions for non-life insurance, accident and health damage insurance, life insurance and fixed return accident and health insurance contracts as follows:

(1) Non-life insurance contract: an insurance contract under which an insurer undertakes to cover any damage that may arise through a certain contingent accident (Ins. Law Article 2(6)) and a non-life insurance contract may be executed for making profits as long as they are rateable as money (Ins. Law Article 3).
(2) Accident and health damage insurance contract: non-life insurance contract under which an insurer undertakes to cover any damage that may arise through an injury or illness of a person (which shall be limited to those to be incurred by the person who suffered such injury or illness) (Ins. Law Article 2(7)).
(3) Life insurance contract: an insurance contract under which an insurer undertakes to pay certain insurance benefits with respect to survival or death of a person (except, however, for a fixed return accident and health insurance contract) (Ins. Law Article 2(8)).
(4) Fixed return accident and health insurance contract: an insurance contract under which an insurer undertakes to pay certain insurance benefits in connection with an injury or illness of a person (Ins. Law Article 2(9)).

181. Two types of personal insurance contract, provided in the Insurance Law, such as an accident and health damage insurance contract and fixed return accident and health insurance contract may be underwritten by both a non-life insurance company and a life insurance company IBL Article 3(4),[54] (5)[55]):

(1) insurance (other than that pertaining solely to death as mentioned in sub-item (c) of the following item) whereby, in consideration of an insurance premium, an undertaking is made to pay a specified sum of insurance claim in connection with survival or death (including a physical condition in respect of which a physician has diagnosed that the remainder of life is not likely to exceed a specified period; this inclusion applying in this and the following paragraph);
(2) insurance whereby, in consideration of an insurance premium, an undertaking is made to pay a specified sum of insurance claim in connection with any of the events mentioned below or to indemnify any loss which may be sustained as a result of such events:

(a) disease;

---

54. Authorization for life insurance business shall be for the business of underwriting insurance mentioned in item (1) below or underwriting it and, additionally, any insurance mentioned in item (2) or (3).
55. Authorization for non-life insurance business shall be for the business of underwriting insurance mentioned in item (1) below or underwriting it and, additionally, any insurance mentioned in item (2) or (3).

(b) any condition arising from injury or disease;

(c) death resulting directly from injury;

(d) events (other than death) designated by Insurance Business Law Enforcement Regulation (IBLER) as being similar to those mentioned in sub-items (a) and (b);

(e) medical treatment (including those designated by IBLER as being similar to medical treatments) which may be carried out in connection with the events mentioned in sub-item (a), (b) or (d).

(3) insurance (other than that mentioned in the following item) whereby, in consideration of an insurance premium, an undertaking is made to indemnify any loss which may arise from certain fortuitous accidents;

(4) insurance mentioned in item (2) of the preceding paragraph;

(5) insurance mentioned in item (1) of the preceding paragraph which is connected with death occurring during the period between the departure from home for the purpose of travelling abroad and the return home (hereinafter called 'overseas travel period') or with death directly resulting from any disease contracted during the overseas travel period.

Chapter 3.   Structure of the Contract

§1.   Formation of the Contract

182. The Ins. Law defines that an insurance contract means an insurance contract, a mutual aid contract or any other contracts whichever name under which one of the parties thereto undertakes to pay financial benefit to the other party subject to the occurrence of such certain event and the other party undertakes to pay insurance premium according to the possibility of the occurrence of such certain (Ins. Law Article 2 item 1), but a contract of insurance itself, as with any contract, is formed when the parties agree mutually (Com. Code 629, 673), and no benefit (payment of premium etc.) is required between the parties to form a contract (11 November 1968, Supreme Court, *Hanreijihou* 541), and also no form is required for making a contract.

In insurance practice, however, the application form is a key factor for establishing the conditions of the insurance as agreed between parties, and payment of premium is also a key factor for indemnification.

§2.   Application Form

183. The Ins. Law stipulates that an insurer shall, at the time of execution of an insurance contract, deliver to an application for insurance contract without delay a document containing certain items (Ins. Law Article 6 – non-life insurance contract, Article 40 – life insurance contract and Article 69 – fixed return accident and health insurance contract), but has no specific stipulation for an application form.

Matters to be described in application form for an insurance contract, and the documents to be attached thereto have to be provided in a document indicating the methods of business that must be submitted to the FSA (IBLER Article 8), so that matters to be described in an application form may be checked by the authority to ensure they do not invade the privacy of an insured unnecessarily.

§3.   Payment of Premium and Commencement of Insurer's Liability

184. It is known that an insurance contract itself is set up theoretically only by the mutual agreement of the parties. In insurance practice, however, the payment of the premium is treated as the necessary condition to commence the insurer's liability under general conditions of insurances.[56]

---

56.   The insurer is not liable for loss, damage or bodily injury sustained unless the premium is paid (general conditions of dwelling house fire insurance). The insurer's liability may commence on conditions of the policy after the insurer agrees to accept an insurance contract and receives a premium (general conditions of life insurance).

§4. INSURANCE POLICY

185. As to an insurance policy, Old Com. Code stipulated that the insurer should, upon demand by the applicant for insurance, furnish him/her with an insurance policy but New Ins. Law provides that the insurer shall, at the time of the execution of an insurance contract, deliver to the applicant for insurance without delay a document containing certain information (Ins. Law Article 6 – non-life insurance contract, Article 40 – life insurance contract, Article 69 – fixed return accident and health insurance contract).

186. The specific items to be informed in an insurance policy are provided in the Insurance Law:

(1) For non-life insurance contract (Ins. Law Article 6):

    (a) the name or trade name of the insurer; (b) the name or trade name of the insurance applicant; (c) the name or trade name of the insured or any other information necessary for identifying the insured; (d) insurable contingencies; (e) the period provided in the non-life insurance contract as the period during which damage from an insurable contingency is coverable; (f) the amount covered (the amount provided in the non-life insurance contract as the maximum amount of the insurance benefits) or, if there is no definite amount covered, the statement thereof; (g) if any subject matter of insurance (the subject provided in the non-life insurance contract as the subject to which an insurable contingency may cause damage) exists, information necessary for identifying such subject matter; (h) if there is an agreed insurable value under the proviso to Article 9, such agreed insurable value; (i) if it is provided that notice under Article 29 (Cancellation Due to Increase of Risk), paragraph 1, item 1 should be given, the statement thereof; (j) the date of the execution of the non-life insurance contract; and (k) the date of the execution of the document.

    (b) The document prepared under the preceding paragraph shall bear a signature or a name and seal impression of the insurer (if it is a corporation or any other organization, the representative person thereof).

(2) For life insurance contract (Ins. Law Article 40):

    (a) The name or trade name of the insurer; (b) the name or trade name of the insurance applicant; (c) the name of the insured or any other information necessary for identifying the insured; (d) the name or trade name of the beneficiary or any other information necessary for identifying the beneficiary; (e) insurable contingencies; (f) the period provided in the life insurance contract as the period of occurrence of insurable contingencies for which insurance benefits are payable; (g) the amount of insurance benefits and the method of payment thereof; (h) insurance premiums and the method of payment thereof; (i) if it is provided that notice under Article 56, paragraph 1, item 1 should be given, the statement thereof; (j) the date of the execution of the life insurance contract; and (k) the date of the execution of the document.

(b) The document prepared under the preceding paragraph shall bear a signature or a name and seal impression of the insurer (if it is a corporation or any other organization, the representative person thereof).

(3)   for fixed return accident and health insurance contract (Ins. Law Article 69):

(a) The name or trade name of the insurer; (b) the name or trade name of the insurance applicant; (c) the name of the insured or any other information necessary for identifying the insured; (d) the name or trade name of the beneficiary or any other information necessary for identifying the beneficiary; (e) grounds for payment (f) the period provided in the fixed return accident and health insurance contract as the period of occurrence of injuries or illness or grounds for payment for which insurance benefits are payable; (g) the amount of insurance benefits and the method of payment thereof; (h) insurance premiums and the method of payment thereof; (i) if it is provided that notice under Article 85, paragraph 1, item 1 should be given, the statement thereof; (j) the date of the execution of the life insurance contract; and (k) the date of the execution of the document.

(b) The document prepared under the preceding paragraph shall bear a signature or a name and seal impression of the insurer (if it is a corporation or any other organization, the representative person thereof).

Chapter 4.   Obligations of the Insured and Applicant

§1.   Non-disclosure and Misrepresentation

187. In executing a non-life insurance contract, a person who is to become the insurance applicant or the insured shall disclose to the insurer-to-be the fact concerning important matters as to the potential for damage to be covered by such non-life insurance contract whose disclosure is required by such insurer-to-be (Ins. Law Article 4). This means that the insurance applicant or the insured has no duty to disclose any matters other than those to be required to disclose by the insurer-to-be.

In life insurance contract and fixed return accident and health insurance contract, the insurance applicant or the insured has same duty mentioned above (Ins. Law Articles 37, 66).

An insurance, in general, may cancel an insurance contract if an insurance applicant or an insured, by wilful misconduct or gross negligence, fails to make disclosure of facts or makes a false disclosure with request to any matters to be disclosed (Ins. Law Articles 28, 55, 84).

188. The right of cancellation of an insurer shall lapse if the insurer fails to exercise the same for one month from the time when it has become aware of the existence of the cause of cancellation (Ins. Law Articles 28, 55, 84). Any cancellation of an insurance contract shall become effective only for the future, and not retroactively (Ins. Law Articles 31, 59, 88).

§2.   Payment of Premium

189. The applicant for the insurance contract is bound to pay the premium to the insurer (Ins. Law Article 2, item 3). Legally, the premium is remuneration for the indemnification of the insurer against any loss. In the case of a mutual insurer, the applicant for the insurance contract is an individual of the mutual company and the premium paid by him/her is accepted as a contribution to becoming an individual of the mutual company.

A contract of insurance may be effected for the benefit of another person. In this case the applicant for the insurance contract is bound to pay the premium to the insurer.

190. There is no specific stipulation in the Ins. Law about the time when the applicant of the insurance contract must pay. In non-life insurance practice, however, the total amount of premium must ordinarily be paid in cash or by cheque before the duration of the insurance may commence.[57]

191. Unless there is any express or implied contract, the applicant for insurance is bound to bear the premium to the insurer or his/her intermediaries (Com. Code Article 516). Insurance intermediaries, however, usually collect premiums at the place

---

57.   It is not permitted to pay a premium by bill at all but it is permitted to pay the premium by credit card for some kinds of insurance contract.

of business or residence of the applicant for the insurance, therefore this is interpreted to be an implied contract between the applicant of the insurance and the insurer that the insurer will collect a premium (Supreme Court, 8 July 1959, *Minsyuh* 13(7)).

The right to claim insurance premiums shall be extinguished by prescription if not exercised for one year (Ins. Law Article 95(2)).

§3.   Obligations in the Case of the Insured Event

192. An insurance applicant or an insured shall notify the insurer of the occurrence of damage from an insurable contingency upon learning thereof without delay (Ins. Law Article 14).

The insurance contractor or the beneficiary under a death insurance contract shall notify the insurer of the death of the insured upon leaning thereof without delay (Ins. Law Article 50).

An insurance applicant, an insured or a beneficiary shall notify the insurer of the occurrence of a ground for payment upon leaning thereof without delay (Ins. Law Article 79).

193. The Insurance Law, in its Article 13, stipulates that an applicant for insurance contract and an insured shall, upon learning of the occurrence of any insurable contingency, make efforts to prevent the occurrence and expansion of damage from such insurable contingency, while the Old Com. Code, only the insured would be responsible to prevent the occurrence and expansion of damage from the insurable contingency, but insurance practice the applicant for insurance contract also had same obligation as those of the insured.

In Old Com. Code provided that the insurer would be responsible for the necessary or advantageous expenses incurred for the purpose as well as for the amount of indemnity even though it exceeds the amount insured, the Ins. Law, however, only provides that an insurer shall bear any expense necessary or advantageous for the prevention of the occurrence or expansion of damage. So that, it may be entrusted to the insurance contract whether the insurer, in case of above mentioned, will be responsible for the amount of indemnity even though it exceeds the amount insured or not.

In the Ins. Law there is no provision for the case that the insured fails to endeavour to prevent a loss; the insurer, however, provides in his/her general conditions that the amount of loss assumed to be prevented may be deducted from the amount of indemnity due.[58]

---

58.   In fire insurance policy for a dwelling house, the replacement cost of chemicals used for fire fighting, the repair or replacement cost of the items used and damaged by fire fighting and the cost for the personnel or apparatus urgently mobilized for fire fighting are paid as loss prevention expenses.

Chapter 5.   Obligation of the Insurer

§1.   OVER-INSURANCE AND PARTIAL INSURANCE

194. Over-insurance and partial insurance, concepts peculiar to non-life insurance, are stipulated in the Ins. Law as follows:

(1) Over-insurance: In the event that at the time of the execution of a non-life insurance contract the amount insured thereunder is in excess of the value of the subject matter of insurance and both the applicant for insurance contract and the insured are in good faith and are not grossly negligent with respect of such exceeding amounts, the applicant for insurance contract may cancel the non-life insurance contract partially as far as such excess is concerned; provided, however, that this shall not apply if there is a certain amount agreed on the insurable value (Ins. Law Article 9).
(2) Partial insurance: In the event that the amount insured is less than the insurable value (the agreed insurable value, if any), the amount of insurance benefits to be paid by the insurer shall be the amount obtained by multiplying the amount of damage to be covered by the proportion of the amount insured to the insurable value (Ins. Law Article 19).

195. Under Old Com. Code, in the event of over-insurance, the insured amount exceeded the value of the insured subject will be void in respect of the excess, and the return of the premium may be demanded of the insurer only where the applicant for insurance contract and the insured have acted bona fide and without gross negligence. Under new Insurance Law, however, only stipulates that in the event that both the applicant for insurance contract and the insured have acted bona fide and without gross negligence with respect to such exceeding amounts, the applicant for insurance contract and the insured may cancel the insurance contract partially as far as such excess is concerned, so that the applicant for insurance contract acquires, as the matter of course, the right of the return of the premium.

196. The general conditions for dwelling house fire insurance contain an 80% co-insurance clause to indemnify the loss in full up to the insured amount, if the insured amount is equal to at least 80% of the insurable value. And also endorsement for value agreement insurance on fire insurances for dwelling houses and their contents was introduced in 1975 in order to cover loss or damage on replacement cost value basis in full up to the insured amount.

For buildings other than dwelling houses, a co-insurance clause, with an agreement for a specific proportion to be insured, is provided for fire-resistant buildings.[59]

---

59.   Specific proportion: 30%–80% of insurable value.

§2. DOUBLE INSURANCE

197. The Ins. Law stipulates, in its Article 20, the amount of insurance benefits borne by an insurer under double insurance as follows:

(1) in the case where damage that should be covered by a non-life insurance contract is to be covered by other non-life insurance contract, the insurer shall be liable to pay insurance benefits with respect to the entire of the amount of damage to be covered;

(2) in the event that the total amount of the insurance benefits to be paid by each insurer of two or more non-life insurance contracts exceeds the amount of damage to be covered (if the amount of damage to be covered calculated pursuant to the respective non-life insurance contracts vary, the highest one) and if one of the insurer has paid insurance benefits beyond its share (the amount obtained by multiplying the amount of damage to be covered by the proportion of the amount of insurance benefits to be paid by each insurer assuming that there is no other non-life insurance contract to the total insurance benefits) and has thereby procured a discharge for common benefit, such insurer shall be entitled to reimbursement only for the proportion that exceeds its own share from other insurers in proportion of their respective shares.

§3. CASE OF INSURANCE EVENTS

198. 'Time of Performance of Insurance Benefits' is stipulated, in Articles 21, 52, 81 in Ins. Law as follows:

(1) if, even in the case where a time limit is fixed for the payment of insurance benefits, such time limited is the day after the day elapsing a reasonable period of time for confirming insurable contingencies, the amount of damage to be covered, immunity reasons of the insurer or any other matters required to be confirmed under a non-life insurance contract – Article 21 (life insurance contract – Article 52, fixed return accident and health insurance contract – Article 81) for the payment of the insurance benefits, such day elapsing the said period shall be the date by which the insurance benefits are payable.

(2) in the event that no time is fixed for the payment of insurance benefits, the insurer shall not be responsible for delay from the time of request for insurance benefits to the expiration of a certain period of time necessary for the confirmation of the insurable contingencies and the amount of damage to be covered in connection with the said request.

(3) if, where the insurer carries out an investigation necessary for making the confirmations mentioned in above (1), (2) the applicant for insurance contract or the insured hinders or fails to cooperate in such investigation without good reason, the insurer shall not be responsible for delay for the period during which it has delayed payment of insurance benefits due to such hindrance or non-cooperation.

199. The Ins. Law stipulates in its Article 22 'liability insurance contract lien' as follows:

(1) a person who is entitled to claim compensation for damage from an insured under a liability insurance contract resulting from insurable contingencies under such liability insurance contract shall have a lien against the insured's right to claim insurance benefits;

(2) an insured may exercise the right to claim insurance benefits from an insured to the extent of the amount repair with respect to the right to claim damages mentioned in (1) above or the amount agreed to by a person who has such right to damages;

(3) the right to claim insurance benefits pursuant to a liability insurance contract may not be transferred pledged or seized except in the case:

(a) where the said right is transferred to the person who has the right to claim damages mentioned in (1) or where the same is seized with respect to such right to damages; or

(b) where an insured is entitled to exercise the right to claim insurance benefits pursuant to the provisions of (2) above.

200. Payment of Expenses (Ins. Law Article 23)

(1) The following expenses shall be borne by an insurer:

(a) any expenses necessary for the calculation of the amount of damage to be covered; and

(b) in the case of Article 13 (Occurrence of Damage and Prevention of Expansion), any expense necessary or valuable for the prevention of the occurrence or expansion of damage.

(2) The provisions of Article 19 (Partial Insurance) shall apply *mutatis mutandis* to the amount of the expenses mentioned in (1)-(b) above. In this case, 'the amount of damage to be covered' in the said Article shall be deemed to be replaced with 'the amount of expenses mentioned in Article 23, paragraph 1, item 2'.

201. Destruction of subject matter of Insurance after Occurrence of Damage (Ins. Law Article 15).
In the event that any damage has occurred from an insurable contingency, the insurer shall cover such damage even if the subject matter of insurance in connection with such damage is destroyed after the occurrence of such damage due to a cause not attributable to the insurable contingency.

202. Special Provision on Damage Coverage by fire Insurance (Ins. Law Article 16):
An insurance of a non-life insurance contract under which fire is an insurable contingency shall cover any and all damage caused to the subject matter of insurance as a result of measures necessarily taken for fire extinction, evacuation or any other fire fighting operation even if no insurable contingency has actually occurred.

203. Refund of Insurance Due Reserves[60] – for life insurance contract – (Ins. Law Article 63).

In the event that a life insurance contract is terminated for any of the following reasons, an insurer shall refund to an applicant for insurance contract the insurance due reserves (meaning the portion of the total insurance premiums received which is equivalent to the amount calculated as the amount that should be used for the payment of the insurance benefits of the said life insurance contract on the basis of the expected mortality rate, assumed interest rate or any other computational foundation generally used for fixing the amounts of insurance premiums or insurance benefits) at the time of such termination, unless the insurer is responsible for the payment of the insurance benefits;

(1) Any of cases set out in respective items (except for item 2) or Article 51;
(2) Cancellation pursuant to the provisions of Article 54 or paragraph 2 of Article 58 prior to the commencement of insurer's responsibility;
(3) Cancellation pursuant to the provision of paragraph 1 of Article 56; or
(4) Cancellation pursuant to the provisions of paragraph 1 of Article 96 or lapse of the said life insurance contract pursuant to the provisions of paragraph 2 of the said article.

§4. OTHERS

204. Request for Cancellation by Insured (Ins. Law Article 34):

(1) In the event that an insured is a person other than a party to an accident and health damage insurance contract, such insured may request an applicant for insurance contract, unless otherwise agreed to with such applicant for insurance contract, to cancel the said accident and health damage insurance contract.
(2) An applicant for insurance contract shall be entitled to cancel an accident and health damage insurance contract if it is requested to do so pursuant to the provisions of the preceding paragraph.

205. Transfer of insurance contracts (IBL Article 135)

The previous IBL provided about transfer of insurance contracts that a transfer of insurance contracts shall cover the whole insurance contracts for which the policy reserve is calculated on the same basis (excluding the insurance contracts specified by a IBLCO, such as those for which an insured event had occurred by the time of public notice (limited to those contracts which would be terminated with the payment of insurance claims pertaining to the insured event)).

The revised IBL (in March 2013) provides transfer of insurance contracts only to exclude the insurance contracts specified by a IBLCO, such as those for which an insured event had occurred by the time of public notice (limited to those contracts

---

60.   Refund of Insurance Reserves – for a fixed return accident and health insurance contract – is stipulated in Art. 92 of the Insurance Law.

which would be terminated with the payment of insurance claims pertaining to the insured event).

Chapter 6.   Subrogation

206. Subrogation for remaining property: in the event that the subject matter of insurance is destroyed in its entirety and an insurer has paid insurance benefits, it shall, as a matter of course, acquire on behalf of an insured the title or other real rights retained by such insured in respect of such subject matter of insurance in accordance with the proportion of the amount of such insurance benefits to the insurable value (agreed insurable value, if any) (Ins. Law Article 24).

207. Right of subrogation against third party:

(1)   in the event that an insurer has paid insurance benefits, it shall, as a matter of course, acquire on behalf of the insured the claims to be obtained by the insured as a result of damage due to insurable contingencies (as regards a non-life insurance contract under which damage that may arise on certain claims from default or otherwise is to be covered, such claims shall be included; hereinafter referred to as the 'insured's claims'), to the extent of lesser of:

(a) the amount of insurance benefits paid by such insurer; or
(b) the amount the insured's claims (if the amount mentioned in the preceding item is less than the amount of damage to be covered, the amount remaining after deducting from the amount of the insured's claims such deficiency).

(2)   if, in the case of the preceding paragraph, the amount mentioned in item 1 of the said paragraph is less than the amount of damage to be covered, an insured shall be entitled to receive repayment of the insured's claims except for the portion acquired by an insurer on behalf of the insured in accordance with the provisions of the said paragraph, in priority to the claims of the insurer thus acquired.

208. In practice, the insurers are basically following these articles of the Ins. Law to the cases of such subrogation.

However, the insurers stipulate, in their general conditions for 'subrogation for remaining property' that the insurer may inform whether he/she acquires the right or not and if the insurer does not inform the insured the right remains to the insured, and for 'right of subrogation against a third party' that both the applicant of the insurance contract and the insured have a duty to cooperate with the insurer to preserve and to exercise the right against the third party, and also cooperate to acquire, at the cost of the insurer, such documents or evidence as may be required by the insurer.

There is no stipulation for violation of such duty in the general conditions; it is, however, accepted that the insurer may reduce the amount from his/her indemnity amount or claim that the insurer may be presumed to acquire in the course of subrogation.

Chapter 7. Duration of the Contract of Insurance

§1. DURATION OF THE CONTRACT

209. The Ins. Law does not refer to the duration of the contract of insurance; the Commercial Code, however, refers those only in case of marine hull insurance for a single voyage (Com. Code Article 821), cargo insurance and prospective insurance (Com. Code Article 822).

In insurance practice, the duration of the contract of insurance is basically provided between the insurer and the applicant for the insurance contract. This must be done even in the case of the insurance contract mentioned above.

So, such stipulations of the Com. Code are accepted to apply only if the duration of the insurance contract between parties is not stated.

210. For operating insurance business, the insurer must submit a statement of the methods of operation to the FSA, and the insurer must provide the maximum duration of the contract of the insurance. So, in insurance practice, the insurer will be restrained in underwriting the limit of the duration[61] of the contract of insurance.

§2. CANCELLATION

211. While the applicant of the insurance contract is able to cancel the contract of insurance at any time and for any reason (unless the right to claim is in pledge), the Ins. Law limits the insurer to cancelling the contract of insurance only if:

(1) For non-life insurance contract:

    (a) Cancellation due to breach of duty of disclosure (Ins. Law Article 28(1)). An insurer may cancel a non-life insurance contract if an applicant for insurance contract or an insured, by wilful misconduct or gross negligence, fails to make disclosure of facts or makes a false disclosure with respect to any matters to be disclosed.

    (b) Cancellation due to increase of risk (Ins. Law Article 29(1)). Even if, in the event that there arises an increase of risk (meaning a situation where the risk in respect of the matters to be disclosed become greater and insurance premiums stipulated in a non-life insurance contract is less than the insurance premiums calculated on the basis of such risk) after the execution of a non-life insurance contract, such non-life insurance contract may be continued if the insurance premiums are changed to the amount which responds to such increase of risk,

---

61. As to an insurance contract underwritten by SASTIP, the duration of the insurance contract whichever life insurance contract or non-life insurance contract has already been stipulated in the IBLCO Art. 1-6.

an insurer shall be entitled to cancel the said non-life insurance contract where the case falls under both of the following requirements:

- if it is provided in the said non-life insurance contract that the applicant for insurance contract or the insured shall, without delay, notify the insurer of any change in the matters to be disclosed in connection with such increase of risk;
- if the applicant for insurance contract or the insured has failed to give such notification as mentioned in the preceding item without delay by wilful misconduct or gross negligence.

(c) Cancellation due to Material Event (Ins. Law Article 30). An insurer may cancel a non-life insurance contract in any of the following events:

- if an applicant for insurance contract or an insured has caused or has intended to cause damage to the insurer in an attempt to make it pay insurance benefits under the said non-life insurance contract;
- if an insured has committed or has intended to commit a fraud in connection with the claim for insurance benefits under the said non-life insurance contract;
- in any other material events than those mentioned in the preceding two items in which the insurer's trust in either of an applicant for insurance contract or an insured is undermined or which makes the continuance of the said non-life insurance contract difficult.

(2) For life insurance contract:

(a) Cancellation due to breach of duty of disclosure (Ins. Law Article 55(1)). An insurer may cancel a life insurance contract if an applicant for insurance contract or an insured, by wilful misconduct or gross negligence, fails to make disclosure of facts or makes a false disclosure with respect to any matters to be disclosed.

(b) Cancellation due to increase of risk (Ins. Law Article 56(1)). Even if, in the event that there arises an increase of risk (meaning a situation where the risk in respect of the matters to be disclosed become greater and insurance premiums stipulated in a life insurance contract is less than the insurance premiums calculated on the basis of such risk) after the execution of life insurance contract, such life insurance contract may be continued if the insurance premiums are charged to the amount which responds to such increase of risk, an insurer shall be entitled to cancel the said life insurance contract where the case falls under both the following requirements:

- if it is provided in the said life insurance contract that the applicant for insurance contract or the insured shall, without delay, notify the insurer of any change in the matter to be disclosed in connection with such increase of risk;

- if the applicant for insurance contract or the insured has failed to give such notification as mentioned in the preceding item without delay by wilful misconduct or gross negligence.

(c) Cancellation due to Material Event (Ins. Law Article 57). An insurer may cancel a life insurance contract (which shall be limited to a death insurance contract in the case of (1) below) in any of the following events:

- if an applicant for insurance contract or a beneficiary has caused or has intended to cause death to an insured intentionally in an attempt to make an insurer pay insurance benefits;
- if a beneficiary has committed or has intended to commit a fraud in connection with the claim for insurance benefits under the said life insurance contract; or
- any other material events than those mentioned in the preceding two items in which the insurer's trust in any of the applicant for insurance contract, the insured or the beneficiary is undermined or which makes the continuance of the said life insurance contract difficult.

(d) Request for Cancellation by Insured (Ins. Law Article 58):

(1) In the event that an insured under a death insurance contract is a person other than a party to such death insurance contract, such insured may request an applicant for insurance contract to cancel the said death insurance contract under any of the following circumstances:
- if any of the events than those mentioned in item 1 and item 2 of the Article 57 occurs;
- in any other material events than those mentioned in the preceding item in which an insured's trust in either of an applicant for insurance contract or a beneficiary is undermined or which makes the continuance of the said death insurance contract difficult; or
- in the event that certain circumstances on which an insured relied in giving his/her consent as set forth in Article 38 have materially changed due to a termination of kinship between an applicant for insurance contract and an insured or for any other reason.
(2) An applicant for insurance contract shall be entitled to cancel a death insurance contract if it is requested to do so pursuant to the provisions of the preceding paragraph.

§3. PRESCRIPTION

212. A claim that has arisen out of a commercial transaction will generally be extinguished by prescription if it is not exercised within five years (Com. Code Article 522). As to the contract of insurance, however, the Ins. Law applies, in Article 95, a specific short-term prescription that:

–   the right to claim insurance benefits, a refund of insurance premiums or insurance due reserve under Article 63 or 92 shall be extinguished by prescription if not exercised for three years;
–   the right to claim insurance premiums shall be extinguished by prescription if not exercised for one year.

Part III. Property and Liability Insurance

Chapter 1.   Fire Insurance

§1.   STATUTORY REGULATION

213.

(1) The Insurance Law has no provision as to the definition of fire or fire insurance. It has only one provision, peculiar to the fire insurance, that stipulates 'an insurer of a non-life insurance contract under which fire is an insurable contingency shall cover any and all damage caused to the subject matter of insurance as a result of measures necessarily taken for fire extinction, evacuation or any other fire-fighting operation even if no insurable contingency has actually occurred'. This specific provision is not an enforceable clause, so that an insurer may be permitted to set up a certain limit, in the insurance contract, to the amount to pay damage caused by fire-fighting operation, as far as the reasonable grounds exist in the calculation of the insurance premium thereof.

(2) Old Com. Code provided such legal exemption risks other than wilful misconduct and gross negligence as war, public disturbances and inherent vice, New Insurance Law, however, provides, as legal exemption risk, that 'an insurer shall not be liable to cover any damage arising from wilful misconduct or gross negligence of an applicant for insurance contract or an insured. The same shall apply to damage arising as a result of war or any other disturbance (Ins. Law Article 17(1))', so the risk of inherent vice may be submitted to each insurance contract conditions.

(3) It was not only fire insurance contract but also other insurance contracts that Old Com. Code required to an insurer, on demand by an applicant for insurance contract, to furnish him/her with an insurance policy, and New Insurance Law, however, does not use a word 'insurance policy' and stipulates an insurer shall, at the time of execution of the insurance contract, to deliver to an applicant for insurance contract without delay a document containing certain items[62] (Ins. Law Article 6). The reason which a word 'document' is used as substitution for an insurance policy, is said that New Ins. Law may be applied to mutual aid contract, etc.

---

62.   Items had to be written in a document: see Part II, Ch. 3. §4. Insurance Policy.

(4) General Conditions and special agreements do not have to be printed on the surface of an insurance policy; most insurers give a booklet to the applicant for an insurance contract in which general conditions and special agreement applicable are printed, and some insurers, according to the selection of the applicant, are showing general conditions and special agreements in their website instead of giving a booklet.

214. The Ins. Law prescribes that the amount of damage to be covered by a non-life insurance contract shall be calculated on the basis of a value[63] at the place and time where and when such damage has occurred (Ins. Law Article 18(1)) and also provides that in the event which there is an agreed insurable value, the amount of damage to be covered shall be calculated on the basis of such agreed insurable value; provided, however, that if such agreed value exceeds the insurable value significantly, the amount of damage to be covered shall be calculated on the basis of such insurable value (Ins. Law Article 18(2)).

And the Ins. Law, in its Article 9,[64] provides that in the event which at the time of the execution of a non-life insurance contract the amount covered thereunder is in excess of the value of the subject matter of insurance and both the applicant for insurance contract and the insured are in good faith and are not grossly negligent with respect to such part of excess, the applicant for insurance contract may cancel the non-life insurance contract partially as far as such excess is concerned; provided, however, that this shall not apply if there is a certain amount agreed on the insurable value.

215. Decrease of Insurable Value

The event that the insurable value has significantly decreased after the execution of the non-life insurance contract, the applicant for insurance contract shall be entitled to require the insurer to reduce, for the future: (i) the amount covered or the agreed insurable value down to amount equivalent to the insurable value after the said decrease, and (ii) the insurance premiums down to the amount corresponding to the amount covered after making reduction of (i) (Ins. Law, Article 10).

Any special agreement violating the provisions of this Article 10 shall have no effect (Ins. Law Article 12).

216. In the event that the amount covered is less than the insurable value (the agreed insurable value, if any), the amount of insurance benefits to be paid by the insurer shall be the amount obtained by multiplying the amount of damage to be covered by the proportion of the amount covered to the insurable value (Ins Law Article 19).

217. Increase of risk and the effect of contract (Ins. Law Articles 29, 31):

(1) Even if, in the event that there arises an increase of risk (meaning a situation where the risk in respect of the matters to be disclosed become greater and insurance premiums stipulated in a non-life insurance contract are less than the insurance premiums calculated on the basis of such risk) after the execution

---

63.   It is practicable to attach an endorsement to estimate insurable value and to cover loss or damage on the basis of replacement cost.
64.   The body of Art. 9 of the Ins. Law is the enforceable clause.

of a non-life insurance contract, such non-life insurance contract may be continued if the insurance premiums are charged to the amount which responds to such increase of risk, an insurer shall be entitled to cancel the said non-life insurance contract where the case falls under both of the following requirement:

(a) if it is provided in the said non-life insurance contract that the applicant for insurance contract or the insured shall, without delay, notify the insurer of any change in the matters to be disclosed in connection with such increase of risk;

(b) if the applicant for insurance contract or the insured has failed to give such notification as mentioned in (a) above without delay by wilful misconduct or gross negligence.

(3) The right of cancellation shall lapse if the insurer fails to exercise the same for one month from the time when it has become aware of the existence of the cause of cancellation. The same shall apply when five years have elapsed from the time when there arises an increase of risk.

(e) Effect of cancellation

Any cancellation of a non-life insurance contract shall become effective only for the future, and not retroactively. In the event that an insurer has cancelled a non-life insurance contract pursuant to the provision of paragraph 1 of Article 29[65] – any damage due to an insurable contingency arising during the period from the time when the increase of risk in connection with such cancellation has occurred to the time of such cancellation (but excluding any damage due to an insurable contingency occurred but not from the event that caused such increase of risk – it shall not be liable to cover any damage (Ins. Law Article 31 (2) item 2).

(c) Decrease of risk (Ins. Law Article 11[66])

In the event that the risk has significantly decreased after the execution of a non-life insurance contract, the applicant for insurance contract shall be entitled to require the insurer to reduce, for the future, the insurance premiums down to the amount corresponding to the risk after such decrease.

218. Insurance contract for the benefit of another person: The Ins. Law stipulates, for a non-life insurance contract executed for benefit of third party, in its Article 8, that in the event that the insured is a person other than a party to the non-life insurance contract, such insured shall, as a matter of course, be entitled to enjoy the benefits under the said non-life insurance contract. Even in this case, the insurer is obligated to pay insurance premium (Ins. Law Article 2 (1) item 3). The Old Com. Code provided, in Article 64, that in case where the applicant for insurance contract has effected, without any mandate, a contract for the benefit of another person and failed to inform the insurer thereof, the contract shall be void. The purpose of this Article was said to

---

65. Articles 29(1) and 31 of Ins. Law are enforceable clauses.
66. Article 11 of the Ins. Law is an enforceable clause.

prevent such an illegal act as to fraud insurance benefits, but in the Ins. Law this Article is deleted with the reason that the insured in a non-life insurance contract has the right to make a claim to insurance benefits, so that an actual damage might not be developed from affirming an applicant for insurance contract to fail to inform the insurer such contract has effected without any mandate.

219. Regarding accidental fire, the Special Code (Law Concerning Responsibility for Fire by Negligence, Law No. 40, 8 March 1889) exempts the person who has started an accidental fire from compensation for damage arising from an unlawful act bounded by Civ. Code Article 709; however, this will not apply where such a fire is caused by a person's bad faith or gross negligence.

§2. INSURANCE PRACTICE

I. Conditions and Rates of Fire Insurance

220. The Non-Life Insurance Rating Organization (hereinafter called 'the Rating Organization'), founded in 1948 under the Law Concerning Non-Life Insurance Rating Organizations (29 July 1948, Law No. 193), produces standard conditions and calculates pure premium rates to submit for reference (advisory pure premium rate) to its members.

From 1 July 1998, insurance companies have to produce their own conditions and to calculate their own premium rates with reference to those of the Rating Organization.

As for the conditions and the premium rates for personal lines, however, the prior approval of the FSA is required, while those for commercial lines and factory lines are only notified to the FSA.[67]

---

67. Main changes to the Rating Organization's fire insurance premium rates:

(1) 29 Jul. 1948: the Law Concerning Non-life Insurance Rating Organizations (hereinafter called 'Rating Organizations Law') was issued and enforced. The premium rates calculated by the Rating Organization were only reference rates for its members. The provisions of the Anti-monopoly Act should not apply to collaborating acts in calculation of the premium rates by the Rating Organization.

(2) 10 Dec. 1951: the Rating Organizations Law was revised and the premium rates calculated by the Rating Organization had to be approved by the Ministry of Finance. When the Rating Organization obtains the approval of the premium rates, it should, without delay, notify its members of such premium rates and member insurance companies were also presumed to obtain the approval of such premium rates.

(3) 1 Apr. 1996: as for the premium rates, the prior approval system was disappeared. So the Rating Organization was only required to notify to the Minister of Finance. The reference premium rates system, where member insurance companies were obliged to use pure premium rates except those applied to the large fire insurance contracts where the sum insured was more than JPY 30 billion, was introduced.

II.   General Conditions

221. There are, broadly speaking, four kinds of general conditions that form the basis of various fire insurance products as shown hereunder:

Category of Risks	Fire Insurance Products:
Dwelling risk (personal line)	Dwelling house fire insurance Householders' comprehensive insurance Apartment house dwellers' insurance Earthquake insurance
General risk (commercial line)	Fire insurance (for general risk) Storekeepers' comprehensive insurance Business interruption insurance Store business interruption insurance Extra expense insurance (Earthquake insurance)
Factory risk	Fire insurance (for factory risk): Business interruption insurance Extra expense insurance
Warehouse risk	Fire insurance (for warehouse risk): Business interruption insurance Extra expense insurance

III.   The Amount of Indemnity in Partial Insurance

222.

(1)   The Insurance Law prescribes in its Article 19 that in the event that the amount insured is less than the insurable value (the agreed insurable value, if any) the amount of insurance benefits to be paid by the insurer shall be the amount obtained by multiplying the amount of damage to be covered by the proportion of the amount insured to the insurable value.
(2)   Dwelling house fire insurance (including householders' comprehensive insurance and storekeepers' comprehensive insurance) contains an 80% co-insurance clause. If the insured amount is equal to at least 80% of the insurable value, the amount indemnified is paid in full up to the insured amount.
(3)   General fire insurance (for commercial risk, factory risk and warehouse risk) is subject to the principle mentioned above in (1).

IV.   Preservation of Mortgagee's Interest

223. One of the following measures is commonly taken to protect the interest of creditors.

A.   Establishment of Pledge on the Right to Claim

224. 214.1. A mortgagee compels the mortgagor have fire insurance on the mortgaged property and preserves his/her mortgage by taking over the right to claim under the policy. This method is that most widely used in Japan.

The mortgagee has, in accordance with the provisions of Civ. Code (Article 303), a right to obtain satisfaction of his/her claim out of the property of the obligor in preference to other obligees.

Civ. Code Articles 304 and 372, however, prescribe that the person having such a preferential right must levy an attachment thereon prior to their payment or delivery.

The order of the priority between the establishment of pledge on the right to claim and mortgagee's right of subrogation shall be on either of the earlier date when the pledgee establishes his/her right or the mortgagee attaches the property.[68]

B.   Mortgagee Clause

225. The mortgagee's interest may be protected by attaching a mortgagee clause to the fire insurance policy on the mortgaged property, which transfers the right to claim to the mortgagee.

C.   Fire Insurance for Mortgagee's Interest

226. This insurance covers the loss of the mortgagee's interest if the mortgaged property suffers loss or damage caused by fire, lightning, bursting and explosion. Under this insurance, the insured is the mortgagee and he/she has to bear the insurance premium.

V.   Subrogation by the Insurer

A.   Subrogation for Remaining Property

227. In the event that the subject matter of insurance is destroyed in its entirety and an insurer has paid insurance benefits, it shall, as a matter of course, acquire on behalf of an insured the title or other real rights retained by such insured in respect of such subject matter of insurance in accordance with the proportion of the amount of such insurance benefits to the insurable value (the agreed value, if any) (Ins. Law Article 24, enforceable clause).

B.   Rights of Subrogation Against Third Party

228. 218.

(1)   The Ins. Law provides the rights of subrogation against third party, in its Article 25 (enforceable clause), that in the event that an insurer has paid insurance benefits,

---

68.   Supreme Court 7 Apr. 1923 (O) 319.

it shall, as a matter of course, acquire on behalf of an insured the claims to be obtained by the insured as a result of damage due to insurable contingencies (as regards a non-life insurance contract under which damage that may arise on certain claims from default or otherwise is to be covered, such claims shall be included), to the extent of the lesser of:

- the amount insurance benefits paid by such insurer;
- the amount of the insured's claim (if the amount mentioned in the preceding item is less than the amount of damage to be covered, the amount remaining after deducting from the amount of the insured's claims such deficiency).

(2) If, in the case of the preceding paragraph, the amount mentioned in item (1) above is less than the amount of damage to be covered, an insured shall be entitled to receive repayment of the insured's claims except for the portion acquired by an insurer on behalf of the insured in accordance with the provisions of the said paragraph, in priority to the claims of the insurer thus acquired.

The cost and expenses for acquiring or exercising the right of subrogation will be borne by the insurer.

VI.   Termination of the Insurance Contract

229. When the amount paid for property loss or damage, per an accident, exceeds 80% or more of the amount insured, the insurance contract will be terminated when the accident to be paid for has occurred.

If the amount paid for property loss or damage, per an accident, is less than 80% of the amount insured (or the amount of the insurance value), the original amount insured is still effective for the policy period remaining.

VII.   Breach of Duty to Disclose and to Give Notice

230. If, at the time when the contract of insurance was effected, the policyholder and the insured, through bad faith or gross negligence, failed to disclose material facts or made a false statement in regard to material facts, the insurer may rescind the contract.

The policyholder or the insured has a duty to give notice to the insurer at the times mentioned below and if he/she does not, the insurer may rescind the contract:

(1) the time of assignment of the subject matter of the insurance;
(2) if the construction of the building insured or the building in which the subject matter insured has been stored and the purpose for which it has been used has been altered;
(3) at the time of a change of location of the subject matter insured.

(4) If the contract has been rescinded, this rescission will take effect only for the future.

VIII. Arbitrator

231. If any difference arises as to the amount of any loss or damage, or the degree of bodily injury, the differences shall independently be referred to the decision of arbitrators appointed by the parties in difference and in case of disagreement between arbitrators, the difference shall be referred to the decision of an umpire who has been appointed by them.

§3. SAVINGS-TYPE (MATURITY-REFUND-TYPE) INSURANCE

I.   Introduction

232. Savings-type insurance related to fire insurance started in the early 1960s. The Insurance Council reported in January 1963:

If building endowment insurance offer refunds to policyholders upon accident-free expiration of a policy period, it would better suit the sentiments of a certain group of fire insurance policyholders. Therefore, we assume that realization of such a type of policy would be significant as an addition to the conventional type of fire insurance policies with no refund upon expiration. In light of the actual needs, it can be said that it would promote the popularization of insurance in Japan and eventually serve to improve the solidity of the non-life insurance industry if such a new type of policy were offered in any appropriate style.

In response to this report, mutual companies started to sell 'fire mutual insurance'[69] and 'building endowment'[70] within the year 1963. In April 1968, stock companies also started to handle 'long-term comprehensive insurance',[71] and 'savings-type family personal traffic accident insurance'[72] was developed in 1974.

233. Non-Life insurance companies proceeded with the improvement and variation of savings-type of insurance according to the further recommendation of the Insurance Council (1981, 1987).

In 1987, a basic endorsement for savings-type was developed by the Tokyo Marine and Fire Insurance Co. Ltd for wide use, so that any conventional product

---

69.   The covered risks of these insurances are very similar to those of householders' comprehensive insurance.
70.   *Ibid.*
71.   *Ibid.*
72.   The covered risks of this insurance are very similar to those of family traffic personal accident insurance.

could easily be transformed into savings-type insurance. Savings-type insurance products meet the needs of the society and expand their premium volume quickly.[73]

234. Premiums for insurance with basic endorsement for savings-type consist of coverage premium (risk premium + premium loadings including agency commission and company profit) and premiums for supplementary saving insurance (saving premium = source of money to be paid to the policyholder, maintenance expense and agency commission).

II.   Characteristics of Savings-Type Insurance

A.   *Maturity Refund and Policyholder's Dividend*

235. When a policy matures with no total loss, the policyholder is entitled to receive a cash refund, the amount of which depends on the kind of insurance and type of policy he/she has held. If the savings elements of a premium yield more than the programmed interest rate, the surplus is paid to the policyholder as a dividend.

B.   *Long Policy Period*

236. The policy period is generally three to twenty years, but in case of the annuity-type personal accident insurance the policy period is up to fifty years and for life in the case of nursing care expenses insurance.

C.   *Total Loss Lapse*

237. The policy is generally lapsed when a certain percentage (80%–100%, depending upon the kind of policy) of the insured amount is paid during a single insurance term.

D.   *Premium Payment Methods*

238. Various types of payment methods can be offered, such as lump sum, annual, biannual and monthly payment. Lump sum payment of part of premium (down payment) is also available for some kinds of policies.

E.   *Automatic Premium Loan*

239. If the premium is paid in instalments, if the premium for the second payment onwards and after is not paid within its payment period (until the end of the month following the month in which the premium is due), that amount is automatically on loan from the cash surrender value.

---

73.   *See* s. III of this chapter. Direct net premiums of all savings-type insurance were JPY 1,346 billion in 2002 (about 15% of all lines of insurance).

F.   Policy Loan

240. When the policyholder temporarily needs a fund, he/she is able to borrow a sum of up to 90% of the cash surrender value without surrendering the policy.

III.   Main Savings-Type Insurance Products

241. Fire insurance related products are the following:

(1)   fire mutual insurance (1963);
(2)   building endowment insurance (1963);
(3)   long-term comprehensive insurance (1968);
(4)   savings-type apartment dwellers' insurance (1984);
(5)   savings-type store business interruption insurance (1984);
(6)   savings-type comprehensive insurance for homeowners (1989);
(7)   savings-type comprehensive insurance for storeowners (1993).

242. Personal accident insurance related products are:

(1)   personal accident mutual insurance (1969);
(2)   savings-type family traffic personal accident insurance (1974);
(3)   savings-type ladies insurance (1984) and new savings-type ladies' insurance (1989);
(4)   savings-type ordinary personal accident insurance (1986);
(5)   savings-type family personal accident insurance (1986);
(6)   savings-type juvenile comprehensive insurance (1988);
(7)   asset-making savings-type personal accident insurance (1988). This insurance was developed to meet the request of the Workers' Asset-Making Promotion Law (Law No. 92, 1 June 1971);
(8)   savings-type married couple comprehensive insurance (1989);
(9)   savings-type income indemnity insurance (1990);
(10) annuity-type personal accident insurance (1992). This insurance is a so-called non-life version of individual annuity products.

243. Other products are:

(1)   savings-type movables comprehensive insurance (1984);
(2)   savings-type nursing care expenses insurance (1990);
(3)   savings-type workers' accident comprehensive insurance (1990);
(4)   savings-type automobile insurance (1999).

Chapter 2.   Consequential Loss Insurance

§1.   CHARACTERISTIC FEATURE

244. Consequential loss insurance generally requires as a condition of cover that material damage must have been caused directly to the subject matter insured, which belongs to the insured. Some consequential loss insurances, however, cover the consequential loss that has been caused by damage to a third party's properties or injury to another person.

§2.   LOSS OF INCOME AND PECUNIARY LOSS

245. In Japan, consequential loss insurance may be roughly divided into two categories (i.e., loss of income insurance and miscellaneous pecuniary insurance).

I.   Loss of Income Insurance

246. Loss of income insurance provides cover for damage owing to loss of income because of an idle business. For instance:

– A manufacturer (insured) may suffer losses, if he/she has to stop business for a certain term because a fire broke out in his/her factory or if parts or accessories of his/her products cannot be supplied because of a fire in the supplier's factory.
– A restaurant (insured) may suffer losses, if it is ordered by the authorities to stop business for a certain term because of food poisoning or an infectious disease at the insured's premises.

Loss of income insurance can be underwritten as an independent insurance or by an endorsement attached to certain insurance policies such as fire insurance, machinery insurance, stores liability insurance or product liability insurance, etc.

II.   Miscellaneous Pecuniary Insurance

247. This pecuniary insurance covers the loss or profit that the insured has to pay following an accident.

Medical expenses insurance and nursing care insurance (see Part V, Chapter 3) are the most popular insurances in this category. There are, however, many other kinds of pecuniary insurance such as event cancellation insurance,[74] sports reward insurance, [75] weather insurance,[76] withdrawal expense insurance,[77]etc., that may be designed to cover the loss or profit on each demand of the insured.

248. As the proportion of elderly person (65 years old and more) in the population increased (26.7% as of September 2015), single-person becomes high proportion and lonely death or suicide are increased. Some insurance companies developed new products to cover such costs and/or losses that in case which lonely death, suicide, death of the crime and the like have occurred, the landlord may suffer loss such as having to pay cost to clean, refurbish the room and also the landlord may lose money because of that new lessee may hesitate to rent or ask for discount of rental fee.

---

74.   Events cancellation insurance covers:

(a)   such expenses as have been disbursed by a producer (insured) as rental fee for a hall or a stadium, working expenditure, advertising or giving publicity, if a sports competition or a concert, etc., is cancelled because of bad weather or illness of players or broadcasters, etc.;

(b)   loss of profit in cases mentioned above.

75.   Sports reward insurance covers rewards, etc., which are given to a person who achieves the specific act contracted between a sponsor and players (for instance, the sponsor of a hole-in-one prize in a professional golf players' tournament may buy this insurance).

76.   Weather insurance covers loss owing to idle business suffered by an owner of a leisure centre, etc., from bad weather.

77.   Withdrawal expense insurance covers expenses from withdrawing products, work or property from the market because of any defect or deficiency therein.

Chapter 3. Transport Insurance

§1. MARINE INSURANCE

I. Introduction

249. In insurance practice, marine insurance consists of hull insurance and cargo insurance and the object of cargo insurance is goods conveyed by sea, land and air, while the Com. Code Article 815 prescribes that 'a contract of marine insurance has for its object indemnification against loss which may arise from a contingency with navigation'.

250. In the Japanese marine insurance market, general conditions in both Japanese and English are used. Usually, both Japanese and English general conditions are used for hull insurance. As for cargo insurance, the Japanese wording is used for domestic transportation cargo insurance contracts and the English wording is used for import and export cargo insurance contracts.

251. According to the IBL Cabinet Order Article 19 and Enforcement Regulations Article 116, foreign insurers with no licence and no branch office in Japan may make the following transport insurance contracts in Japan:

(1) insurance contracts which cover vessels having Japanese nationality used for international marine transportation and cargos in the process of being internationally transported by such vessels and the liabilities arising therefrom, or any of them;

(2) insurance contracts which cover aircraft having Japanese nationality used for commercial airline business and the cargos being internationally transported by such aircraft and the liabilities arising therefrom, or any of them;

(3) insurance contracts which cover launches into cosmic space, transported cargos relating to such launches (including satellites) and means of transportation of such cargos and the liabilities arising therefrom, or any of them;

(4) insurance contracts which cover cargos that are located in Japan and are being internationally transported (excluding those contracts mentioned above in (1) and (2)).

II. Hull Insurance

252. In Japan, the subjects of hull insurance business are insurance companies, fishing vessel mutual insurance associations, small vessel mutual insurance associations and the Ship Owners' Mutual Protection and Indemnity Association. They are formed under respective special laws.[78]

253. The objects of hull insurance written by these fishing vessel mutual insurance associations are limited to Japanese flag fishing vessels of under 1,000 gross tons. These fishing vessel mutual associations also write 'savings-type hull insurance for fishing vessels', 'fishing vessel PI insurance', 'personal accident insurance for ship owners on board' and 'liability insurance for pleasure boats under 5 tons'.

The government subsidizes the pure risk premium to the owners of fishing vessels of under 100 tons, in certain cases where all fishing vessels registered in a certain area are insured as a whole, etc.

254. A small vessel mutual insurance association writes hull insurance not only on wooden vessels (excluding fishing vessels) but also on small steel vessels of under 300 gross tons and the Ship Owners' Mutual Protection and Indemnity Association writes protection and indemnity insurance on all kinds of ship except wooden ones.

A.   Hull Insurance of Insurance Companies

255. The objects of hull insurance written by insurance companies are not only such vessels as stipulated in Com. Code Article 684 (definition of vessel) but also vessels under construction or repair at dockyards, barges, mobile drilling rigs, fixed platforms and other offshore structures used in offshore oil exploration and production.[79]

256. If a vessel is insured, any accessories without regard to entering in the ship's inventory appurtenances, fuel, provisions and other stores of such vessel can be insured, while the Com. Code (Article 685) stipulates that any article entered in the ship's inventory of appurtenances is presumed to be an accessory to the ship.

257. The insured of hull insurance is the owner of the insured ship in usual. The demise-charterer is not treated as an insured under the policy, but in the case of bareboat charter, the charterer who may provide such consumables as fuel, provisions, etc., is also treated as the insured on those provided.

B.   Insured Value

258. Hull insurance policy is a valued policy. And the value agreed on between the contracting parties taking the cost of reconstruction, the market price, the book value and other elements into consideration at the time of the insurance contract is final.[80]

---

78.   For insurance companies – the IBL; for fishing vessels mutual insurance associations –fishing vessel damage, etc. Indemnity Law (Law No. 28, 1952);for small vessel mutual insurance association and P & I Club – Ship Owners Mutual Insurance Association Law (Law No. 177, 1950).

79.   Com. Code Art. 684: 'A ship within the meaning of this Code is one which is made available in navigation for the purpose of engaging in commercial transactions. The provisions of this Book shall not apply to small boats or to any vessel propelled only or chiefly by oars.'

80.   Com. Code Art. 818 (insurable value of ship insurance): 'In the insurance of a ship, the insurable value shall be the value of the ship at the time when the liability of the insurer commences.'

C.   Hull Insurance Clauses

259. The Japan Hull Insurers' Union (JHIU) had standardized general conditions and other clauses but at present there are no standard conditions and clauses since the JHIU disbanded in 1997 according to the revision of the IBL in 1995.

Insurance companies, however, still use the same conditions and clauses in general, so it can be said in a sense that there are still the same standard conditions and clauses.

In Japan, most hull insurance contracts have been written under Japanese clauses, but recently the use of foreign clauses such as British or American clauses has increased.

The general conditions of hull insurance (time insurance, voyage insurance, port risks insurance) is always supplemented by following six kinds of special clauses and currently special clause class No. 2, class No. 5 and class No. 6 are used in general:

(1)   special class No. 1 (TLO);[81]
(2)   special class No. 2 (FAA S/C) or (FAA S/C, 4/4 RDC);
(3)   special class No. 3 (FPA absolute but including 4/4 RDC);
(4)   special class No. 4 (FPA unless caused by sinking, fire or collision with 4/4 RDC excess PA);
(5)   special class No. 5 (FPA unless caused by sinking, fire or collision with 4/4 RDC);
(6)   special class No. 6 (full conditions, 4/4 RDC).

D.   Term of Insurance

260. The Com. Code (Article 821, commencing and terminating points of ship insurance) stipulates that:

(1)   if a ship is insured for a single voyage, the liability of the insurer shall commence at the time when the loading of the goods or of ballast commences;
(2)   if a ship is insured after goods or ballast have been loaded, the liability of the insurer shall commence at the time of the formation of the contract;
(3)   in the cases mentioned in the preceding two paragraphs, the liability of the insurer shall terminate upon the completion of the unloading of the goods and ballast at the port of destination; provided, however, that it shall terminate at the time when

---

81.   TLO = total loss only, FAA = free from all average, S/C = salvage charge, RDC = running down clause, FPA = free from particular average. Total loss means both actual total loss and constructive total loss. Actual total loss means such loss as when the insured ship was lost into the unsalvageable deep sea or sustained unrepairable loss or damage from collision, fire, etc., and the general conditions of hull insurance sustain terms of the constructive total loss such as following:

(1)   where each or total amount of repair cost, general average contribution or suing and labouring expenses exceeds the insurable value;
(2)   where the insured ship shall be deemed to be missing for sixty days;
(3)   where the insured shall not be able to possess and/or use of the insured ship for a continuous 180 days.

their unloading should have been completed, in cases where such unloading has been delayed otherwise than by reason of force majeure.

In practice, insurers issue two types of policy to vessels, that is, a time policy or a voyage policy. Time insurance (insurance for a definite period, which is usually one year) is the most popular one for ordinary steel vessels in Japan.[82]

For a voyage policy:

the Company's liability shall commence, unless otherwise specially agreed, at the time when the Vessel has commenced either casting off mooring or weighing anchor, whichever shall first occur, at the port of departure specified in the Policy and shall terminate upon expiry of 24 hours after either she has dropped her anchor or she has been moored, whichever shall first occur, at the port of destination specified in the Policy.

If, however, the Vessel has either commenced loading of cargo or other preparations for the departure for another voyage or she has commenced casting off moorings or weighing anchor, the Company's liability shall terminate at the time of any such occurrence even if it is within the said 24 hours (General Condition Article 10(2)).

E. Kinds of Hull Insurance in the Japanese Market

261. In the Japanese market, these insurances are underwritten in the category of hull insurance business:

(1) time insurance;
(2) voyage insurance;
(3) port risks insurance;
(4) builders' risks insurance;
(5) repairing risks insurance;
(6) ship repairers' risks insurance;
(7) repairing expenses insurance;
(8) war and SR and CC risks insurance;
(9) mine risks insurance;
(10) loss time insurance;
(11) protection and indemnity insurance for dredgers, barges and the like.[83]

F. Rating Organization

262. The rates of hull insurance were changed from the union tariff to the Rating Organization tariff subject to the Law concerning Non-Life Insurance Rating Organization enacted on 29 July 1948 (Law No. 193).

---

82. According to the demand of the insured, the period of insurance may be extended to commence twenty-four hours before the time of the departure.
83. The Japan Ship Owners' Mutual Protection and Indemnity Association has not underwritten for dredger, barge and the like formerly. So insurance companies issue their policies for P and I risks together with hull risk coverage.

In 1962, however, the revised IBL changed the union tariff again (both the union tariff and the Rating Organization tariff were excluded from application of Law Concerning Prohibition against Private Monopoly and Preservation of Fair Trade (Law No. 54, 1947), hereinafter called 'Monopoly Law').

The new IBL (in force from 1 April 1996) makes marine insurance apply Monopoly Law. The Japanese Hull Insurers' Union was disbanded in 1997 complying with this change.

So, the rates of hull insurance in Japanese market are at present free rates.

III. Cargo Insurance

263. Cargo insurance in the Japanese insurance market is made up of marine cargo insurance, inland transit insurance and air-borne cargo insurance. Marine cargo insurance is compounded from export and import cargo insurance and coastwise cargo insurance (or domestic marine cargo insurance). Air-borne cargoes can be written under both marine insurance and aviation insurance, and under the marine insurance field, air-borne cargoes in international transportation may be written under export and import cargo insurance while air-borne cargoes in domestic transportation may be written under inland transit insurance.

264. The domestic marine cargo insurance and the inland transit insurance are subject to Japanese law and written in yen-based policies.

Export and import cargo insurance is written in foreign-currency-based policy. This insurance is subject to English law and practice only as to liability for and settlement of any and all claims, and the insurance policy or certificate of insurance is also issued with English wording.

265. There are two general conditions in English for the export and import insurance.

The first is the form drafted on the model of the marine policy form prevailing as companies' combined policy in the London market, together with various cargo clauses of the Institute of London Underwriters and the other is so-called New Institute Policy and the Institute Cargo Clause (A), (B) and (C) which were prepared by the Institute of London Underwriters from 1 January 1982 to comply with international criticism on the hard reading of the policy form.[84]

A. Duration of Risks for Export and Import Cargo Insurance

266. As for the period insured, the Com. Code (Article 822(1)) stipulates:

in cases where the cargo has been insured or in cases where prospective profit or remuneration to be earned upon the arrival of the cargo have been insured, the liability of the insurer shall commence at the time when the cargo has left the land and terminate at the time when its unloading has been completed at the port of unloading, and general conditions in the policy body also provide that the liability of the insurer

---

84. Japanese insurers are still continuing to use the traditional cargo policy form, together with the old Institute cargo clauses, unless a letter of credit requires the new policy form with the new Institute clauses attached on export and import cargoes.

is 'beginning the Adventure upon the said Goods and Merchandises from the loading thereof abroad the said ship, and shall so continue and endure, until the said Goods and Merchandises shall be arrived at (name of the port of unloading) and until the same be there discharge and safely landed'.

This restriction of the period of insured, however, may not be adapted to the business procedure, so the insurers may amend the period of insurance, with Institute cargo clause (transit clause and craft clause), to include transit risk by the craft at the port of loading and inland transit risk from warehouse to warehouse under certain conditions. And moreover, additional clauses such as an FOB attachment clause and/ or FAS warehouse, etc., may be adopted to suit the individual requirements of each deal.

B.   The Domestic Marine Cargo Insurance and Inland Transit Insurance

267. Domestic marine cargo insurance usually covers incidental land transportation, and inland transit insurance is able to cover incidental marine transportation (by ferry boats, for instance). In case of some kinds of insured subject (the post, currency, note, securities, for example), only inland transit insurance covers marine transportation.

The general conditions in Japanese, used for both of domestic marine insurance and inland transit insurance, are drafted with the same wording apart from the title.

268. General Conditions, for both Domestic Marine Insurance and Inland Transit Insurance, cover the goods from warehouse to warehouse against all risks, or alternatively against specified risks such as fire, explosion or collision, overturning, derailment, falling, forced landing, sinking, grounding or stranding of conveyances, according to the agreement between the insurer and the insured. In both cases of all risks cover and specified risks cover, the insurer will pay, in addition, for such expenditure as loss preventing charges, salvage charges, forwarding charges and general average contribution.

C.   General Average

269. The Com. Code stipulates general average with twelve articles (from Article 788 to Article 799). These provisions are, however, seldom applied in an actual case of general average, because these provisions are not mandatory and therefore cannot be forcibly applied to the case where any special agreement as to applicable rules exists in the contract of affreightment and/or marine insurance.

Bills of lading and insurance policies issued in Japan uniformly contain, with only a few exceptions, a clause to the effect that general average shall be adjusted according to the York – Antwerp Rules 1974. So, it can be said that the York – Antwerp Rules 1974 play a role as 'living law' of the general average in Japan.[85]

D.   Term of Insurance

270. The Com. Code stipulates the duration of the policy for inland transit insurance that in the absence of any special agreement, the insurer is bound to make indemnification against any loss which may arise between the time when the carrier receives the goods and the time when he/she delivers them to the consignee. In fact, however, the general conditions of domestic marine insurance and inland transit insurance provide the following and there are some endorsements to amend the duration of policy according to the conditions of each deal (e.g., an endorsement to limit the duration of policy only from the time the goods are taken in the place of storage to the time the goods are loaded to the marine conveyance or an endorsement to extend the duration of policy to include the term that the subject matter insured is being processed in a factory):

(1)   The liability of the insurer: commences from whichever is earlier of the time the goods are taken out from the place of storage stipulated in the policy or the time the loading of the goods onto the conveyance begins at such place of storage for the commence of the transit, continues during the ordinary course of transportation, and terminates at whichever is later of the time the goods are taken into the place of storage appointed by the consignee at the place of destination named in the policy or the time the goods are unloaded from the conveyance at such place of storage (this paragraph is applied to any part of the goods as that part is taken out or the loading of that part begins, or as that part is taken in or unloaded). However, the duration of insurance after arrival of conveyance at the place of storage appointed by the consignee at the destination ceases at the latest at noon of the day following the day on which the conveyance arrived.

(2)   In cases to cover storage risks at the port of loading or unloading: the duration of insurance before loading of the goods onto the marine conveyance is limited to fifteen days (or thirty days if the place of departure is a place outside the port of loading) counting from 00:00 hours of the day following whichever is earlier of the day on which the taking out of the goods from the place of storage at place of departure stipulated in the policy began or the day on which the loading of the goods onto the conveyance at such place of the storage began, and the duration of insurance after unloading of the goods from the marine conveyance at the port of unloading is limited to fifteen days (or thirty days if the place of destination

---

85.   The provisions, with respect to general average, in the Com. Code still maintain the legal value of existence in such cases:

(1)   in cases of the coastal transit of goods for which a bill of lading is rarely issued, general average is sometimes adjusted in accordance with the provisions;

(2)   in cases not stipulated in the York–Antwerp Rules 1974, the provisions remain operative so far as these matters concerned (Art. 798 provides for the period of prescription of the claims arising from general average).

is a place outside the port of unloading) counting from 00:00 hours of the day following the day on which the unloading of the goods was completed.

§2. MOVABLES COMPREHENSIVE INSURANCE

I.   Statutory Regulation

271. For the category of this movables comprehensive insurance, there are no standard conditions; however, the general conditions adopted by domestic insurers are more or less similar.[86]

II.   Features of this Insurance

272. This insurance, produced in 1961 on the model of inland marine floaters practised in the US market, covers all risks on movables in all situations, whether in storage, in use, in carrying or in transit within the territory specified in the policy, subject to some exclusions.

273. The subjects eligible for this insurance are all kinds of movables except the following:[87]

(1) movables to be insured only when stored in a specific place;
(2) movables under processing or manufacturing (excluding repairing);
(3) automobiles;
(4) vessels (excluding sailing-yacht, private motorboats under twenty gross tons, etc.);
(5) aircraft;
(6) movables to be insured only while in transit between specific places.

---

86.   There are several types of insurance in the category of this insurance such as the following:

(1) ordinary type of movables comprehensive insurance (mentioned in this section);
(2) long-term movables comprehensive insurance with maturity refund;
(3) yacht and motorboat comprehensive insurance;
(4) computer comprehensive insurance;
(5) banker's blanket policy;
(6) franchise-chain comprehensive insurance.

87.   These exceptions are to avoid possible confusion in the fields and rating between this insurance and other classes of insurance such as fire, machinery, hull (marine and aviation), cargo and inland transit, etc.

III. Exclusions

274. There are two types of exclusion, that is, 'absolute exclusions', which may not be overridden by any means, and 'relative exclusions', which can be overridden by special endorsements.

The main absolute exclusions are:

(1) loss or damage caused by wilful act or gross negligence on the part of policyholder, the insured or beneficiary;
(2) loss or damage resulting from wear and tear of the property insured or rust, mould, deterioration or similar degradation due to the inherent nature of the insured property;
(3) loss or damage resulting directly or indirectly from war, civil war, revolution, rebellion or any similar incident;
(4) loss or damage caused by radioactive, explosive or other hazardous features of nuclear fuel materials or used nuclear fuel materials;
(5) loss or damage occurring after the commencement of processing (exclude repair) and/or similar works of the insured property;
(6) loss or damage caused by the accident (to be covered under this insurance) occurring before the premium had been paid.

The main relative exclusions are:

(1) loss or damage resulting from operational error or faulty workmanship in the course of repair, cleaning or similar works done to the insured property;
(2) loss or damage resulting from electrical or mechanical breakdown;
(3) loss or damage due to flood, high sea, etc., caused by typhoon, windstorm, heavy rain, etc.;
(4) loss or damage resulting directly or indirectly from earthquake, volcanic eruption or tidal wave arising therefrom.

IV. Insurance Practice

275. This insurance covers not only property loss or damage but also extraordinary expenses, debris removal expenses and expenses incidental to repairing.

A. *Payment of Loss*

1. Property Loss or Damage
276. The indemnity amount for property loss or damage shall be calculated with following formula:

the amount to be paid = (amount of property loss or damage – deductibles) × (amount insured ÷ value of the insured property at the time and place of loss occurrence or the agreed value).[88]

2. Extraordinary Expenses

277. Thirty per cent of the indemnity amount for property loss or damage shall be paid as extraordinary expenses (up to JPY 3 million per accident), even if the total amount of payment for extraordinary expenses and other indemnity amounts exceeds the amount insured.

3. Debris Removal Expenses

278. Ten per cent of the indemnity amount for property loss or damage shall be paid as debris removal expenses (up to the amount actually incurred by the insured), even if the total amount of payment for extraordinary expenses and other indemnity amounts exceed the amount insured.

4. Expenses Incidental to Repairing

279. When the subject insured sustained damage caused by fire, lightning, bursting or explosion, necessary or useful expenses borne by the insured (e.g. expenses to inspect the origin of the accident, expenses for temporary repair or expenses to rent substitutional equipment for the subject insured damaged) shall be paid. This indemnity amount, however, shall not be paid when the subject insured is mainly kept at a warehouse or a dwelling house.

Thirty per cent of the indemnity amount for property loss or damage shall be paid as expenses incidental to repairing (up to JPY 10 million per accident for commercial risk and JPY 50 million for factory risk), even if the total amount of payment for expenses incidental to repairing and other indemnity amounts exceeds the amount insured.

B.   No Claim Return and Good Result Return

280. In case of no claim during the policy period, a no claim return (up to 20% of the premium) may be paid in general.

To a large account, showing a loss ratio of under 20% or so a good result return may be paid (up to 15% of the premium paid) in general.

---

88.   If the amount insured exceeded the value of the insured property, the amount insured may be presumed to be the same as the value of the insured property. In case of total loss, deductibles shall not be applied. Necessary or useful expenses incurred by the insured to prevent or minimize the loss or damage or to preserve or exercise his right of claim against a liable third party may be included in the amount of property loss or damage.

Chapter 4.   General Liability Insurance

§1.   GENERAL LIABILITY INSURANCE

I.   Introduction

281. Liability insurance is designed to pay for the financial loss suffered by an insured who becomes legally liable to pay the damages to other parties. 'General liability insurance' may be underwritten as a branch of insurance independent from other types of liability insurance in Japan. The examples of other types of liability insurance are compulsory automobile insurance, voluntary automobile insurance, nuclear energy liability insurance, employers' liability insurance and the liability section under the aviation insurance and the like.

282. There are four types of liability insurance policies in Japan as follows:

(1) comprehensive type policies (commercial general liability insurance), to be underwritten under the comprehensive general conditions;
(2) separate-type policies (general liability insurance); to be underwritten under the general conditions coupled with the special conditions that are designed to provide specific liability cover such as for premises, contractors, elevator/escalator, bailees, garage-keepers, products, hotel owners, personal, doctor, lawyer and the like;
(3) independent-type policies to be underwritten under the general conditions designed for the each purpose such as directors' and officers' liability insurance, insurance brokers' liability insurance, environmental liability insurance, etc.;
(4) umbrella liability insurance.

II.   Statutory Regulations

283. The Civ. Code has the closest relation to the general liability insurance, since the insurer is liable to indemnify the insured when the insured becomes legally obliged to pay damages to the claimant for his/her wrongful acts (Civ. Code Article 709) and his/her impossibility of performance (Civ. Code Article 415).

Under old Com. Code, there was no provision for a liability insurance contract except the insurance contract, for fire risk, made by person holding another's property. However, considering the situation that a liability insurance contract has become to play an important role in the economic activities of individuals and corporate of the day. From the viewpoint to protect a victim, insurance benefits paid to the insured of liability insurance contract must be prevented from being used up repaid to another creditor before being paid to the victims thereof. So, the Ins. Law stipulates, in its Article 22(1) and (2), that a person who is entitled to claim compensation for damages from an insured under a liability insurance contract resulting from insurable contingencies under such a liability insurance contract shall have a lien against the insured's right to claim insurance benefits (Ins. Law Article 22(1)) and an insured may exercise the right to claim insurance benefits from an insurer to the extent of the amount repaid with respect to the right to claim damages mentioned in the preceding paragraph or the amount agreed to by a person who has such right to damages (Ins. Law Article 22(2)). The insurer being exercised the right of lien may assert against the victim such right (e.g., insurer's immunities provided in the insurance contract, limit of the amount payable) as having against the insured.

Other insurance contract lien; CALI contract lien (the ALSL Article 16(1)), Nuclear liability insurance contract lien (the Law relating to the Liability for Nuclear Damage Article 9(1)).

284. For product liability insurance, there is a Product Liability Law that is based on the so-called strict liability on manufacturers' defective products for the purpose of protecting consumers; it came into force on 1 July 1995.

III.   Basic Features of Cover

285. Liability insurance is designed to cover the financial loss suffered by a third party resulting from bodily injury or property damage due to the insured's negligence. The cover generally excludes defamation, infringement of the right of privacy and wrongful detention, contractual liability and further pure financial loss which does not involve any physical damage to property.

286. Liability insurance covers damages and expenses as shown below:

(1)   damages which the insured is legally liable to pay the claimant generally, including:

   (a) medical expenses, hospital room charges and financial compensation for absence from work due to bodily injury; and
   (b) costs and expenses incurred for repair or replacement of damaged property and loss of use;

(2)   expenses paid by the insured to provide first aid to the injured at the time of the accident;
(3)   reasonable expenses incurred by the insured in preventing or minimizing damages and in preserving or exercising the right of recovery where damages are recoverable from other persons;
(4)   legal expenses paid by the insured with prior consent from the insurer such as court expenses, remuneration for an attorney in defence of a claim and necessary expenses pertaining to arbitration, mediation and settlement; and
(5)   reasonable expenses incurred by the insured to cooperate with insurer in circumstances whereby the insurer opts to exercise his/her right to settle the claim directly with the claimant or to sue in the name and on behalf of the insured.

§2.   LIABILITY INSURANCE FOR ENTERPRISES

287. Both commercial general liability insurance and general liability insurance are available for enterprises to cover the liability of companies and persons to third parties in the course of business.

These policies are generally based on the loss occurrence principle. Product liability insurance, however, is usually based on the claim-made principle.

288. Commercial general liability insurance also covers liability on account of libel, slander, piracy, invasion of privacy and infringement of human rights, while general liability insurance does not cover such liability.

289. There are three types of special conditions in general liability insurance for enterprises:

(1)   special conditions to cover the liability caused by the insured's wrongful act: premises liability, elevator/escalator liability, contractor's liability, product liability, etc.,
(2)   special conditions to cover the liability caused by the insured's impossibility of performance: bailees' liability, garage-keepers' liability, etc.,
(3)   special conditions to cover both the liabilities mentioned above: hotel owners' liability, LP gas dealers' liability, etc.

I.   Persons Insured

290. The policy generally covers not only the company itself but also its employees acting in the course of business. Its agents, partners, subcontractors and suppliers, etc., can be covered as additional insureds under the same policy.

Insurers waive recourse directly or indirectly against the insured (including additional insured).

The cross-liability clause is generally applied to the liability among persons insured.

II.   Main Exclusions

291. These are:

(1)   liabilities due to wilful misconduct of the insured;
(2)   liabilities due to war, civil war, insurrection, rebellion, riot, strike or lock-out;
(3)   liabilities due to earthquake, eruption, flood or tidal wave;
(4)   liabilities to any of the insured's family members or relatives who live in the same household as the insured;
(5)   liabilities arising out of drainage, exhaust or smoke (this does not apply to liabilities arising out of drainage and others that may be due to sudden and accidental causes);

(6) liabilities to any employee of the insured for bodily injury arising out of and in the course of employment;[89]
(7) liabilities assumed by the insured under a contract with another party;
(8) liabilities for damage to property under care, custody or control of the insured.[90]

III. Product Liability

292. This insurance covers liability for bodily injury or property damage to a third party arising out of products sold or distributed by the insured which may occur after the physical possession of such products has been relinquished by him/ her to others, or works performed by the insured which may occur after such works have been completed and delivered by him/her to the others.

293. Some insurance companies may be selling product liability insurance with the special endorsement to cover re-call expenses.

A.   Product Liability Law (Law No. 85, 1994)

294. The manufacturer etc.,[91]shall be liable for damages caused by the injury, when he/she injures someone's life, body or property by the defect in his/her delivered products. However, the manufacturer, etc., is not liable when only the defective product itself is damaged (Article 3).

The manufacturer, etc., shall not be liable, if he/she proves (Article 4):

(a) that the state of scientific or technical knowledge at the time when the manufacturer, etc., delivered the product was not such as to enable the existence of defect in the product to be discovered; or
(b) in the case where the product is used as a component or raw material of another product, that the defect is substantially attributable to compliance with the instruction concerning the specifications given by the manufacturer of the said other product, and that the manufacturer, etc., is not negligent on occurrence of the defect.

---

89. This type of liability is specifically covered under the workers' accident comprehensive insurance or the government workmen's compensation system.
90. This type of liability can be covered under the special conditions (bailees', garage-keepers').
91. Article 2 provides that 'manufacturer, etc.,' means any one of the following:

(a) any person who manufactured, processed, or imported the product as business (hereinafter called just 'manufacturer');
(b) any person who, by putting his name, trademark or other feature on the product presents himself as its manufacture, or any person who puts the representation of name, etc., on the product in a manner mistakable for the manufacturer;
(c) any person who, by putting the representation of name, etc., on the product, may be recognized as its manufacturer-in-fact, in the light of a manner concerning manufacturing, processing, importing or sales, and other circumstances.

The right for damages shall be extinguished by prescription if the injured person or his/her legal representative does not exercise such right within three years from the time when he/she becomes aware of the damage and the liable party for the damage. The same shall also apply upon the expiry of a period of ten years from the time when the manufacturer, etc., delivered the product (Article 5(1)).[92,93]

295. In many cases, manufacturers and trading firms exporting goods particularly to the US are required to take out product liability insurance in Japan.

Insurers offer product liability insurance policy in English, modelling the policy on the wording used in the US market.

§3. PROFESSIONAL LIABILITY INSURANCE

296. Several types of professional liability insurance have been successively developed since 1963. Professional liability insurance covers professional people such as doctors, dentists, accountants, architects, lawyers, pharmacists, travel agents, data processors, public tax accountants, nurses, surveyors, administrative scriveners, emergency life-saving technicians, social insurance labour consultants, insurance brokers and civil engineering consultants etc., for negligence and errors or omissions in the course of their professions.

297. The word 'professional' is defined in the statement of the methods of operation, which should be submitted to the FSA at the time of the application for authorization to do business, as below:

(1) There is a certain Act which regulates the qualification to do such business.
(2) The Act mentioned above forbids doing such business without the qualification.
(3) The Act mentioned above provides criminal punishment against the person doing such business without the qualification.
(4) The qualification provided in the Act mentioned above has to belong to the individual.

298. There are three types of coverage according to the professions such as the following:

(1) Some insurance such as 'accountants' liability insurance, lawyers' liability insurance and public tax accountants' liability insurance, etc.' covers pure economic damage.
(2) Doctors' liability insurance and architects' liability insurance, etc., covers bodily injury claims and damage to property.

---

92. The period (ten years) shall be calculated from the time when the damage arises, where such damage is caused by the substances which are harmful to human health when they remain or accumulate in the body, or where the symptoms for such damage appear after a certain latent period (Art. 5(2)).
93. The English translation of this law is found in the book of *Article by Article Products Liability Law* [*ChikujoKaisestuSeizobustuSekinin-hou*] written by the Economic Planning Agency Consumer Administration s. 1 (published by Shoji-Homu Kenkyusha in 1994).

(3) Some insurance such as travel agents' liability insurance covers both pure economic damages, and bodily injury and property damage claims.

§4. Environmental Liability Insurance

299. The Solid Contamination Countermeasures Act (Law No. 53, 2003) has stipulated, in Article 7, that in case when the landowner intends to change the character of land over a certain size, he/she has to notify the prefectural governor thereof, and if there is apprehensions about soil contamination the prefectural governor may order to investigate soil contamination. Environmental impairment liability insurance was introduced in early 1990s, and some insurers underwrite this insurance. Insurers, however, are generally showing negative attitude to writing this insurance because of its counter selection from the insurer's point of view.

300. This insurance provides coverage (on a claim-made basis) for:

(1) liability arising out of drainage, exhaust or smoke which is excluded under the general conditions of other liability insurance;
(2) losses resulting from either sudden or gradual pollution incidents;
(3) cleaning up costs which the insured spends in accordance with legal obligations imposed by laws and regulations;[94]
(4) loss of use of tangible property which is not physically damaged;
(5) loss of fisheries.

301. A co-insurance clause may be attached in all cases.

302. A new Act, 'Provision Act for Ground Pollution', came into force on 1 January 2003. This Act makes landowners obliged to examine the ground and to clean up the ground if it has been polluted when he/she makes plans to develop the site of factory, etc., into a residential area or park, etc.

§5. Liability Insurance for Private Individuals

303. There are some private individual liability insurances such as the following:

(1) personal liability insurance;
(2) golfer insurance;
(3) hunter insurance;
(4) tennis player insurance;
(5) skier and skater insurance, etc.

304. Personal liability insurance covers the policyholder (named insured), spouse, any member of the named insured's or spouse's relatives living at home under the same livelihood and unmarried children living elsewhere but under the same

---

94.   Responsibility to bear expenses to prevent pollution (25 Dec. 1970, Law No. 133).

livelihood with the named insured or spouse. This insurance covers legal liability for bodily injury or property damage to a third party on account of:

(1) any accident arising out of the ownership, use or control by the named insured of the dwelling house (including movables and immovables being in the same premises) specified in the policy; or
(2) any accident occurring in the daily life of the insured.

305. Other private individual liability insurance mentioned above generally covers not only liability but also personal accident and damage of goods.

306. Golfer insurance has an endorsement to cover the celebration expenses of 'hole-in-one' or 'albatross'. In Japan, there is a custom among the golfers that when a golfer has succeeded in making a hole-in-one or albatross in the course of playing golf, he/she holds celebration parties inviting his/her friends, gives souvenirs to them and sometimes plants a tree in the golf course in commemoration of his/her achievement of a hole-in-one or albatross.

307. For hunters, the law concerning the protection of birds and animals and hunting (Law No. 32, 4 April 1918) prescribes that the licensed hunters should take out liability insurance, etc., which will be sufficient to cover the damage of death or bodily injury caused to the third persons by hunting (Article 8-3), Reg. Article 18). Hunter insurance has an endorsement to cover loss sustained by death of the hound while it is engaged in hunting.

Chapter 5. Aviation Insurance

§1. Aviation Insurance

308. The Ins. Law does not specify aviation insurance as a separate subject. Aviation insurance offers considerably broad coverage in the forms of aviation hull insurance, legal liability insurance for third parties and passengers, personal accident insurance and insurance for air cargoes, etc., (such as airport owner's and operator's/ hangarkeeper's/manufacturer's and repairer's liability insurance, shipper's interest insurance, search and rescue insurance, etc.).

Given the importance of reinsurance, aviation insurance has been generally accepted in English clauses based on the Lloyd's policy.

309. The IBL, according the special nature of aviation insurance, exempts insurance companies from applying the Law relating to the Prohibition of Monopoly and the Method of Preserving Fair Trade, and permits industry-wide cooperation in the form of the pooling system.

The Japanese Aviation Insurance Pool is formed as a reinsurance pool and consists of Japanese domestic insurance companies carrying on aviation insurance business.

Individual member companies are generally obliged to cede to the pool 100% of the businesses they accept domestically under aviation insurance, except for those businesses which are deemed inappropriate for acceptance by the pool.

All businesses, once ceded to the pool, are partly or totally retained by the pool member companies in accordance to their individual participating shares which are determined for each underwriting year. Any excess beyond the pool's retention is passed over to overseas reinsurers.

310. Drone began to be used in such ways as agrochemical-spraying, aerial photographing, aerial surveying, disaster response and/or crime prevention support, so as to define the flight rule for unmanned aircraft such as drone, Aviation Law has been amended and gone into effect in December 2015.

In addition, the Ministry of Land, Infrastructure and Transport announced the guidelines for the safe flight of unmanned aircraft, and in that there is a recommendation to prepare insurance for third-party liability. Some insurance companies, in relation with the guidelines, have started offering insurance to cover hull (repair costs, search & rescue costs), third-party liability and the like.

§2. Satellite Insurance

311. Satellite insurance covers loss or damage to insured satellites or rockets. It also covers the expenses incurred by the insured in a failed launch, as well as the insured's legal liability for bodily injury or property damage directly caused by the satellite or the rocket.

At each stage of the satellite operation, the following three forms of coverage are prepared:

(1) pre-launch insurance: the coverage provides for loss or damage to the satellite during construction, loss of the expected revenue as a result of the loss or damage, continuing operating cost and third-party liability;

(2) launch insurance: the coverage provides for loss or damage to the launched satellite, loss of the expected revenue and additional expenses incurred as a result of the loss or damage, as well as liability to third parties;

(3) in-orbit insurance: the coverage provides for loss or damage to the satellite, loss of the expected revenue and additional expenses incurred as a result of the loss or damage, liability to third parties and can also be able to applicable for incentives or penalties.

Chapter 6.   Burglary and Theft Insurance

§1. BURGLARY AND THEFT INSURANCE

312. The Ins. Law does not regulate burglary and theft insurance as a separate subject.

I.   Scope of Coverage

313. This insurance covers the property loss or damage resulting from burglary, theft or robbery while the insured property has been accommodated in the premises mentioned in the policy. Property loss or damage caused by fraud and embezzlement is not covered.

II.   Main Exclusions

314. The property loss or damage caused by a shoplifter or a person who has not trespassed on the building accommodating the property insured is not covered. If, however, such a person behaves violently or threateningly, the property loss or damage is covered.

The property loss or damage arising from a burglary, theft or robbery, while any 15-year-old or other normal person has not been in the premises for continuous seventy-four hours or more, is not covered.

Property loss or damage caused by one's relatives and own staff, etc., is not covered.

III. Subrogation by Insurer

315. The Ins. Law provides that 'If, in cases where the subject matter of the insurance has been totally destroyed, the insurer has paid losses, the insurer shall automatically acquire the proprietary rights and other real rights possessed   by the insured on the subject matter, by the ratio of the amount of losses paid to the insurable value (in case where it is the agreed value, it shall be the agreed value)' (Ins. Law Article 24).

Under this insurance, however, in cases where the subject having been stolen is recovered within one year from the date when the insurance money was paid, the insured is able to demand that the insurer return the subject on condition that the insured refunds the insurance money.

§2. INSURANCE FOR CREDIT CARDS

316. This Insurance covers the credit card holder's loss that has been caused by iniquitous use of a credit card, which the credit card holder lost because of stealing, fraud or embezzlement.

Only loss that has happened during forty-one days (ten days before the date the card issuer received the information that the credit card holder had lost the card and another thirty days after such date) is covered. The forty-one days can be changed with special endorsements to 121 days maximum, eleven days minimum.

Cash dispenser cards (deposits can be withdrawn through a dispenser machine by using this card) can also be the object of this insurance.

Chapter 7.   Fidelity and Guarantee Insurance

§1.   FIDELITY AND CREDIT INSURANCE

I.   Fidelity Insurance

317. Fidelity insurance (or dishonest employee insurance) covers employers against loss resulting from the dishonest acts of their employees. Almost all employers in Japan protect themselves against this loss by means of individual sureties.

In fact, however, the liability of the individual surety is very restricted by the Law concerning Fidelity Guarantee (Law No. 42, 1 April 1933), which stipulates a limited period of suretyship contract for fidelity, the right to cancel the contract in certain cases and the limited liability of the surety.

Fidelity insurance was developed as a substitute for individual suretyship for fidelity but this insurance has not been popular in the Japanese market.

II.   Credit Insurance

318. Non-Life insurance companies in Japan write the following credit insurances:

(1) Instalment sales credit insurance: all risks of failure to collect instalment sales debts are covered under this insurance. The insured is indemnified for 50% of the eventual loss; that is, the amount overdue less any recovery subsequently made, including the value of the goods recovered, plus the cost incurred of effecting the recovery.
(2) Employee's housing loan credit insurance:

   (a) basic cover covers losses suffered by employers or creditors, who supply housing loans to their employees as a part of employees' benefit program, in consequence of the failure of the employee or debtor to repay the loans;
   (b) guarantee liability covers (by way of an endorsement) losses suffered by employers in consequence of being compelled to repay, as guarantor for their employees, housing loans to financial institutions in case of the failure of their employees to repay the loan.

(3) Employee's general loan credit insurance: the 'general loan' means all kinds of personal loan other than housing loan, such as education, leisure, marriage, birth, etc., Basic cover and guarantee liability cover are the same as those of the above insurance.
(4) Personal loan credit insurance: this insurance is available to financial institutions that supply unsecured loans (or overdraft facilities) to private individuals.

§2.   Guarantee Insurance

I.   Guarantee Insurance

319. Guarantee insurance is a variation of the surety bond, taking the form of insurance.

There are some kinds of guarantee insurance such as the following:

(a)   Bid and Performance Guarantee Insurance

This insurance covers loss suffered by the insured (or the obligee) due to the default of the policyholder (or the principal): (1) in the case of bid guarantee insurance, in concluding the contract in spite of his/her successful bid; or (2) in the case of performance guarantee insurance, in performing obligations under the contract after it is concluded. The amount of indemnity payable by the insurer is: (1) in the case of bid guarantee insurance, the difference between the reasonable contract price (second bidding price in general) and the bidding price submitted by the policyholder; or (2) in the case of performance guarantee insurance, the difference between the contract price of the new successful bidder and the original contract price for the uncompleted part of the construction, supply, etc. If the amount of damages has been previously agreed on between the insured and policyholder, the amount of indemnity payable by the insurer is equal to that amount.

The insurer is subrogated, to the extent of the amount paid by him/her, to the insured's right of claim for compensation against the policyholder.

(b)   Housing Loan Guarantee Insurance

This insurance covers loss suffered by the insured (or financial institutions) due to default of the policyholder (debtor of housing loan) in performing his/her obligations under the housing loan contract.

The insurance contract is deemed to become null and void when the property put out by the policyholder as a collateral for the loan is completely destroyed or heavily damaged due to war, civil war, earthquake or the like.

A first mortgage on the real property purchased by the loan must be placed with the insurer or the financial institution (the difference between the insurer and the financial institution is based on differences in the method of making the housing loan).

(c)   Exclusive Sales Agents Guarantee Insurance

This insurance covers loss suffered by the insured (distributor of petroleum or cement) in the event of his/her cancellation of the sales agency contract for the reason that the policyholder (exclusive sales agent) fails to pay the insured any of his/her debt under the sales agency contract.

II.   Surety Bonds

320. Japanese insurers are able to write various types of surety bond such as bid bonds, performance bonds, maintenance bonds, advance payment bonds, labour and material bonds, supply contract bonds, lease contract bonds, licence and permit bonds, fiduciary bonds, judicial and court bonds, customs bonds and other miscellaneous bonds.

Chapter 8.   Livestock Insurance

§1.   INTRODUCTION

321. In Japan, there are two systems to cover loss as a result of livestock dying.
The first is the livestock mutual aid system based on the Agricultural Disaster Compensation Act (Law No. 185, 15 December 1947), which is operated by mutual agricultural cooperation societies and supported, by way of reinsurance, by prefectural federations of the above societies and also supported, by way of subsidy for a part of premium and retrocession, by the national government. And the other is animal insurance operated by non-life insurance companies.

I.   The Livestock Mutual Aid System

322. The mutual agricultural cooperation society operates the mutual aid systems for farm products (paddy rice, wheat, potato, soybean, small bean, etc., specified by the government ordinance), fruit and fruit tree (apple, orange, peach, grape, pear, etc., also specified by government ordinance) and stock (horse, cattle, pig, etc.).

These systems for livestock cover loss or damage (including deterioration) arising from fire, earthquake, volcanic eruption, windstorm, flood, drought, cold weather, blight and insects, disease, injury, dying, etc.

§2.   PRIVATE ANIMAL INSURANCE

323. Private animal insurance may be underwritten by some insurance companies and SASTIP. Insurance companies and SASTIP only cover, as usual, losses as a result of the death of animals insured.

However, insurance companies and/or SASTIP established quite recently are likely to underwrite such animal insurance as cover losses caused by not only death but also medical examination, treatment and surgical operation, etc.

324. Subject matters of insurance was mainly racing horse, but some insurance companies and/or SASTIP established quite recently, are likely to underwrite domestic animals[95] (i.e., dog, cat, ornamental fishes like tropical fish, reptile, etc.).

325. A certain insurance company has recently developed, for livestock trader, a new product which compensates feed cost for feeding the alternative livestock and labour cost, etc., required for the re-production, when livestock death (including waste and culling) due to infectious disease or natural disaster have been become.

---

95.   Some automobile insurance policy has its special endorsement to cover damages for injury accident of domestic animals while they are riding in the automobile insured.

Chapter 9.   Catastrophe Insurance

§1.   GENERAL

326. The Disaster Relief Act (Law No. 119, 1957) may be invoked in the event that many families lose their living place or if the life and health of many persons are harmed or seriously threatened. This Act does not provide insurance and/or compensation system.[96]

327. There are certain pieces of legislation for offering some compensation for victims.

They are the Act Concerning Earthquake Insurance (enacted in 1966 after the terrible experience of Niigata earthquake in 1964), which provides support for the government's reinsurance scheme, the Law relating to the Compensation Contract for Nuclear Damage enacted in 1961, the Indemnification Act against Oil Pollution Liability enacted in 1975 (Law No. 95), the Supporting Act for Reconstruction of Victims' Life enacted in 1998 (Law No. 66), and so on.

§2.   NUCLEAR RISKS

328. The system, in Japan, relating to the liability for nuclear damage is made up of two acts that are the Law relating to the Liability for Nuclear Damage (Law No. 147, 1961, hereinafter referred as 'the liability Law') and the Law relating to the Compensation Contract for Nuclear Damage (Law No. 148, 1961, hereinafter referred as 'the Compensation Contract Law'[97]). The damage developed from operation of a nuclear reactor is provided by the Liability Law as such:

(a)   a nuclear operator has concentrically to bear the liability whether or not such liability is caused from the operator's wilful misconduct or gross negligence (Liability Law Article 3);
(b)   any person other than a nuclear operator does not bear the liability (Liability Law Article 4);
(c)   the Liability Law does not provide the limit of liability of a nuclear operator (it means the operator has to bear unlimited liability).

Precautions to ensure compensation: A nuclear operator shall be obliged to take measures to ensure compensation for nuclear damage (the Liability Law Articles 6–10), so that a nuclear operator makes a contract for nuclear energy liability with insurance company, and for nuclear energy compensation contract with the government. Nuclear

---

96.   'Disaster' is defined in the Fundamental Law of Countermeasures for Disaster (Law No. 223, 1961).
97.   The government may entrust an insurance company with a part of the service of the compensation contract (Compensation Law Art. 18).

energy liability insurance covers so-called general liability and a nuclear energy compensation contract covers liability broken out in connection with earthquake, volcanic eruption/tidal wave and normal operation of nuclear energy plant.

Other risks such as social disturbance and unnaturally huge convulsion of nature may be compensated by the government (Liability Law Article 17). In case that the legal liability of a nuclear operator may exceed the limit of a measure taken by the nuclear operator, the government will assist the nuclear operator (the Liability Law Article 16).

329. The IBL exempts insurance companies from applying the Law relating to the Prohibition of Monopoly and the Method of Preserving Fair Trade, and permits all the Japanese non-life insurance companies and some foreign insurance companies doing business in Japan to cooperate to form an industry-wide underwriting system (the Japan Atomic Energy Insurance Pool) specifically to provide coverage for nuclear energy business.

330. The Japan Atomic Energy Insurance Pool is the only direct insurance pool in Japan and was authorized by the Prime Minister with the consent of the Fair Trade Commission to perform the approved 'concerted acts'.

The approved 'concerted acts' are exempted from the application of Japan Anti-monopoly Act and they are: (a) soliciting; (b) determination of premium rates and insurance policy conditions; (c) determination of claim settlement; (d) transacting direct insurance and reinsurance; and (e) study and research.

I.   Classes of Insurance

331. Nuclear energy liability insurance includes:

(a) nuclear energy site liability insurance (compulsory insurance);
(b) nuclear transport liability insurance (compulsory insurance);
(c) liability insurance for nuclear energy vessel (compulsory insurance).

Nuclear material damage insurance is voluntary.

II.   Insurer's Liability Limit

332. Nuclear energy site liability insurance includes:

(a) limit for nuclear accident – insured's liability limit per premises required by the law is JPY 4,000 million, JPY 24,000 million or JPY 120,000 million, according to the kind and scale of nuclear installation;
(b) the limit for conventional accidents is determined automatically by a certain percentage of the limit for nuclear accidents within the range from JPY 4,000 million to JPY 120,000 million;
(c) liability insurance for nuclear energy vessels – insured's liability limit per vessel by law is JPY 120,000 million.

Nuclear transport liability insurance has a limit during a fixed period required by law of JPY 4,000 million for non-irradiated fuel and JPY 24,000 million for the spent fuel.

§3. Oil Risks

I. Oil Pollution Liability Insurance

333. In December 1974, a large quantity of heavy oil accidentally flowed into the Seto Inland Sea from a tank on the premises of the oil refinery company in Okayama prefecture, causing heavy damage to fishermen on the coast. The company was obliged to pay approximately JPY 50 billion as damages, including expenses for cleaning up the oil from the sea. This accident was taken up in the Diet as a serious social issue in February 1975. In complying with the social requirements, all the Japanese direct insurers and the foreign direct insurers then operating in Japan formed a pool in May 1975 to cover the huge liabilities and expenses incurred by oil refineries and other such installations. This insurance is written by attaching the oil pollution liability special conditions to the general conditions of general liability insurance.

§4. Natural Catastrophes

I. Introduction

334. It is said that Japan is one of the natural disaster-prone countries in the world.

Insurance to cover loss or damage from natural disasters such as earthquake, flood or windstorm always has problems due to its high frequency of occurrence, claims spreading across wide areas and potentiality for the huge accumulation of claims. In the circumstances, the insurers cannot help placing restrictions on their policy conditions in writing such policies.

II. Earthquake Risks

A. Earthquake Insurance for Business Risks

335. Earthquake insurance for business risks started in November 1956, written by way of attaching an extended coverage endorsement to the ordinary fire insurance policy. For the purpose of controlling the accumulation of the insured amount of such earthquake insurance, the insurers usually divide the whole country into twelve zones, the insurers applying the limited indemnity system (i.e., partial insurance).

As a consequence, the actual indemnity for loss or damage caused by earthquake is always limited to a certain percentage of the insured amount.[98]

B.   Earthquake Insurance for Dwelling Houses

336. This insurance started in June 1966 for the purpose of covering the dwelling risks only after the experience of Niigata earthquake in 1964. Although this insurance has its own general conditions, it must be sold with a main fire insurance policy. The insured may choose not to effect the earthquake insurance by notice and signature on the application form to describe his/her wish not to do so. This insurance is run with the support of the government's reinsurance scheme.

1. Subject Insured[99]

337. The subjects are limited to dwelling houses and/or household goods only.

'Dwelling house' includes 'buildings' under construction that will be a dwelling house after completion, a second house which can be used as dwelling house at any time (excluding one for rent), a dwelling house which is empty but ready for use and also includes gate, fence, shed, garage, etc., when the house itself is insured.

All household goods have to be insured as a package. However, the following matters are excluded from subject insured:

(1)   precious metals, precious stones jewellery and works of art that are worth over JPY 300,000 per piece or pair;
(2)   manuscripts, designs, patterns, documents, accounts, and the like;
(3)   automobiles;
(4)   cash, securities, bank books, revenue stamps, postage stamps and the like.

2. Cover Limit

338. The cover limit of the earthquake insurance must be decided, at the insured's option, within 30% to 50% of the amount of main fire insurance insured, but up to JPY 10 million for household goods and up to JPY 50 million for a house.

The aggregate limit of indemnity payable by all insurers to all claimants in respect of any earthquake is JPY 11,300 billion.[100]

All earthquakes that occur within seventy two hours from the first one are regarded as one and same earthquake.

3. Coverage

339. This insurance covers total loss, half loss and minor loss caused by fire, destruction, burying or washing away following not only earthquake and/or volcanic eruption but also a tidal wave following an earthquake or volcanic eruption.

The way in which the insured is indemnified is as follows:

---

98.   Zone 5, Tokyo, Kanagawa and Chiba area, is the densest area in the accumulation of insured value for earthquake insurance. Consequently, the indemnity limit is, in general, up to 15% of the actual insured value.
99.   The number of policies; 16,489,482 (as of March 2015).
100.   If the total amount of claims per earthquake exceeds the limit, payments shall be reduced in the proportion of JPY 11,300 billion to the total amount of claims. The aggregate limit of indemnity payable by all the insurers must be approved by the Diet every year.

(1) Dwelling house: total loss is more than 50% damage in cash value – to the main structural part of the house or more than 70% of total floor space burnt or washed away – 100% of the amount insured is paid; half loss is 20% to 50% damage or under in cash value to the main structural part of house or 20% to 70% of total floor space burnt or washed away – 50% of the amount insured shall be paid; minor loss is 3% to 20% damages in cash value – to the main structural part of house or a flood coming up above the floor level or 45 cm from the ground – 5% of the amount insured shall be paid.

(2) Household goods: total loss – no less than 80% damages of cash value occurred to household goods – 100% of the amount insured shall be paid; half loss – 30% to 80% damages of cash value occurred to household goods – 50% of the amount insured shall be paid; minor loss – 10% to 30% damages of cash value occurred to household goods – 5% of the amount insured shall be paid.

C.   Earthquake Fire Expense

340. In case of half loss of dwelling house (subject of insurance contract) or total loss of household goods (subject of insurance contract) caused by fire following earthquake, volcanic eruption and/or tidal wave following the earthquake or volcanic eruption, fire insurance may cover 5% of the sum insured as extraordinary expenses up to JPY 3 million per accident and premise.

D.   Dwelling House Earthquake Expense Insurance: Underwritten by SASTIP

341. SASTIP shall not be permitted to underwrite dwelling house earthquake insurance itself; however, SBISSI Co. Ltd,[101] one of SASTIP, has been registered as the SASTIP that may underwrite the specific insurance – Dwelling house earthquake expense insurance – which can be payable fixed amount benefits for the expenses to re-establish the life of the insured who had his/her own dwelling house damaged from earthquake.

Dwelling house earthquake expense insurance can be underwritten separately while dwelling house earthquake insurance must be sold with a main fire insurance policy.

This insurance pays benefits at total loss, half loss (large) and half loss (normal) of the insured's own dwelling house caused by fire, destruction, burying or washing away following not only earthquake and/or volcanic eruption but also a tidal wave following an earthquake or volcanic eruption. However, this insurance, different from the dwelling house earthquake insurance, does not pay benefits at partial loss. The amount insured of each total loss, half loss (large or normal) is fixed for five types of amount according to a number of lives (one to five persons or more) in the household – for instance, in case of total loss and five persons or more; the sum insured shall be

---

101. After the occurring of earthquake, a local government shall survey damages of each building, according to the criteria for surveying degree of damage provided by the government. So SBISSI Co.Ltd, will pay its insurance benefits, without its own survey, according to the degree of damage being surveyed by the local government.

obtained by multiplying JPY 3 million by number of lives of the household (up to JPY 9 million).

III. Wind, Storm and Flood Insurance

A. *Wind, Storm and Flood Insurance for Business Risks*

342. Wind, storm and flood insurance began to be written in 1938, and covers loss of or damage to property caused by typhoon, windstorm, rainstorm, high seas, flood, etc. However, with the development of the wind, storm and flood risks coverage endorsement of fire policies in 1956 and of various type of comprehensive policies covering wind, storm and flood risks as one of covered risks, on dwelling houses, stores and contents therein in 1961, wind, storm and flood insurance for business risks is generally written by way of attaching coverage endorsement to the ordinary fire insurance or by way of comprehensive policies.[102,103,104]

B. *Wind, Storm and Flood Risks for Dwelling Houses*

343. Wind and storm risk can be covered only when the amount of loss or damage exceeds JPY 200,000 per building or per premises under both dwelling house fire insurance and dwelling house comprehensive insurance.

Water risk may be covered under dwelling house comprehensive insurance only when insured property suffers loss or damage by floodwater, flood by thaw, high sea, landslide, etc., in consequence of typhoon, windstorm, heavy rain, etc. And the indemnity amounts for loss or damage may be calculated in the same way as those of the storekeeper's comprehensive insurance mentioned above.

---

102. If multiple buildings are located in the same premises, all buildings or contents must generally be insured.
103. Co-insurance endorsement can be applicable.
104. Under the storekeepers' comprehensive insurance: for wind risks, if the amount of loss or damage to the subject insured exceeds JPY 200,000 per building or per premises the amount of loss or damage is paid. Flood risks – (1) if the amount of loss or damage to the insured building is 30% or more of the insurable value, the amount of indemnity is 70% of the amount damage. (2) If the amount of loss or damage to the insured building is 15% or more and less than 30% of the insurable value as a result of flood above the floor level (or flood of over 45 cm high above the ground) 10% of the insured amount is paid but not exceeding JPY 2,000,000 per accident per premises. (3) If the amount of loss or damage to the insured building is less than 15% of insurable value as a result of flood above the floor level (or flood of over 45 cm high above the ground), or in case of loss or damage to the insured property such as installation, utensils, merchandise and the like caused by flood, 5% of the insured amount is paid but not exceeding JPY 1,000,000 per accident per premises.

Chapter 10.   Technical Insurance

§1.   GENERAL TECHNICAL INSURANCE

I.   Introduction

344. The main technical insurances in Japan are the following:

(1) contractor's all risks insurance:

   (a) contractor's all risks (building works) insurance;
   (b) contractor's all risks (civil engineering works) insurance;
   (c) civil engineering completed risks insurance;

(2) machinery insurance;
(3) boiler and turbo-set insurance;
(4) erection insurance.

A.   Standard Construction Contract

345. There are two standard construction contracts in Japan. One is for the contracts of government and local municipalities, and the other is for contracts between private enterprises.

The Central Council of Contractors made the former standard construction contract on 21 February 1950 (for contracts of government and local municipalities) and four associations (the Architectural Institute of Japan, the Architectural Association of Japan, the Japan Institute of Architects and the National General Contractors of Japan) cooperated to draw up a standard construction contract in February 1951 (for contracts between private enterprises).

§2.   CONTRACTOR'S ALL RISKS INSURANCE

I.   Contractor's All Risks (Building Works) Insurance

346. The contractor usually applies this insurance. However, if building materials are supplied and possessed by the principal, the principal may apply this insurance to protect both his/her and the contractor's interests. Subcontractors, manufacturers of building materials, and other related parties may also be co-insured under the policy if required.

A.   Property Insured

347. This insurance covers the following property at the construction site:

- buildings;
- materials for construction; and
- temporary frameworks, scaffolding, field offices, workmen's quarters and other temporary structures set up for construction purposes.

B.   Loss or Damage to Be Covered

348. This insurance is an all risks insurance covering loss or damage to the property insured caused by an unforeseeable and sudden occurrence during the course of construction at the building site.

Indemnity is provided under this insurance for the costs required to restore the property insured to its pre-loss condition. The necessary expenses incurred in preventing or minimizing loss or damage are also included in the loss amount to be indemnified. And extraordinary expenses incidental to property loss or damage caused by insured perils and debris removal expenses are covered, even if the total amount of these expenses plus property damage or loss exceeds the sum insured.

C.   Third-Party Liability Coverage

349. Any legal liability of the insured for bodily injury or property damage caused to a third party arising from an accident during construction works may be covered by attaching a specific endorsement.

D.   Main Exclusions

350.

(1) The main exclusions are loss or damage resulting from wilful acts, gross negligence or violation of laws or regulations by the insured parties or the superintendent at the construction site;
(2) costs or expenses incurred in rectifying defects in design or workmanship;
(3) loss or damage caused by cold weather, frost, ice or snow.

Loss or damage caused by flood, high sea, earthquake, volcanic eruption, etc., are excluded in the general conditions and insurers provide specific endorsements to cover such perils. However, insurers are usually very careful to extend cover to those perils.

E.   Period of Insurance

351. The period of insurance, in general, starts at the commencement of construction works and terminates when the works are delivered (or completed).

There is a specific endorsement to cover all construction contracts by one policy (introduced in July 1984 mainly to provide covers to the smaller contractors such as wooden house builders). In this case, the period of insurance is generally one year.

II.   Contractor's All Risks (Civil Engineering Works) Insurance

A.   Introduction

352. The basic features of this insurance are similar to those of the contractor's all risks (building works) insurance with some differences.

B.   Property Insured

353. This insurance covers loss or damage to the following property located at the civil engineering site:

(1)   civil engineering works, including temporary supporting works such as frameworks, access roads, cofferdams, temporary bridges and diversion tunnels;
(2)   materials and temporary buildings for the works mentioned above (1);
(3)   temporary facilities for installation of machinery and equipment for civil works such as conveyors, cranes and bulldozers (those mentioned in (3) are covered under a specific endorsement).

C.   Third-Party Liability

354. Third-party liability cannot be covered under this insurance. It may be covered under the separate policy, if necessary.

D.   Main Exclusions

355. In addition to the main exclusions specified in the CAR (building works) insurance, the following loss or damages are also excluded unless otherwise specifically agreed by the insurer:

(1)   loss or damage due to faulty design;
(2)   costs or expenses incurred for blocking or draining water which springs up out of the earth; and
(3)   loss or damage due to unexpected bombs or mines in the earth or water.

III.   Civil Engineering Completed Risks Insurance

356. Property insured is structures such as tunnels, bridges, railway, dams, embankments, waterways, water pumps, housing lots and factory lots.

A. Loss or Damage to Be Covered

357. This insurance is an all risks insurance covering loss or damage to the property insured caused by an unexpected and sudden occurrence, such as those caused by following perils:

(1) subsidence, upheaval, landslide or rockslide; and
(2) windstorm, typhoon, whirlwind or other natural phenomena of a similar nature.

B. Main Exclusions

358. In addition to the main exclusions specified in the CAR (building works) insurance, the following loss or damages are also excluded unless otherwise specifically agreed by the insurer:

(1) loss or damages caused by electrical or mechanical breakdown of the property insured;
(2) costs or expenses incurred for rectification of settlement of the property insured due to consolidation;
(3) costs or expenses incurred for such extra works as reclamation, banking and land grading resulting from consolidation of the insured property;
(4) loss or damage to lawn, trees or other vegetation;
(5) loss due to burial or upheaval on dredged areas of dredging works;
(6) loss or damage caused to rubble-mound, riprap, concrete block for wave dissipation or any other property of the like kind due to scour, settlement or movement thereof;
(7) loss by swelling, shrinking or freezing of the property insured caused by change of temperature or humidity;
(8) loss or damage caused by unexploded bombs or mines;
(9) loss or damage to any part of the property insured which has been under extension, reconstruction, repair or other construction.

§3. MACHINERY INSURANCE

359. Loss or damage covered by this insurance includes physical loss of or damage to the subject matter of insurance by an unexpected and fortuitous accident while the subject matter is in a workable condition.

360. Loss of profit due to business interruption as a consequence of material damage to machinery is covered under machinery business interruption insurance.

361. Blanket coverage is designed to cover collectively all the machinery on the same premises under a single insured amount. Blanket coverage is available only for certain kinds of equipment and machinery (office building equipment, machinery in motor car repair shops, electric apparatus in factories, etc.).

362. Robot (industrial use) comprehensive insurance is written by way of an endorsement to machinery insurance policy.

§4.   BOILER AND TURBO-SET INSURANCE

363. In Japan, the First Engine and Boiler Insurance Co. Ltd was founded in 1908 to write boiler insurance exclusively. Their portfolio was transferred to the Yasuda Fire and Marine Insurance Co. Ltd (SONPO JAPAN Insurance Inc., at present) in 1944. Boiler insurance has been solely written by that company in the Japanese market ever since.

364. The physical loss or damage caused by explosion, collapse, etc., of the boilers or pressure vessels is the basic cover of the boiler insurance. And the policy may be extended, for an additional premium, to cover business interruption, employees' personal accident and third-party liability due to boiler accidents.

365. Boiler insurance provides the insured not only with insurance coverage but also with technical services mainly from the standpoint of preventing industrial accidents. SOMPO Japan Insurance Inc. is authorized to conduct on behalf of the authority, inspections of boilers and pressure vessels which are required by the Occupational Safety and Health Act.

366. Turbo-set insurance covers loss or damage caused by disruption, breakdown or overheating of turbo-sets or engines. Turbo-set insurance may also be extended, at an additional premium, to cover business interruption, employees' personal accident and third-party liability due to boiler accident. Engineering services are also provided under this insurance. However, the insurer is not authorized to conduct inspections of turbo-sets and engines on behalf of the authority.

§5.   ERECTION INSURANCE

367. This insurance provides so-called all risks coverage for loss of or damage to structures while they are in the process of erection or installation.

The coverage begins from the unloading, at the work site, of the materials, parts and components needed to erect such structures, and the coverage ends at the time the structures are delivered to the principal after the completion of the necessary commissioning test or test-run.

368. This insurance can also provide optional coverage for a third party's liability exposure that may be associated with the erection or installation works.

369. The main exclusions are:

(1)   loss or damage caused by wilful act or gross negligence of the policyholder, the insured or the site overseer;
(2)   earthquake, volcanic eruption or tidal waves arising therefrom;
(3)   war, strike, riot or civil commotion;
(4)   nuclear accident;
(5)   cost of eliminating defects in design, faulty casting, material or workmanship;
(6)   liability to the principal for non-fulfilment of the erection contract such as delayed delivery.

Chapter 11.   Miscellaneous Insurances

§1.   GLASS INSURANCE

370. Breakage of glass fixed to buildings resulting from fortuitous accident is covered by extended coverage of fire insurance or by glass insurance.

In the case of extended coverage of fire insurance, all glass fixed to the building (i.e., the subject matter of fire insurance) must be insured all together and the amount insured for glass must be calculated into the insured amount of fire policy.

In the case of glass insurance, the glass to be insured must be specified individually and distinguished from others in the policy and the insured amount of each piece of glass is also specified individually. Glass insurance also covers accidental damage to frames, handles, etc., attached to the glass.

§2.   SHIP'S PASSENGER ACCIDENT LIABILITY INSURANCE

371. This insurance covers losses that the insured (i.e., owner or operator of a ship) may become legally liable to pay as damages for death of or bodily injury to passengers in connection with transportation. This insurance was developed in 1953 for the purpose of securing the financial responsibility of passenger carriers. The Japan Passenger Boat Association was established for the purpose of improving and developing the business of domestic marine transportation of passengers, and the Association has been effecting this insurance, for ensuring stability of all its members' business, as a group insurance, which forms the major part of this class of business.

§3.   COMPUTER INSURANCE

372. This insurance is a comprehensive type insurance that covers physical loss or damage, by any risks such as fire, lightning, explosion, theft, breakage, getting wet or electronic or mechanical disturbance, to data processing equipment's information media (magnetic tapes, magnetic disks, program data, documents, etc.) and also covers loss of business interruptions.

Recently, some insurance companies have developed a special endorsement to compensate for such liability as caused by information leakage and/or inhibition of other people's business caused by cyber-attacks on computer systems, and the endorsement to compensate for the profit damage due to the stop or suspension of computer network caused by cyber-attacks has also been developed.

§4.   WARRANTY AND INDEMNITY

373. Recently, Japanese companies have been increasing cases to merge and acquire foreign companies, so that some insurance companies started to sell Warranty and Indemnity Insurance to cover loss of the buyer due to the breach of the representations and warranties at that time.

Part IV. Automobile Insurance

Chapter 1. Compulsory Automobile Liability Insurance (CALI)

§1. INTRODUCTION

I. Origin of the System

374. There has been a remarkable growth in motorization since the 1950s. In line with this rapid progress in motorization, the number of accidents increased dramatically. That resulted in the serious problem that victims of traffic accidents were unable to obtain compensation due to a lack of financial resources on the part of the wrongdoer or arising from a lack of legal knowledge on liability on the both parties.

To ensure financial relief to such victims of traffic accidents, the ALSL was enacted in 1955, and the CALI took effect in December 1955.

Insurer

375. Insurers who can accept CALI are non-life insurance companies (stipulated in the IBL Article 2, paragraph 4) and foreign non-life insurance company, etc. (stipulated in the IBL Article 2, paragraph 9).

Furthermore, agricultural cooperatives and a federation of agricultural cooperatives (established under the Agricultural Cooperative Society Act) and consumer cooperatives and a federation of consumer cooperatives (established under the Consumers' Livelihood Cooperative Act) and common facility cooperatives and a federation of common facility cooperatives (established under the Act of cooperatives of Small and Medium Enterprises, etc.) are carrying on the same insurance business as CALI, but this business is called CALMA, because under the IBL insurance business can only be carried out by stock or mutual companies, and so other name are required to denote insurance business operated by other entity.

II.   Outline of the Automobile Liability Security Law

376. One of the purposes of the ALSL for automobile bodily injury accidents is to remove the difficulty of the proof of assailant's responsibility from the victim's side. If a person operating an automobile for his/her benefit causes death or bodily injury to any other person through such operation, he/she is liable to compensate the victim for damages, unless he/she proves all three conditions: (1) neither he/she nor the driver failed to exercise due diligence in operating the automobile; (2) there was intent or negligence on the part of the victim or a third party other than the driver; (3) the automobile had no structural defect or functional disorder) (ALSL Article 3).[105]

A.   Basic Amount of Indemnity to Be Secured by Compulsory Insurance

377. Under the CALI system, any automobile which is not insured by an automobile liability insurance contract specified under the ALSL secures a basic amount of indemnity for the victims of automobile accidents, and ALSL also stipulates that an automobile for which a contract of CALI is not concluded shall not be operated (Article 5 of ALSL). This secures a compensation means on the assailant's side.

At its inception, the insured amount (i.e., the limit of liability for the insurer) required by the law was JPY 300,000 for death, JPY 100,000 for serious injury and JPY 30,000, for slight injury. As a result of economic growth, the maximum limit of liability (the limit for death or permanent disability of the most serious degree) now stands at JPY 30,000,000.

Separate from voluntary insurance, CALI is established and has been operated under the law, and obliges all automobile use to be covered by CALI in order to secure funds for compensation.

B.   The Government Compensation Plan

378. The victim of an automobile accident has basic compensation taken from CALI. Benefit from CALI cannot be taken when an assailant is unknown and an assailant's automobile was without CALI coverage. (There are automobiles without CALI because some automobiles such as motorbikes are exempted from periodical vehicle inspection system even though they are required to be insured under CALI by law.)

The victim of 'hit and run' accidents can be indemnified under the Government Compensation Plan.

---

105. If the driver of an agricultural cooperative association lent a car in the association's possession without notice, and the driver caused an accident, the owner of the car would be assumed the person operating the automobile for his/her benefit (Supreme Court decision, 11 Feb. 1964, *Minroku*, Vol. 18, Part 2).

If a wife who was injured while she was in the car that her husband was operating, she would be the 'other person' of ALSL Art. 3 (Supreme Court decision, 30 May 1972, *Minroku*, Vol. 26, Part 4).

§2. OUTLINE OF CALI

I. Coverage

379. CALI provides indemnification for damages only if the insured injures the body of another person or kills another person. The coverage does not provide for physical damage.
Subrogation

380. The government, in its turn, is subrogated to the right owned by the victim against the liable party (the policyholder or the insured) to the extent of the amount paid by the insurer (ALSL Article 76 paragraph 2).

II. Limit of Liability

381. The limits of liability are applied to each victim without any total limit per occurrence under Article 2 of the Enforcement Ordinance. A payment for a claim does not reduce the limit of the Insurer's liability for the rest of the insured period as the limit of liability is automatically reinstated.

382. The limits of insurer's liability currently in force are JPY 30,000,000 for death and JPY 40,000,000 for permanent disability requiring nursing care at all time, JPY 30,000,000 for permanent disability requiring nursing care as needed and each degree of permanent disability (other than above) with a range of JPY 30,000,000 for the 1st grade and JPY 750,000 for the 14th grade, and JPY 1,200,000 for other injuries.

III. Exclusions

383. Under CALI, which ensures finance relief to victims of traffic accidents, the insurance company is only allowed to exclude loss caused by malicious intent on the part of the policyholder or the insured (Article 14 of ALSL) and dual insurance (Article 82(3) ALSL).

IV. Duty of Disclosure and Notification

384. Insofar as the liability insurance contract is concerned, the material facts or matters as stipulated in Article 20 of the ALSL are the motor vehicle registration number.

385. Under Article 22 of ALSL, if the policyholder or insured is aware of an increase of risks during the insurance period, he/she must notify the insurance company without delay after the occurrence of the following:

(1) change of type and use or registration number (including any number) of the insured automobile;
(2) the fact that the person effecting the insurance or the insured does not possess the automobile any longer;
(3) the fact that the automobile is not operated; or
(4) any other change of the items designated in the CALI policy.

V. Insurer's Obligation to Provide Insurance

386. Under Article 5 of the CALI, any automobile which is not insured by an automobile liability insurance contract as specified under ALSL (or by automobile liability mutual aids) must not be operated.

Every automobile has an obligation to be insured by CALI, through the introduction of a liability system that forces a wrongdoer to secure funds to pay for damages at any time.

387. As this is a compulsory insurance system, the following regulations are written in the CALI law:

(1) The insurer is prohibited from refusing any application for a CALI contract, except in the case of justifiable reasons as specified in the law (Article 24 ALSL).
(2) In case of failure to produce a CALI certificate, the automobile is prohibited from being operated (Article 8 ALSL).
(3) A valid CALI certificate must be produced both at the time of initial registration of an automobile and each vehicle inspection carried out periodically by administrative authorities (Article 9 ALSL).
(4) Any automobile, except for motorcycles, which are exempted from periodical vehicle inspections, is prohibited from being operated, in the event of failure of such inspections.

Mutual Pool

388. The mutual pool system is formed by all insurers participating in the CALI (and CALMA) schedule for the purpose of preventing deterioration in the underwriting results of insurers because of the obligation to accept any applicants regardless of their risk.

VI. Claim for Indemnity

389. The following three payments are accepted under CALI:

(1) Payment of the actual amount paid by the insured: the insured is entitled to claim against the insurance company only up to the amount of damages that have actually been paid by him/her to the victim (Article 15 of ALSL).

(2) Victim's direct claim payment: the victim is entitled to the right of direct claim against the insurance company with which the automobile is insured for the amount of damages within the limits described above the insurer's liability (Article 16 of ALSL). Direct claim by claimant-for-damage was introduced for the special purpose of social policy.

(3) Provisional payment: this system is a measure to ease the financial burden of the victim, since it often takes a long period of time to finalize the payment for the damage.

A.   *Relief of Victims Suffering from Permanent Disability from Traffic Accidents*

390. The number of victims who suffer from permanent disability from traffic accidents in Japan has an upward tendency according to the increase of traffic, and exceeded JPY 1 million for the first time in Japanese history in 1999. The cost of permanent disability that needs nursing is to increase drastically from April 2002 (e.g., the cost of the permanent harm that always needs nursing will increase to JPY 40 million from JPY 30 million).

B.   *Assessment of the Amount of Claim or Damages*

391. The fixed-form and fixed amount method of calculation in order to make prompt and impartial handling of claims has been adopted for CALI. Under this CALI scheme, the amount of loss suffered by victims of traffic accidents is assessed in a standardized manner in accordance with the Loss Assessment Manual for CALI (hereinafter referred to as the Assessment Manual).

C.   *Role of Claims Survey Office*

392. After an accident, an insurance company goes through all aspects of handling claims (December 1980, High Court, Tokyo). However, under CALI, which is characterized by its function as a basic compensation system to provide relief to victims of traffic accidents, a high degree of fairness, objectivity and uniformity are required in handling claims, and for that reason a significant part of claim handling procedures, including appraisal of validity of claim and assessment of loss, is carried out by AIRO's claim survey offices. AIRO is a non-profit organization independent of insurance companies and established under the Law Concerning General Insurance Rating Organizations. AIRO merged with the Fire and Marine Insurance Rating Association of Japan, and the GIROJ was established on 1 June 2002.

GIROJ continues to work for the claim service of CALI as its main business.

393. The amount paid, which is first referred for evaluation by the survey office, and then decided by an insurance company, is paid to the victim or the claimant.

The number of the survey offices is fifty-five as of April 2016 through Japan, and they handle about 1,330,000 claims annually. The results of such surveys are utilized to establish basic premium rates for CALI.

394. In case of any objection to assessment made by the survey office, the matter is inspected by GIROJ's survey office. If there is further objection to it, GIROJ's head office then inspects the matter. It can therefore be taken into deliberation twice at different offices.

395. In some special cases, CALI's Inspection Committee for Liability or CALI's Inspection Committee for Permanent Disability, which are both established in the home office, may make inspections.

Special cases are:

(1)   no liability for death;
(2)   gross negligence for death;
(3)   objection to assessment of grades for permanent disability.

§3.   PREMIUM RATES FOR CALI

I.   No-Loss, No-Profit Rule

396. Since the function of CALI is to ensure financial relief to victims of traffic accident, under Article 25 of ALSL, it is stipulated that premium rates should be set at the lowest level possible to cover the cost of insurance incurred under efficient management, and it is also construed that no profit should be made from the operation of CALI. The premium rates for CALI are based on a 'no-loss, no-profit' basis.

II.   Premium Rates

397. Premium rates need permission from the FSA, according to Article 26. Premium rates are calculated by GIROJ, completely independent from other insurance companies.

III.   The Structure of the Premium Rate

398. The CALI premium rate consists of a pure premium, which is used to cover the payment and loading premium, which would be used to the expenses of the insurance company (i.e., sales cost, claim cost, agent commission, etc.). The pure premium plus loading premium is the full premium rate for CALI, but does not include any profit. Under the CALI law, it is prohibited to make profit from operation of CALI, and this is called a 'no-loss, no-profit' rule.

§4. GOVERNMENT REINSURANCE SYSTEM

399. The government reinsurance system was introduced in 1955, from the establishment of the CALI system, for two reasons.

As CALI is a compulsory insurance, the government thought it had better intervene in the insurance company's operation by using reinsurance.

There was insecurity about the proper premium rating which could result from an insurer's unexpected huge loss since this was a new compulsory insurance. It was considered that the government should therefore reinsure parts of the risk.

400. There was an argument about whether it was necessary for the government to reinsure.

As a result, by a revision to the ALSL in June 2001, the government reinsurance system was abolished. From April 2002, the insurance company insures 100%.

§5. NEW CALI SYSTEM (EFFECTIVE FROM APRIL 2002)

I. The Abolition of the Government Reinsurance System

401. Under the old system, the government would assume 60% of CALI from the risk hedge viewpoint. After revision, the government no longer assumes this and the insurance company assumes 100%.

II. A Supervision System for Appropriate Claims Payment

402. There is an inspection of important matters (Article 16(6) revised CALI law). The government checks all payment assumed through reinsurance currently, but would abolish this and only inspect for important matters such as death.

403. CALI has a social security-like nature. Because of that, if the payment standards were different in each company this would cause lack of fairness, so it is important that loss to be calculated by standards written in law (Article 16(3) revised CALI law).

404. The information service to the victim is as follows (Article 16(4) to (5) revised CALI Law):

(1) The insurance company assigns various duties such as the insurance payment to the victim and so on.
(2) It issues a document of the amount of loss paid and grade of permanent disability, including the reason of certification.
(3) It issues the reason in writing if the accident is a case of exclusion.
(4) It explains details in writing if the victim wants an explanation about the loss payment.

405. Introduction of an offer system against government (Article 16(7) revised CALI Law):

(1) When the loss payment is against the standard, claimant can make an offer to the government.
(2) When that fact is recognized as the result of a government investigation, directions for the modification can be shown to the insurance company.

III. Introduction of Dispute Management (Article 23(5) to 23(21) Revised CALI Law)

406. When a dispute of loss payment occurs, settlement by the court would take long time, so organization of dispute settlement by a third party would be established and would be settled by fair neutral specialist, speedily.

Chapter 2.   Voluntary Automobile Insurance

§1.   INTRODUCTION

407. Automobiles were imported for the first time in 1900, and automobile insurance was permitted at 1914. However, at that time there were only 1,000 vehicles in Japan. The main business of automobile insurance was reinsurance from the US.

408. Automobile insurance spread after 1955. In 1995, the ALSL, which aimed at the relief of victims of automobile accidents, was enacted. The next year, CALI became compulsory and the diffusion rate of automobile insurance increased rapidly.[106]

409. Highways opened and the roads were expanded on the occasion of the Tokyo Olympics in 1969, and the number of cars increased rapidly. As a result, traffic accidents increased dramatically in proportion to the number of the cars. As for automobile accidents, 6,871 persons died and 1.16 million persons were injured in 2005, and it is still a social problem.[107]

§2.   COVERAGE

I.   Bodily Injury Liability Coverage

410. The insurance policy covers the insured for his/her legal liability for bodily injury, including death, due to automobile accidents when the injured person is in another automobile, driving together, or walking, in excess of the loss payment by CALI.

II.   Self-Inflicted Personal Accident Coverage

411. The insurance policy covers accidents in which no other vehicle is involved, such as an accident where the insured's vehicle hits a telephone pole or falls down a cliff and causes bodily injury to or the death of the insured or the passengers, which is not indemnified for his/her own loss caused by the injury under either CALI or the Government Compensation Plan.

III.   Protection Against Uninsured Automobile Coverage

412. Those who are seated normally in the insured automobile are all covered by this policy when they are killed or sustain permanent disability arising out of the

---

106.   Bodily injury liability's diffusion rate is 70.9% (2002).
107.   Number of cars: 72.6million cars, 2000: 76.1 million cars, 2012.

ownership, maintenance or use of an 'uninsured vehicle', which is not insured against bodily injury under a voluntary automobile insurance policy or an automobile for which any coverage under its voluntary insurance excludes coverage for the accident in question, or an automobile whose limit of liability for bodily injury is lower than the limit under the insured's own policy.

IV.   Physical Damage Liability Coverage

413. The insurance policy covers the insured for his/her legal liability for an accident arising out of the owner's automobile.

V.   Passenger's Personal Accident Coverage

414. Those who are seated normally or are inside the insured automobile are all covered by this policy if they are killed or suffer from bodily injury due to a sudden and external accident.

VI.   Property Damage Coverage

415. This coverage indemnifies any accidental loss to the insured vehicle on an all risk basis, including collision or impact, fire, explosion, theft (excluding two-wheel automobiles and motorcycles), typhoon, flood, tidal wave and so on.

416. The standard policy conditions are composed of the above six types of coverage.

§3.   TYPES OF POLICY

417. In Japan, there are following four types of policies according to general policy conditions, which are combined with the said six types of coverage:

(a)   special automobile policy;
(b)   private automobile policy;
(c)   basic automobile policy;
(d)   paper driver policy.

§4. SPECIAL AUTOMOBILE POLICY (SAP)

I. Contents

418. This package policy provides all the six types of coverage; that is, bodily injury liability coverage, self-inflicted personal accident coverage (protection against automobile own injury), protection against uninsured automobile coverage, property damage liability coverage, passenger's personal accident coverage and physical damage coverage:

(1) If a claim for damages for a bodily injury accident or a property damage accident is brought against the insured, the insurance company must, in order to ascertain the particulars of the damages for which the insured is legally liable, cooperate or assist, to the extent that the insurance company is liable to indemnify the insured, in negotiation, settlement or proceedings as to conciliation or legal action to be made or taken by the insured.
(2) When the insured becomes legally liable for damages because of a bodily injury accident, the claimant for damages may file a claim with the insurance company for payment of the amount of damages.
(3) According to general conditions, own damage always deducts a certain amount of payment in case of accident, but contracts with a deductible amount special clause do not deduct the amount in certain cases.

II. Insured Automobile Applicable to this Package

419. The following kinds of automobile can be insured with an SAP policy:

(1) private passenger automobile (standard or small size, light four wheel);
(2) private light four wheel truck;
(3) private truck (small size).

III. Duty of Notification

420. The insurance company may cancel a policy if the person effecting the insurance (the named insured or any of their representatives) either intentionally or by gross negligence has failed to disclose any known fact or made misrepresentations about any fact regarding the matters required to be started in the application form at the time of entering into this contract (Commercial Law Article 644, paragraph 1).

421. The person effecting the insurance is required to declare to the insurance company the following items:

(1) information about the insured automobile;
(2) name/type/specification of the insured automobile;

(3) license plate no.;
(4) serial no.;
(5) original month of registration;
(6) type and use of the insured automobile;
(7) total number of automobiles that the insured person owns;
(8) driver's age limit, if any;
(9) discount and addition of premium;
(10) special clauses applied;
(11) named insured, owner of insured vehicle;
(12) any other effective insurance, coverage, accidents, if any;
(13) whether any insurance company has declined or cancelled an insurance contract in the past year;
(14) for private trucks:

> (a) possibility of commercial use;
> (b) possibility of loading of dangerous objects or towing a truck loaded with such objects.

422. Material increase in the hazard during the policy period is defined according to Commercial Law Article 656 or 657. General Condition Article 14 duty of notification is based on this and the following clauses are written:

(a) change of type and use or registration number (including any like number) of the insured automobile;
(b) use of the insured automobile for racing (including racing practice), stunts or testing;
(c) loading on the insured automobile of hazardous goods (meaning high-pressurized gas, gunpowder, hazardous goods, combustibles or inflammable materials), or trailing by the insured automobile of a trailer with hazardous goods loaded thereon;
(d) in addition to the above items, occurrence of a fact which would cause a material change regarding the matters described in this policy or the application form and involve material increase in the hazard;
(e) other insurance or mutual contracts insured to the same insured automobile.

423. Duty of notification in the case of accident is written in commercial law Article 658, but general condition Article 16 orders notification within sixty days from the accident, and in case of delay insurance company will not indemnity.

§5. PRIVATE AUTOMOBILE POLICY (PAP)

I. Coverage

424. This package policy provides all the five specified coverages; that is, bodily injury liability coverage, self-inflicted personal accident coverage (protection against own injury), protection against uninsured automobiles, property damage liability coverage and passenger's personal accident coverage. All the coverage has to be taken together. Coverage for physical damage may be covered under this package as an applicable special clause.

II.   Difference from Special Automobile Policy

425. In case of a property damage accident, any direct claims by a claimant for damages are not acceptable. Under protection against uninsured automobile coverage, the insured is limited to any person while riding on regular riding equipment fitted on the insured automobile (any place where it is partitioned so that a person cannot proceed through the partition is excluded).

If a claim for damages in a property damage accident is brought against the insured, the insurance company must not cooperate or assist in negotiation, settlement or proceedings as to conciliation or legal action to be made or taken by the insured.

§6.   BASIC AUTOMOBILE POLICY (BAP)

I.   Coverage

426. This policy provides any coverage required, except for protection against own injury coverage, which is covered together with bodily injury liability coverage. Under this package, a passenger's personal accident must be covered as an applicable special clause to bodily injury liability coverage or physical damage coverage. Protection against uninsured automobile coverage is not provided under this package.

II.   Difference from Special Automobile Policy

427. If a claim for damages on a property damage accident is brought against the insured, the insurance company must not cooperate or assist in negotiation, settlement or proceedings as to conciliation or legal action to be made or taken by the insured. In a property damage accident, any direct claim by the claimant for damages is not acceptable.

§7.   PAPER DRIVER POLICY (PDP)

I.   Contents

428. If people do not own an automobile, but have a driver's licence, there could be occasions where they drive a car rented from a friend, etc. The kinds of coverage applied to PDP are bodily injury liability coverage, self-sustained personal accident coverage, property damage liability coverage and passenger's personal accident coverage endorsement (this cover is available as an additional endorsement together with bodily injury or property damage).

429. The insured is only limited to the named insured driving a borrowed car, who shall not be changed during the policy period. To change the named insured during the policy period is prohibited. In a property damage accident, any direct claim by a claimant for damages is not acceptable.

§8. RATING SYSTEM

I.   Rating System

430. Major risk segments of the GIROJ tariff are as follows:

(1)   number of automobiles:

   (a) fleet (ten or over);
   (b) non-fleet (less than ten), with 1 to 20 grades which are determined by number of non-claim years;

(2)   automobile model; there are 1 to 9 classes for physical damage coverage, bodily injury liability, property damage liability and passenger's personal accident of a private passenger automobile according to the loss ratio of each automobile model.
(3)   initial year registered; new car or others
(4)   limitation to pay; sum insured, amount of own expense, etc.
(5)   driver's age; all ages, twenty-one years or over and twenty-six years or over. In case of twenty-six years or over, the age of insured may be considered.
(6)   definition of drivers; the named insured and his/her spouse, family all drivers
(7)   use and types of automobiles; private, business, truck, etc.
(8)   history of driving (non-fleet); 1~20 classes (a fresh contract start from 6-class)

431. Risk-segmented rates are regulated to approve the following nine categories:

(a)   driver's age; any number of categories allowed, but differentials between the highest and lowest rated groups to be within a range of 300%.
(b)   sex; segmentation allowed, but differentials between male and female to be within a range of 150%.
(c)   history of driving; any kind of segmentation allowed.
(d)   autousage; usage such as commercial, personal, commuting leisure.
(e)   pattern of usage; annual mileage and other pattern of use.
(f)   area; maximum division up to seven regions specified in the Act, differentials between regions to be within a range of 150%.
(g)   type of vehicle; any kind of segmentation allowed.

(h) vehicle safety features; discount can be applied depending on availability of safety features such as air bags and anti-lock brake systems.
(i) number of automobiles possessed or insured (multi-car ownership); discount can be applied based on the number of automobiles insured.

II. Deregulation and Tariff Rating

432. In 1996, the Japanese government perceived the necessity of deregulation, and started immediate reform under political leadership in the so-called financial field, including insurance and securities.

433. In the non-life insurance field, the IBL and Rating Organization Law were revised, and in the automobile insurance, range rates and special additional rates were deregulated, in April 1997. Therefore, insurance companies can now use their own tariffs more easily and rating competition expanded. However, as each insurance company still has duty to use the reference tariff calculated by the Rating Organization, there are opinions that deregulation has not gone far enough.

434. In December 1996, the Japan–US insurance talks reached an official conclusion, which contained:

(1) approval of the Financial System Reform Bill to revise the law concerning General Insurance Rating Organization of Japan which remove their member insurers from an obligation to use advisory pure premium rates calculated by GIROJ;
(2) approval of risk-segmented rates under the Ministry of Finance's guidelines in September 1997.

The talks ended with liberalization of automobile insurance, entrusting the details of contents to the Council.

435. Insurance-related reform was discussed by the Council, the MOF's advisory organization, which then submitted a report to the MOF. A reform Bill was proposed by the MOF.

In June 1997, the Council submitted a report on the Rating Organization, which contained the following:

(1) to repeal an obligation of observance of the premium rates by AIRO, and to refer to reference loss-cost rates (in other words, advisory pure premium rates) calculated by them;
(2) the rating organization should only calculate and advise reference pure premiums (advice of full premium, that is, including loading cost premium, is not acceptable); and should take effect by July 1998.

436. Following the approval of the financial system reform Bill, the law concerning the Non-Life Insurance Rating organization was considerably revised as follows:

(1)   The General Insurance Rating Organization of Japan only calculates reference loss-cost rates for voluntary automobile insurance, and these can be used by the member insurers but are not obligatory.

(2)   The General Insurance Rating Organization of Japan must file the advisory pure premium rates with the FSA, and then present the approved rates to insurance companies.

(3)   Each insurance company has to obtain approval for its own rates from the FSA; rates are calculated by adding each insurance company's loading such as expenses, commissions and profits to them.

(4)   However, since CALI is originally designed for protection of victims of accidents and does not correspond to liberalization of rating, the same rates apply and the Anti-monopoly Law does not apply to CALI.

437. In July 2000, the General Insurance Rating Organization of Japan applied to the FSA for another approval of new advisory pure premium rates as follows:

(1)   it abolished the four types of general conditions that are SAP, PAP, BAP and PDP, and made the reference to general conditions according to the types of coverage;

(2)   it revised the pure premium rate;

(3)   it subdivided the risk segmentations;

(4)   it revised the rules of coverage (introducing flexible deductible amounts, etc.).

This promoted competition for each insurance company to make its original products.

III.   Segmented Risk Type Automobile Insurance

438. The American Home Insurance Company launched a segmented risk type automobile insurance in 1998 as the first insurance company by telemarketing in Japan. The telemarketing of automobile insurance was first kicked off by Direct Line, London in 1984, providing such insurance upon receipt of a telephone inquiry, which has attracted the attention of the whole world.

439. In Japan, however, the non-life insurance industry did not much react to new business overseas, as there was a steady agency system, the premium rates were compulsorily calculated by GIROJ, and the solicitation of insured with good results was criticized.

Then, the segmented risk type automobile insurance was eventually introduced due to the deregulation resulting from the Japan–US talks and the utilization of IT.

As of August 2001, there are eight insurance companies in Japan that provide the telemarketing of automobile insurance, two of which are Japanese firms, three foreign-affiliated and one Japanese-foreign joint enterprise.

We do not know the exact market share of direct business in automobile insurance, because the data are not disclosed.

The reason for the slow growth of this new business in Japan is:

(a)   the strong connection between insured and agents;

(b) the insured's anxiety about insufficient network and services for claim settlement;
(c) less name value as a brand in spite of costly advertising fees.

It is considered that in five years the portion of telemarketing automobile insurance business may reach 10%–20% in Japan.

§9. Trends in New Product Development of Automobile Insurance

440. In July 1998, deregulation of products and rates for automobile insurance stimulated each insurance company to develop its own products. This trend has created some new products that meet the insured's needs beyond the previous traditional conception.

The two main products are as follows:

I. Comprehensive Automobile Insurance (CAI)

441. CAI is a package policy with bodily injury liability coverage, property damage liability coverage, passenger's personal accident coverage, physical damage coverage and personal injury compensation insurance coverage.

442. Personal injury pays benefits (i.e., death benefit, residual disability and medical benefit), in case of accidents with other automobiles while riding on an automobile or walking, and the named insured, his/her wife/husband and their family sustains bodily injury (JPY 30 million to JPY 200 million). The insurance company need only indemnify if the other automobile is a private use passenger automobile or private use freight small/light automobile.

If a contractor himself/herself becomes a victim, an indemnity can be paid by the assailant, but when the fault lies with both parties, it is limited to the part of an assailant's fault, it was only a contractor's self-burden that an indemnity was paid by an assailant. This new product would cover all the damage, including the contractor's own fault that would not be paid by the assailant.

443. Own damage insurance would cover not only damage vehicle itself, but also expenses such as car rental if the vehicle was impossible to use.

444. Originally, one insurance company introduced this new product. However, as a new product that matched consumer needs it was heavily subscribed and therefore many insurance companies introduced this coverage in their own products.[108]

II. Long-Term Insurance with Maturity Funds of Automobile Insurance

445. As the Japanese are said to like savings, Japanese's rate of saving is the highest in the main countries. This is the same for non-life insurance, and according

---

108. Insurance companies are introducing new products. For example, a certain insurance company introduced 'nursing coverage' special clauses.

to a research agency, many customers are dissatisfied with ordinary 'no return funds' non-life insurance products.

Even in non-life insurance, customers' needs are very strong for 'safe management of funds and with return funds', so automobile saving insurance was introduced.

446. This insurance has a period of two to three years with an 'insurance coverage function' and 'saving function'.

Asa concrete example, an insurance company would make a maturity repayment and according to the yield on investment, they would pay the policyholder a dividend (the maturity repayment would be paid independent of the number of accidents).

This is incidental to CAI and it has return funds without regard to the number of accidents in the insurance period. Also, if you have a plan to trade an old car for a new one or need a renewal vehicle inspection, you may have intermediate return of funds, if this is agreed in the contract.

Part V. Personal Insurance

§1. Introduction: Insurance Law Regulations for Accident and Health Insurance Contract

447. As for the personal insurance, the Ins. Law issued in 2008, instead of the traditional classification, that is, personal accident insurance contract and life insurance contract, has set new regulations based on the new concept of life insurance contract, accident and health damage insurance contract and fixed return accident and health insurance contract:

– Life insurance contract; an insurance contract under which an insurer undertakes to pay certain insurance benefits with respect to survival or death of a person (except, however for a fixed return accident and health insurance contract) (Ins. Law Article 2(4) item 7);
– Accident and health damage insurance contract; a non-life insurance contract under which an insurer undertakes to cover any damage that may arise through an injury or illness of a person (which shall be limited to those to be incurred by the person who suffered such injury or illness) (Ins. Law Article 2(4) item 9);
– Fixed return accident and health insurance contract; an insurance contract under which an insurer undertakes to pay certain insurance benefits in connection with an injury or illness of a person (Ins. Law Article 2(4) item 8).

As regarding life insurance contract, accident and health damage insurance contract and fixed return accident and health insurance contract, in the event that an insured is a person other than party, such insured may request an applicant for insurance contract to cancel the said insurance contract under certain circumstances (Ins. Law Articles 34, 58, 87).

448. As regarding the classification of insurance contracts such as life insurance contract, accident and health damage insurance contract and fixed return accident and health insurance contract there are following differences in the Ins. Law and IBL in Table 2.

Table 2 Differences in the Insurance Law and Insurance Business Law[109]

	Insurance Law	*Insurance Business Law*
Accident and health insurance (to cover actual loss)	Accident and health damage insurance contract	–
Accident and health insurance excluding death case	Fixed return accident and health insurance contract (to pay fixed amount)	Accident and health insurance contract (so-called third field insurance)
Insurance benefit– death by accident – (to pay fixed amount)	Fixed return accident and health insurance contract (to pay fixed amount)	–
Insurance benefit – death by disease – (to pay fixed amount)	Fixed return accident and health insurance contract (to pay fixed amount)	Life insurance contract

449. IBLER was revised, in 2009, to make limit on the sum insured of death insurance contract for a minor who shall obtain the consent of his/her legal representative for doing insurance contract. Therefore, an insurance company shall make its office regulations to restrict the sum insured for an insured below the age 15[110] or a policy without the consent of his/her legal representative.

A non-life insurance company, concerning personal accident insurance contract, restricts, in general, the sum insured underwritten for an insured below the age of 15 up to JPY 10 million, and for an insured the age 15 or over also up to JPY 10 million except the case that the said insurance contract with the consent of the insured.

A life insurance company restricts the sum insured of insurance contracts except those of single premium permanent life policy and/or single premium endowment policy, for an insured below the age 15 up to JPY 10 million and no restriction for an insured in the age of 15 or more.

450. Both of 'accident and health damage insurance contract' and 'fixed return accident and health insurance contract' are defined in the Ins. Law Article 2 that:

Accident and health damage insurance contract; a non-life insurance contract under which an insurer undertakes to cover any damage that may arise through an

---

109. Under the Insurance Law, the accident and health damage insurance contract which covers losses arising from injury or disease properly belongs to the non-life insurance contract, the IBL, however, permits a life insurance company to underwrite the said insurance contract as one of the third field insurance contract in spite of its provision prohibiting a person to obtain both business licence of life insurance and non-life insurance.
110. Any person who has attained full 15 years may make a will (Civ. Code Art. 961).

injury or illness of a person (which shall be limited to those to be incurred by a person who suffered such injury or illness);

Fixed return accident and health insurance contract; an insurance contract under which an insurer undertakes to pay certain benefits in connection with an injury or illness of a person.

From the viewpoint of IBL, a health insurance contract may pay a fixed amount of insurance claims or compensate for damage to an individual in connection with the following reasons:

(a) an individual contracted a disease;
(b) state of an individual due to a disease;
(c) treatment concerning those listed in (a) or (b).

As for the health insurance, in twentieth century of Japan market, a life insurance company was selling a product under which an insurer undertakes certain insurance benefits in connection with an illness of a person while a non-life insurance company was not permitted to sell such products and only could be selling for an overseas traveller a product under which an insurer undertakes to cover damage that may arise through an illness of a person.

451. Early in 1970's cancer insurance was permitted to a certain life insurance company to underwrite in Japanese market. This insurance was the first product that paid insurance benefits upon a specific individual disease.

For a non-life insurance company, the insurance product – medical expense insurance (see Part V, Chapter 3) – under which an insurer undertakes to cover damage that may arise through paying of medical expenses.

452. According to the amendment of IBL in 1995, both of a life insurance company and a non-life insurance company may underwrite a health insurance. Some foreign-affiliated insurance companies, however, depend relatively heavily on the so-called third field insurance (personal accident, nursing care, cancer, etc.) underwriting activity; the said circumstance might bring a drastic change in the management environment pertaining to the specified insurance company. So that the third field insurance products were not permitted, according to the supplementary provisions[111,112] of IBL, to underwrite at the time of the amendment of IBL. However, nowadays, many insurance companies, life insurance as well as non-life insurance, are underwriting various third-field insurance products.

453. In Japan, when an employee sustains any injury or suffers from disease due to occupational duty, the employer has to assume the following responsibilities to:

(1)   make compensation according to the Labour Standards Law (7 April 1947, Law No. 49);
(2)   give supplementary benefits compensation, which is instituted voluntarily by the employer under the labour agreement or its office regulation; and
(3)   pay damages that the employee may be entitled to under the Civil Code.

454. The compensation required under the Labour Standards Law is covered by the workmen's compensation insurance provided exclusively by the government.

The Labour Standards Law sets the minimum standard of compensation that an employer is legally required to meet when he/she compensates his/her employee for the injury sustained or disease contracted through work-related activities.

The workers' accident compensation insurance offered by the non-life insurance companies may cover supplementary benefits compensation and the damages awarded by the Civil Code.[113]

---

111.   Supplementary provisions Art. 1-2:

In case of an applicant for the license set forth in Art. 3(1) (limited to the case where the business to be licensed includes the insurance undertaking activity listed in Art. 3(4), item 2 or Art. 3(5), item 2: the same shall apply in the following paragraph), the Prime Minister may, for the time being, attach any necessary condition to such license pursuant to the provision of Art. 5(2) for ensuring that the license will neither bring a drastic change in the management environment pertaining to the specified insurance business activity (referring to the insurance underwriting activity listed in Art. 3(4), item 2 or Art. 3(5), item 2; hereinafter the same shall apply in this Article) of Specific Insurance Company (referring to an insurance company or foreign insurance company, etc. the management of which depends relatively heavy on the insurance activity listed in Art. 3(4), item 2 or Art. 3(5), item 2; hereinafter the same shall apply in this Article) nor pose any risk to the prudentiality in the business of the Specific Insurance Company.

112.   IBL Art. 5(2):

The Prime Minister may, when and to the extent that he/she finds it necessary for the public interest in light of requirements for examination prescribed in the preceding paragraph, impose conditions on the license referred to in Art. 3(1) or change them.

113.   The Workmen's Compensation Insurance Law: 7 Apr. 1947, Law No. 50.

Chapter 1.   Workers' Accident Comprehensive Insurance

455. Worker's accident comprehensive insurance comprises two categories. Category A covers supplementary benefits compensation and category B covers employer's liability.

456. By the amendment of the Occupation Safety and Health Act, a business firm with fifty or more employees has to inspect employees, by doctor and/or public health nurses, to grasp their psychological burden (stress check)(business firm of less than fifty employees has made efforts to do so). After stress check, the business firm has to give the chance to take consultation of doctor to the employee who has the wishes to do so. The business firm, according to the doctor's advice, shall take appropriate measures such as conversion of work, shortening working hours and/or decreasing late-night work, etc., if necessary. And the business firm should not treat the employee as disadvantageous for the reason that the employee insisted on the need of doctor's consultation.

457. Relation with this amendment of the law, special endorsements to cover employee's liability attributable to employee's depression and death from overwork, and discrimination and various harassments have been developed.

§1.   Supplementary Compensation Cover (Category A)

I.   Scope of Coverage

458. The supplementary compensation benefits payable are limited to death, permanent disability, varied in classes of permanent disability from 1 to 14, and benefits for the loss of income. The amount of each benefit may be agreed upon between the insurer and the insured within the limits provided in the labour agreement. There are two different bases for determining the amount.

The first is based on the fixed amount of money and the other is based on the average daily wage per employee.

II.   Exclusions

459. General conditions have the following several specific exclusions in addition to the common exclusions such as wilful acts of the policyholder and/or the insured, earthquake, war, riot, civil commotion, radioactivity or explosion of nuclear fuel materials, etc.:

(1) injuries sustained or diseases contracted by subcontractors of the insured and their employees;
(2) endemic diseases;
(3) occupational diseases;

(4) injuries sustained or diseases contracted by an employee due to his/her own wilful act or gross negligence;
(5) injuries sustained by an employee while he/she is driving an automobile without a driver's license or under the influence of alcohol, narcotics, opium, drugs, etc.; and
(6) injuries sustained by an employee as a result of his/her own criminal act.

III. Coverage Endorsements

460. Various endorsements can be attached to expand or limit the scope of cover. Some of the main endorsements are:

(1) subcontractors' cover endorsement;
(2) portal-to-portal cover endorsement (supplementary benefits compensation is payable for injuries sustained by an employee while commuting to or from his/ her office);
(3) occupational disease cover endorsement;
(4) overseas cover endorsement (injuries sustained by an employee who is working abroad are payable);
(5) contingent expenses cover endorsement (in the event of death or permanent disability of the first to the seventh classes, additional amounts are payable as contingent expenses to cover funeral expenses or other expenses);
(6) conditional war risk cover endorsement (for injuries sustained by an employee due to war, civil war, riot, civil commotion and the like). However, in the event of a considerable increase in the risk exposures during the policy period, the insurer may charge an additional premium or withdraw the endorsement by giving a twenty-four hour notice to the insured;
(7) retired employee endorsement (supplementary benefits compensation for an employee who had to retire from the company as a result of his/her permanent disability sustained or suffered from occupation-related diseases due to his/ her occupational duty, are payable in addition to the permanent disability benefit already provided under the basic coverage).

§2. Employer's Liability Cover (Category B)

I. Liabilities to Be Covered

461. The employer's liabilities covered by this section are those imposed by the Civ. Code but not covered by the government's workmen's compensation insurance. They are excess liability to the employer if the amount of compensation that the employer is liable for under the Civ. Code exceeds the total amounts of following, and they include liability for consolation money:

(1) the amount of benefit given under the government workmen's compensation insurance;
(2) the amount of indemnity provided by the compulsory automobile liability insurance, if any; and
(3) the amount of compensation payable by the insured to the employee under the labour agreement in terms of supplementary benefits compensation (this amount shall be paid under Category A).

II.   Expenses Payable

462. In addition to the amount of liability stated above, the following expenses incurred by the employer are also payable:

(1) expenses for preserving or exercising the employer's right of recovery from a third party, if any;
(2) legal expenses incurred; and
(3) expenses incurred for the purpose of the insured's cooperation with the insurer in preventing or minimizing losses.

III.   Exclusions

463. In addition to the exclusions provided in the supplementary benefits compensation coverage, the following liability and/or expenses are excluded from coverage:

(1) contractual liability assumed under the labour agreement or office regulation;
(2) if the insured is an individual, liability for, or expenses paid to, relatives living with the named insured in the same household;
(3) liability for first three days during the term in the event of the employee, who sustains injury or suffers from disease due to his/her occupational duty, being deprived of income as a result of disability.

IV.   Deduction

464. The amount of the deduction may be decided at the insured's option, and a premium discount can be adjusted according to the amount deducted.

Chapter 2.   Personal Accident Insurance

§1.   INTRODUCTION

465. The IBL of Japan has an article authorizing both a life insurance company and a non-life insurance company to underwrite bodily injury insurance. According to this Article (Article 3), a non-life insurance company may underwrite the following insurances:[114]

(1)   (Article 3(4) item 2); insurance whereby, in consideration of an insurance premium, an undertaking is made to pay a specified sum for an insurance claim in connection with any of the events mentioned below or to indemnify any loss which may be sustained as a result of such events:

(a) disease;
(b) any condition arising from injury or disease;
(c) death resulting directly from injury;
(d) events (other than death) designated by a Prime Minister's Office Ministry of Finance ordinance as being similar to those mentioned in sub-items (a) and (b);
(e) medical treatments (including those designated by a Prime Minister's Office Ministry of Finance ordinance as being similar to medical treatments) which may be carried out in connection with the events mentioned in sub-item (a), (b) or (d);

(2)   (Article 3(5) item 3); insurance which is connected with death occurring during the period between the departure from home for the purpose of travelling abroad and the return home (hereinafter called 'overseas travel period') or with death directly resulting from any disease contracted during the overseas travel period.

466. As for personal accident insurance, the GIROJ has produced six standard conditions (mentioned below) and calculated pure premium rates to submit for reference to its member companies.

Non-life insurance companies have produced various types of personal accident insurance products on the basis of these standard conditions:

(1)   ordinary personal accident insurance (1911);
(2)   domestic travellers' personal accident insurance (1947);
(3)   traffic personal accident insurance (1963);
(4)   family personal accident insurance (1982);
(5)   family traffic personal accident insurance (1973);

---

114.   Insurance to pay a specified sum of insurance claim in connection with survival or death is authorized only for life insurance companies (except overseas travel insurance).

(6) overseas travel personal accident insurance (1974).[115]

§2. SCOPE OF COVERAGE AND BENEFIT

I. Coverage

A. *Ordinary Personal Accident Insurance and Family Personal Accident Insurance*

467. Bodily injury suffered by the insured due to a violent external accident in Japan or abroad is covered. Bodily injury includes any symptom of poisoning or intoxication caused by accidental inhaling, absorbing or taking in of poisonous fumes or any other poisonous substance.

B. *Personal Traffic Accident Insurance and Family Traffic Accident Insurance*

468. These insurances provide the insured with benefits for bodily injury caused by traffic accidents in Japan or abroad, and they cover the following kinds of injury:

(1) injury suffered by the insured while he/she is not riding on a vehicle due to:

   (a) his/her collision or contact with a vehicle under operation or articles loaded thereon;
   (b) collision, contact, fire, explosion, etc., of a vehicle under operation.

(2) injury suffered by the insured as a passenger. The words 'passenger' include not only a person driving a car or riding on or in a vehicle but also a person who is on the premises within the ticket barriers of a traffic station;
(3) injury suffered by the insured while he/she is walking on the road due to:

   (a) collapse of building, scaffolding, etc., or falling of any object therefrom;
   (b) andslide or falling of earth, sand, rock, etc.;
   (c) fire, bursting or explosion of any object;
   (d) collision or contact with an engineering car such as mobile crane, power shovel, etc., used for only as machine tool and collision, contact, fire, explosion, etc., of such a car.

(4) injury suffered by the insured due to fire in a building.

---

115. Overseas travel personal accident insurance is explained in §5.

C.   *Domestic Travellers' Personal Accident Insurance*

469. This insurance, which is written by way of an endorsement to ordinary personal accident policy covers bodily injury suffered by the named insured in an accident during domestic travelling (from the time of leaving the residence to the time of returning thereto).

II.   Benefit

470. There are basically five kinds of benefit, that is, death benefit, permanent disability benefit, hospitalization medical expenses benefit, surgical operation expense benefit and non-hospitalization medical expenses benefit:

(1)   Death benefit: in the case of accidental death of the insured within 180 days from the date of the accident, the sum insured will be paid as a lump sum.
Permanent disability benefit: if the insured sustains permanent disability within 180 days from the date of the accident, 3% to 100% of the sum insured according to the degree of permanent disability will be paid. The occupation of the insured is not taken into consideration.
(2)   Hospitalization medical expenses benefit: if the insured is entirely disabled from participating in daily life or performing occupational duties and requires treatment by a physician, the amount stated in the policy for each day for such period as the insured is so disabled and treated, but not exceeding 180 days from the date of the accident. This period may be extended to 365 days or 730 days by an endorsement.
(3)   Surgical operation expenses benefit: if the insured has an operation as mentioned in the policy within 180 days from the date of the accident, 1,000% to 4,000% of such amount for each day as provided for hospitalization medical expense benefit will be paid, corresponding with the kind of the operation.
(4)   Non-hospitalization medical expenses benefit: if the insured is partly disabled from participating in daily life or performing occupational duties and requires treatment by a doctor attending a hospital or clinic, the amount stated as the non-hospitalization medical expenses benefit in the policy for each day for such period as the insured is so disabled and treated, but not exceeding ninety days within the period of 180 days from the date of the accident.

III.   Option to Combine the Benefits

471. All five of these benefits are basically insured together. However, certain combinations of benefits can be available, that is, (1), (2), (3) and (4), (1) and (2), (3), (4) and (5), (3) and (4).

§3. SCOPE OF THE INSURED

472. Family accident insurance and family traffic accident insurance cover personal accidents suffered by any of the following family members:

(1) the named insured or the principal who is expected to be the person maintaining his/her family's livelihood;
(2) the principal's spouse;
(3) relatives living with the principal or with the principal's spouse in the same household;
(4) unmarried sons or daughters of the principal in the same household who live apart from the principal or the principal's spouse.

§4. MAIN EXCLUSIONS

473. Bodily injury caused by the following is not covered:

(1) wilful acts of the policyholder or the insured;
(2) wilful acts of the beneficiary (if the beneficiary is entitled to receive a part of death benefit, this exclusion does not apply to the amount which any other beneficiary is entitled to receive);
(3) suicide, criminal act or act of fighting of the insured;
(4) accidents occurring while the insured is driving an automobile or a motorcycle without having qualification to drive it or driving it under the influence of alcohol, narcotics, hemp or the like, to the extent the insured may not be able to control the vehicle;
(5) brain disease, sickness or insanity of the insured;
(6) pregnancy, parturition, premature parturition, miscarriage or surgical or any other medical treatment of the insured;
(7) execution of a sentence of the insured;
(8) earthquake, volcanic eruption or tidal wave resulting therefrom;
(9) war, civil war, revolution, civil commotion, riot, etc.;
(10) accidents caused by nuclear reactions;
(11) any accident incidental to exclusions (8) (10) above, or any accident arising from the disturbance of good order incidental thereto.

474. The insurer is in no case liable for cervical syndrome (so-called whiplash injury) or back pain, from any cause, without objective symptoms.

475. Unless otherwise specially agreed and an additional premium being paid, the insurer is not liable for bodily injury sustained:

(1) while the insured is conducting hazardous athletic sports such as mountain-climbing (using ice axe, climbing irons, climbing rope, hammer, etc.), luge or bobsleigh riding, sky diving, etc.;

(2)   while the insured is participating in contests, racing, exhibitions to test cars, motorcycle or motorboat (bodily injury sustained while such performance is made on public roads can be covered);
(3)   while the insured is operating an aircraft other than a scheduled or unscheduled commercial aircraft flying over a regular air route.

§5.   Overseas Travel Personal Accident Insurance

I.   Statutory Regulation

476.   Insurance to indemnify the loss that may result from 'cases where an individual contracts a sickness' and 'the death of an individual directly resulting from sickness', in principal, has to be treated as life insurance business.

The IBL, however, provides that non-life insurance business is able to write such insurance as 'connected with death occurring during the period between the departure from home for the purpose of travelling abroad and the return home (referred to hereinafter in this item as 'overseas travel period') or with death directly resulting from any disease contracted during the overseas travel period (IBL Article 3(V)(3)).

477.   A foreign insurer which has no branch office in Japan, in principle, must not enter into an insurance contract with respect to a person who has an address or a residence in Japan (IBL Article 186).

Overseas travel personal accident insurance, however, is stipulated among the insurance contracts that may be entered into by a foreign insurance company with no branch office in Japan (IBL Enforcement Regulation Article 116(3)).

II.   Scope of Coverage

478.   Bodily injury coverage under the basic policy condition covers the following:

(1)   death and permanent disability benefit – the same as those under ordinary personal accident insurance;
(2)   medical expenses benefit – as defined below, those which are actually incurred as a direct result of bodily injury within 180 days from the date of accident are paid up to the insured amount for medical expenses for bodily injury coverage specified in the policy for any one accident:

   (a) expenses for medical examination, treatment and surgical operation by a doctor of medicine;
   (b) expenses for medicines, medical supplies and use of medical appliances as a result of treatment or prescription by a doctor of medicine;
   (c) expenses for repair of an artificial arm and an artificial leg;
   (d) expenses for X-ray examinations, laboratory tests and use of operating room;
   (e) expenses for employment of a professional nurse;

(f) charges by a hospital or a clinic for room;

(g) hotel room charge, when the insured, otherwise necessarily confined in a hospital or a clinic, shall be under care of a doctor of medicine in an accommodation facility such as hotel, owing to unavailability of hospital or clinic by reason of capacity or distance or any other circumstance beyond control of the insured;

(h) unforeseen hotel room charges such as when the insured is under care of a doctor of medicine and ordered to take rest in the hotel by a doctor of medicine;

(i) expenses incurred for an ambulance service to carry the insured to a hospital or a clinic for emergency medical treatment;

(j) transportation expenses for hospital confinement or hospital visits;

(k) expenses incurred to move the insured to another hospital or clinic by reason of unavailability of specialists or of the difficulty in receiving appropriate treatment at the hospital or the clinic in which the insured is confined, including expenses incurred for attendance, if necessary, of a doctor of medicine or professional nurse to afford treatment during the transportation;

(l) expenses for employment of an interpreter as necessitated for treatment;

(m) the following expenses, when the insured is confined in a hospital or clinic, but up to JPY 200,000 per accident:

(1) the expense for communication such as international calls, etc.;

(2) expense for buying personal effects (up to JPY 50,000);

(c) the following transportation expenses and accommodation expenses, when the insured is necessitated to leave from the original leg of a trip as a direct consequence of hospital confinement:

(1) transportation expenses and accommodation expenses to return to the original leg of a trip;

(2) transportation expenses and accommodation expenses to return home directly.

479. There are various endorsements such as the following:

(1) sickness coverage endorsement – there are two endorsements such as death by sickness coverage and medical expenses for sickness coverage;

(2) personal liability coverage;

(3) baggage coverage;

(4) rescuers' expenses, etc., coverage;

(5) automobile driver's liability coverage.

§6. Modification of the Risk

480. The policyholder has a duty to inform the insurer of any of the following circumstances:

(1) Change of occupation or the activities related to the occupation, and leaving or retiring from the job. When the insurer receives this information, the insurer is able to change premium, if necessary. If insured does not inform the insurer of the change or pay an additional premium, the liability of the insurer will be determined by the proportion which the rate having been applied bears to the rate to be newly applied.

(2) Double insurance – when the insurer receives this information, it is able to cancel its own insurance contract.

§7. TERMINATION OF THE INSURANCE

481. The insurance contract will be terminated in the following circumstances:

(1) expiry date of the policy period;
(2) the death of the insured;
(3) the total amount of disablement benefit to have been paid runs up to the sum insured;
(4) cancellation by the policyholder or the insured;
(5) cancellation by the insurer.

The insurer will only have the right to cancel the policy in the event of double insurance or the discovery of any fraud in obtaining insurance money and the like.

Chapter 3.   Medical and Nursing Care Expenses Insurance

§1.   MEDICAL EXPENSES INSURANCE

I.   Introduction

482. In Japan, people being under a medical doctor for injury or disease can be indemnified against expenses for the doctor's treatment under the public health insurance system (compulsory insurance). These systems are based on Health Ins. Law (Law No. 70, 22 April 1922), National Health Ins. Law (Law No. 192, 27 December 1958), Seamen's Ins. Law (Law No. 73, 6 April 1939), Government Official Benefit Association Act (Law No. 128, 1 May 1958) or the Local Government Official Benefit Association Act (Law No. 152, 8 September 1962).

483. Those insured under the Health Ins. Law are so-called salaried workers (including their dependants) and those insured by the National Health Insurance based on the National Health Ins. Law are independent shop owners, independent lawyers, independent accountants and the like.

484. On 14 August 1984, these Health Insurance Laws were revised and it came into force on 1 October 1984 that the insured had to bear a certain amount of medical expenses or expenses for hospitalization (in the case of Health Insurance, the principal insured had to bear 10% of the amount; 20% today, 30% from April 2003). And expenses for highly advanced medical care such as electromagnetic wave thermotherapy for cancer, an artificial tympanum, an operation to implant an artificial tooth, an operation to the brain with an endoscope, etc., are not covered under public health insurance.

485. Medical expenses insurance was developed to cover hospitalization expenses shared by the insured on public health insurance scheme, in December 1985 (business was started in April 1986).

II.   Coverage of Medical Expenses Insurance

486. Those insured under public health insurance and their dependants may become the insured of this insurance.

487. There are three kinds of coverage in this medical expenses insurance. The following coverage (B) and (C) must be purchased as a package:

(a) Medical treatment expenses coverage – covers a part of medical treatment expenses, incurred during hospitalization, to be borne by the insured in the indemnity period (180, 365 or 730 days at the insured's option) under public health insurance, subject to the deductible amount of JPY 5,000 per hospitalization. If the insured receives an additional benefit (most large enterprises' health insurance associations usually pay an additional benefit), the insurer deducts it from his/her payment.

(b) Expenses for hospitalization, etc., coverage. The following insured's practical expenses, which are not covered under public health insurance, are also covered with a certain of payment:

(1) surcharge for a special room used with the approval of the hospital;
(2) expenses for employment of a professional attendant while it is considered necessary by the doctor;
(3) expenses for attendance of the relatives while it is considered necessary by the doctor:

(a) expenses for attendance of the relatives;
(b) transportation for attendance of the relatives;
(c) hire of bed-linen;

(4) expenses for employment of a housekeeper;
(5) sundry expenses for hospitalization;
(6) transportation for entering, changing and leaving the hospital.[116]

(c) The following expenses for highly advanced medical care are covered:

(1) expenses for highly advanced medical care;
(2) transportation for entering, changing and leaving the hospital for highly advanced medical care.

The indemnity period of coverage (C) is same as case of coverage (B), and the payable limit of benefit is 200 times as much as the basic payable benefit per day as set out under the coverage (B). However, a deduction is not applied.

488. The coverage of this insurance is available only when both disease or bodily injury and start of hospitalization occurred during the policy period, and hospitalization due to a disease occurring within the first sixty days of the new policy period shall not be covered because of the difficulty of determining when a disease is caused.

489. At the time of making an application for this insurance, the insured must submit to the insurer a declaration of his/her health conditions in the prescribed form. It is said that a medical examination by a doctor is one of the important ways of

---

116. The limit shall be calculated with the following method:
(1) in case of the deductible days (the basic payable benefit per day) × [(the number of days in the hospital) – (the number of the deductible days)].
(2) in case of the deductible amount (the basic payable benefit per day) × (the number of days in the hospital) – JPY 5,000 per hospitalization.
The basic payable benefit per day shall be selected in the range from JPY 1,000 to JPY 20,000 per each insured.
The indemnity period shall be 180, 360 or 730 days at the insured's option.
The deductible days shall be 4, 7, 14 or 30 days at the insured's option.

underwriting this type of insurance; insurers (i.e., non-life insurance companies), however, do not adopt this method because of simplification of marketing procedures.

III.   Main Exclusions of Medical Expenses Insurance

490. The main exclusions are as follows:

(1)   hospitalization due to disease or bodily injury caused by:

(a) wilful act or gross negligence of the policyholder or the insured;
(b) suicide, criminal act or act of fighting of the insured;
(c) use of narcotics, opium, hemp or other stimulants;
(d) war, civil war, etc., or nuclear materials, etc.;

(2)   hospitalization due to bodily injury caused by:

(a) driving of automobile or motorcycle without license or in a heavily drunken condition;
(b) earthquake, volcanic eruption or tidal wave;

(3)   hospitalization due to:

(a) mental disease, weak-mindedness or other mental disorder;
(b) pregnancy or delivery (except that covered under the public health insurance);
(c) whiplash or lumbago without objective symptoms;

(4)   hospitalization due to bodily injury suffered while (this exclusion can be deleted by way of an endorsement and at an additional premium):

(a) the insured is doing dangerous sports enumerated in the general conditions of this insurance;
(b) the insured is participating in the racing of or having a test drive in an automobile, motorcycle or motorboat.

§2.   NURSING CARE EXPENSES INSURANCE

I.   Introduction

491. In Japan, the average life expectancy is 83.99 years for females and 77.10 years for males (in 1999). So, people over 65 years of age are expected to jump up from 416 million (4.9% of population) in 1950 to 3,312 million (27.4% of population) in 2025.

Accordingly, this structural problem of a rapidly aging society makes people consider health and life in old age (i.e., how to take care of old people who are under the care of others in daily life – to be called 'old people in a condition needing nursing').

492. In the 1987 *Report of the Insurance Council*, remarks are found that it is important and desirable to proceed with the creation of insurance, which covers nursing care expenses. This nursing care expenses insurance which all Japanese non-life insurance companies started to sell in October 1989 covers various expenses incurred when nursing care is needed as a result of being bedridden or senile, and this insurance has different features from other non-life insurance such as a lifelong policy, use of the mortality table for premium calculation, etc., A maturity refund-type policy has been also marketed since 1990.

493. Public nursing care insurance (compulsory insurance) based on the Nursing Care Ins. Law (Law No. 123, 1 April 1997 came into force on 1 April 2000) and started to supply benefits in April 2000.

The insurer of this insurance is local self-government. Benefits of this public insurance may be classified as nursing care benefit, preventive benefit and local self-government special benefit, and they are also classified, from another point of view, welfare-at-home benefit and expenditure benefit such as the following:

(1) welfare-at-home benefit – the insurer (local self-government), for instance, sends a qualified person to the insured for nursing care such as helping to bathe, rehabilitation, and the like;
(2) expenditure benefit – the insurer pays, for instance, costs to repair a house (e.g., costs for providing a stair rail), expenses to buy specific supporting goods (supporting equipment for having a bath or using the lavatory) or expenses to enter nursing care institutions, etc.

II.   Coverage of Nursing Care Expenses Insurance

494. The Non-Life Insurance Rating Organization provides standard general conditions and some standard endorsements of this insurance. This insurance covers expenses to be borne by the insured because of needing nursing care condition due to being in a bedridden or senile state for a period exceeding 180 days. Basically, expenses arising both from being bedridden and senile are covered; it is, however, possible to cover each of them separately.

495.

(1) Recognition of bedridden condition: the insured is kept in his/her bed all day long; and

(a) the insured cannot walk by himself/herself even with the aid of equipment; and
(b) the insured cannot eat, use the lavatory, bathe or dress by himself/herself even with the aid of equipment.

(2) Recognition of senile condition: the insured is, generally and continuously, failing in his/her intellectual ability by the acquired disease or injury caused in the brain (for instance, Alzheimer's dementia); and

> (a) the insured cannot walk, eat, use the lavatory, bathe or dress by himself/ herself even with aid of equipment; or
> (b) the insured does any abnormal action, for instance, wandering, losing his/her way, toying with faeces, eating something strange, etc.

496. There are three kinds of packaged coverage in this insurance:

(1) Medical expenses and expenses for nursing care institutions coverage: covers, generally, the following expenses to be borne by the insured in the indemnity period. If the insured can receive benefit from other sources, the insurer deducts them from the payment:

> (a) expenses for hospital or clinics;
> (b) expenses for nursing care institutions (in case the insured stays there more than continuous eight days).

The insurance company pays expenses each month up to the agreed limit of monthly indemnity, which is determined, in general, within the range from JPY 100,000 to JPY 200,000 per month. No deduction is applied in this coverage.

(2) Expenses for nursing care, etc., coverage: the insurer pays an agreed amount (generally, JPY 100,000 or JPY 200,000 per month) for nursing care, etc. The amount payable, however, varies according to the type of nursing care:

> (a) in case of nursing care at home or free-charging elderly peoples' homes – 100% of the agreement amount;
> (b) in case of nursing care at hospital or clinic – 50% of the agreed amount;
> (c) in case of nursing care at nursing institutions for eight days or more – 15% of the agreed amount.

(3) The extra expenses borne by the insured shall be covered up to the agreed amount, in general, within the range from JPY 1,000,000 to JPY 2,000,000. No deduction is applied under this coverage.

III. Main Exclusions

497. The condition of needing nursing care in the following cases is excluded:

(1) by wilful act or gross negligence of the policyholder or the insured;
(2) inherited disorder of the insured;
(3) suicide, criminal act or strife of the insured;

(4) use of narcotics, opium, hemp or other stimulants;
(5) alcoholism or medical poisoning of the insured;
(6) earthquake, volcanic eruption, tidal wave, war, civil war or nuclear fuel materials;
(7) driving of an automobile or a motorcycle without license or in a severely drunken condition.

IV. Others

A. Insured

498. The insured has to be 20 years old and over but not exceeding 70 years. Double insurance is prohibited.

B. Policy Period

499. This insurance terminates at the death of the insured.

Chapter 4.   Income Indemnity Insurance

§1.   INTRODUCTION

500. In Japan, for income compensation during disability periods, there are, in effect, two kinds of public insurance systems operated by the government based on law.[117] And there are also private supplementary systems (i.e., income indemnity insurance and long-term income indemnity group insurance).

501. Although the main coverage of the government workmen's compensation insurance is pensions and lump sum compensation for on-the-job death or permanent disability, it also covers 60% of pre-disability income during a disability period with a waiting period of the first three days.

Under public health insurance in case of disability due to off-the-job personal injury or disease, 60% of pre-disability income is paid for up to eighteen months.[118]

§2.   INCOME INDEMNITY INSURANCE

502. Income indemnity insurance was developed and started to be sold in April 1974; it provides coverage for occupational and non-occupational disability and for employees, professionals and self-employed people.

503. This insurance covers loss of income suffered by the insured due to inability to work, which is stated in the policy, in direct consequence of sickness or accidental bodily injury during the policy period. This insurance has an exemption period.

If a policy has a benefit period of over two years, after benefits have been paid for twenty-four months, it is necessary for the insured to be unable to perform his/ her duties of any occupation at all for which he/she is reasonably fitted by ability or experience.[119]

---

117.   The government workmen's compensation system and public health insurance.

118.   The government workmen's compensation insurance is not available to some professionals such as lawyers, medical doctors, accountants and also self-employed person and does not apply either to the executive officers of large firms.

119.   Benefit is to be paid for the disability period in excess of the first 7, 14, 30, 60, 90, 180 or 365 days at the insured's option.

The benefit period is limited according the insured's age:

15 to 60 years old – one, two or five years;

61 to 63 years old – one or two years;

64 years old or over – one year only.

I.   Amount of Benefit

504. The amount of benefit is determined on the basis of a certain percentage of the insured's average monthly income over the last twelve months.[120]

II.   Exclusions

505. The exclusions of this insurance are approximately the same as those of ordinary personal accident insurance. There are two particular cases excluded in case of disease: (a) disability or mental disorder, (b) disability as a result of the insured's pregnancy, delivery or abortion.

III.   Additional Coverage

506. Additional coverage is available, at the insured's option, for death and disability due to accidental bodily injury within 180 days after the accident occurs. The scope of coverage is almost the same as that for ordinary personal accident insurance.

IV.   No Claim Return

507. Twenty per cent of premium is refunded to the insured who has made no claim for the policy period. The policy period is one year only.

§3.   LONG-TERM INCOME INDEMNITY GROUP INSURANCE

508. The coverage of this insurance is approximately the same as those of income indemnity insurance. The policy period is also one year only, but the benefit period can be set for a long-term period. The insurance contract must be concluded between the insurer and the group such as company, union, association, etc.

509. There are two methods of making this insurance contract:

(1)   blanket contract – individuals of the group must come to the insured all together;
(2)   optional participation contract – each individual of the group is able to be insured at his/her own choice.

510. The benefit period can be set up to when the insured is 70 years old.

511. The number of insured must be more than twenty persons, in general. And the exemption period must be set at more than ninety days; however, in a blanket

---

120.   The insurer determines the amount of benefit by reference to the public health insurance or workers' compensation insurance applicable to the insured.

contract where all the insured belong to the same company or the same political office the exemption period can be set at more than thirty days.

Chapter 5. Life Insurance

§1. Statutory Regulation

512. Ins. Law constitutes the statutory framework for life insurance in Japan and it defines life insurance contacts and also stipulates basic items with regard to a life insurance contract on another person's life, obligation to give a health statement and other matters. Also, as life insurance is a type of 'contract', it is subject to the general provisions of the Civil Code.

Further, in order to ensure the healthiness and appropriateness of the insurance business operation, having the nature of public welfare, the IBL also governs this insurance.

Since these laws provide broad and general guidance, specifics are left to insurance policy provisions made by insurers, except as the above laws enforce.

Matters not stipulated in the policy provisions are normally governed by order of the Ins. Law and Civ. Code.

§2. General Items

I. Definition of Life Insurance Contracts

513. 'Life insurance' is not defined by either the Ins. Law or the IBL. The Ins. Law defines the life insurance contract and the IBL defines life insurance business.

Life insurance contracts are defined as 'an insurance contract under which an insurer undertakes to pay certain insurance benefits with respect to survival or death of a person (except, however, for a fixed return accident and health insurance contract) (Ins. Law Article 2(8)) and life insurance business is defined, in the IBL Article 3(4), as 'business to underwrite insurance listed under items (1) to (3) below':

(1) insurance (other than that pertaining solely to death as mentioned in sub-item (1) of the following item) whereby, in consideration of an insurance premium, an undertaking is made to pay a specified sum of insurance claim in connection with survival or death (including a physical condition in respect of which a physician has diagnosed that the remainder of life is not likely to exceed a specified period; this inclusion applying in this and the following paragraph);

(2) insurance whereby, in consideration of insurance premium, an undertaking is made to pay a specified sum of insurance claim in connection with any of the events mentioned below or to indemnify any loss which may be sustained as a result of such events:

(a) disease;

(b) any condition arising from injury or disease;

(c) death resulting directly from injury;

(d) events[121] (other than death) designated by IBLER as being similar to those mentioned in sub-items (1) and (2);

(e) medical treatments (including those[122] designated by IBLER as being similar to medical treatments) which may be carried out in connection with the events mentioned in sub-item (1), (2) or (3).

(3)   reinsurance on insurance defined in the above two items.

Item 2 above can be underwritten by property/casualty insurance company also and so this class of business is called 'third area' insurance.

The amount of insurance fluctuates based on the investment performance in variable insurance and nevertheless, it is classified as life insurance as it has nothing to do with property damage, which is the subject of property/casualty insurance, and also the amount of insurance is still objectively determined and so it has the character of fixed amount insurance.

II.   Type of Life Insurance

514. Life insurance is typically classified in the following three groups for the type of insurance risks:

(1)   Death insurance – to pay the insured an amount for death of the insured. The purpose is to protect the living standard of the bereaved family after the insured's death.

(2)   Survival insurance – to pay the insured amount if the insured survives at the expiration of the period set forth in the contract. The purpose is to prepare for financial needs after a certain point of time.

(3)   Combination of death and survival insurance – death benefit is paid for the death of the insured within the insurance period and maturity benefit is paid for the survival of the insured at the expiration of the insurance period. Thus, this is a combination of (1) and (2) above.

---

121.   Childbirth and the physical condition of an individual resulting therefrom;

Physical conditions which require a constant care resulting directly from senility (IBL Enforcement Regulations Art. 4).

122.   Midwifery performed by midwives as provided for in Art. 3 of the Law Concerning Health Nurses, Midwives and Nurses (Law No. 203, 1948):

– therapeutic arts performed by judo repositionists (*judo seifukusi*) as provided for in Art. 2 of the Judo Repositionists Law (Law No. 19, 1970);

– therapeutic arts performed by *anma* massagers and chiropractors, acupuncturists or Moxa-Cautery therapists under the Law Concerning *Anma* Massagers and Chiropractors Acupuncturists and Moxa-Cautery Therapists (Law No. 217, 1947) (limited to those performed as per medical direction). (IBL Enforcement Regulations Art. 5).

Life insurance can also be classified from dividend features as follows:

(1) participating products;
(2) participating in investment profit only, every five years;
(3) non-participating products.

In a mutual company, non-participating products are regulated as 'non-member contracts' and they are separately administered from participating ones and the class of business must be limited to 20% in terms of the total amount of insurance (IBL Article 63, IBLER Article 33).

These rules are not applied to stock companies. The above-described insurance contracts are traditional ones. Life insurance companies have been marketing so far primarily whole life products with a large amount term rider, with automatic renewal features; however, due to the stagnation of the Japanese economy and also to the ageing population, consumers have started to re-examine the type of life insurance they have been carrying.

Along with this, the so-called third area insurance covering disease or accident, hospitalization, surgery or cancer coverage has started to be developed and has penetrated the market in recent years.

Due to low investment yield, life insurance companies have been faced with difficulty in allocating investment interest, which is scheduled by an assumed interest rate, to existing policies and also due to the continuous bankruptcy of life insurance companies, the IBL was revised so that the insurance company may report to the Prime Minister to the effect that it will modify the clause of its contract, such as a reduction in the amount of insurance claims and other modifications to contract clauses with regard to insurance contracts pertaining to the said insurance company in the case that there is a probability that the continuation of the said insurance company's insurance business will be difficult in the light of the state of its business or property (IBL Article 240–2(1)).

Concerning the assumed interest rate that is modified by the modification of contract conditions, from the standpoint of the protection of insurance policyholders, etc., the assumed interest rate shall not be less than the rate specified by a Cabinet Order (3% per year), taking into account the insurance company's property operating situation and other circumstances (IBL Article 240–4(2),IBLCO Article 36–3).

III. Contract Parties to Life Insurance and Other Related Parties

515. Contract parties to life insurance include the insurer and policyholder, and other related parties include the insured and beneficiary. The relationship of these parties is considered like below:

(1) If the policyholder and beneficiary are the same, the contract is an 'own life insurance contract' and if they are different, the contract is a 'life insurance contract for another'.

(2) If the policyholder and the insured are the same, the contract is an 'insurance contract on own life' and if they are different, the contract is an 'insurance contract on life of another'.

IV. Life Insurance Contract for Third Party (Insurance Law Article 42)

516. In a life insurance contract which designates other than contract parties, as beneficiary, the benefit on the insurance contract goes to the beneficiary as a matter of course. In this case, the beneficiary gains the right to claim without any expression of receiving benefit. The right to request a reduction in the amount of insurance and a change of beneficiary belong to the policyholder.

In the event the insurance applicant intends to change a beneficiary, it shall be made by a declaration of intention to an insurer. Change of a beneficiary by will, however, may not be asserted against an insurer unless, when the will comes into effect, an heir if an insurance applicant notifies the insurer of that fact (Ins. Law Article 44). No change of a beneficiary under a death insurance contract shall become effective without the consent of an insured (Ins. Law Article 45).

V. Insurance Contract on Life of Third Party (Insurance Law Article 38 etc.)

517. A life insurance contract making a third-party person other than the policyholder the insured can be taken out for illegal purpose and in order to prevent this, the following rules apply:

(1) the insurer must give consent (Ins. Law Article 38);
(2) under a death insurance contract, the insured's consent is required in case of the change of a beneficiary (Ins. Law Article 45);
(3) under a death insurance contract, the insured's consent is required in case when the transfer of the right to claim insurance benefits pursuant to a life insurance contract or creation of a pledge on such rights (excluding those executed after the occurrence of an insurable contingency) (Ins. Law Article 47);
(4) under a death insurance contract, the insured may request a policyholder to cancel the said insurance contract under any of the following circumstances (Ins. Law Article 58):

   (a) if a policyholder or beneficiary has caused or has intended to cause death to an insured intentionally in an attempt to make an insurer pay insurance benefits;
   (b) if a beneficiary has committed or has intended to commit a fraud in connection with the claim for insurance benefits under the said life insurance contract;
   (c) in any other material events than those mentioned in the above (a) and (b) in which an insured's trust in either of a policyholder or a beneficiary is undermined or which makes the continuance of the aid death insurance contract difficult;

(d) in the event that certain circumstances on which an insured relied in giving his/her consent as set forth in Article 38 (consent by insured) have materially changed due to a termination of kinship between a policyholder and an insured or for any other reason.

The above consent is valid if it is given either verbally or in writing and, in practice, such requests are made by written application with the insured's signature and seal.

VI. Underwriting Decision of Life Insurance

518. Life insurance is a bilateral contract and so the insurer, when it receives the application, makes underwriting decisions and ratings based on the application, health statement and physicians' report, etc., in order to operate life insurance systems properly.

The information and format of information used for risk selection are determined by each insurer for factors like age, sum insured, etc.

Typical tools for risk selection are:

(1) statement on health condition and occupation made by the policyholder and the insured;
(2) medical reports on the insured;
(3) interviewer reports by a licensed interviewer and further, as additional information, ECGs (electrocardiograms) or blood tests are commonly used. In order to provide protection from improper handling of life insurance, a visit to the policyholder or insured to confirm the contents of the health statement or to confirm that the policyholder or insured are the right person is also made either before or after the policy is issued.

From a medical perspective, examination to detect Acquired immune deficiency syndrome (AIDS) or Human immunodeficiency virus (HIV) infection is widely adopted in many parts of the world; however, such tests are not performed in Japan for life insurance risk selection as the impact of the disease is not yet significant and also no consensus is as yet established as to the way to handle such examinations.

Further, use of genetic information in underwriting is still at the stage of discussion and study involving government, industry and the academic community, particularly with regard to privacy issues.

As to lifestyle, such as smoking and drinking habits, preferred risk insurance has just started, primarily using smoking habit information.

VII. Inception of Contract; Inception of Insurer's Liability

519. The inception of the insurer's liability is defined in policy provisions as the day all of the following conditions are met, subject to the approval of application by insurer:

(1)   receipt of application;
(2)   receipt of insured's health statement;
(3)   receipt of initial premium.[123]

VIII. Cooling-Off

520. The IBL (Article 309) stipulates 'a cooling-off' period whereby the policyholder can make the application void by submitting a request in writing within eight days from the date of application or date of initial premium receipt, whichever the latter. This does not apply to the following cases:

(1)   if the insurance period is less than one year;
(2)   if the contract is obliged by law;
(3)   if the applicant know the occurrence of incident for claims of death or other benefit;
(4)   if the medical examination by physician is completed;
(5)   for change of contract terms (increase of face amount, after issue addition of rider, etc.);
(6)   if the policyholder is a corporation;
(7)   if the contract is a mortgage for obligation, etc.

IX.   Statement Obligation and Cancellation of Insurance Contract

A.   *Duty of Disclosure*

521. An applicant for life insurance contract or the insured shall disclose to the insurer the fact concerning important matters, requested to disclose by such insurer, as to the potential for an insurable contingency (a death of the insured or his/her survival at a certain point of the time) (Ins. Law Article 37).

If the applicant for life insurance contract or insured, by wilful misconduct or gross negligence, fails to make disclosure of facts or makes a false disclosure with respect to any matters to be disclosed, an insurer may cancel a life insurance contract (Ins. Law Article 55(1))

In the event that an insurer has cancelled a life insurance contract, it shall be liable to pay no insurance benefits in connection with any insurable contingency arising

---

123.   The Ins. Law does not specify the format of insurance application and normally it is made by submitting the application form set forth by the insurer filled out with signature and seal. As to the health statement, the insured must fill out the form sent out by the insurer and sign to confirm the contents. For cases which require a physician's examination, the examining physician fills out the form according to the statement of the insured and has the insured confirm and sign. The initial premium is commonly received by the solicitor at the same time as he receives the application form. Other methods like bank account withdrawal or credit card settlement are also used.

no later than the time of cancellation (but excluding any insurable contingency occurred but not form the facts mentioned in Article 55(1) (Ins. Law Article 59(2) item 1).

Any cancellation of a life insurance contract shall become effective only for the future, and not retroactively (Ins. Law Article 59(1)).

B.   Cancellation Due to Increase of Risk (Ins. Law Article 56(1))

522. Even if, in the event that there arise an increase of risk (a situation where the risk in respect of the matters to be disclosed become greater and insurance premiums stipulated in a life insurance contract is less than the insurance premiums calculated on the basis of such risk) after the execution of a life insurance contract, such life insurance contract may be continued if the insurance premiums are charged to the amount which responds to such increase of risk, an insurer shall be entitled to cancel the said life insurance contract where the case falls under both of the following requirement:

(1)   if it is provided in the said life insurance contract that the policyholder or the insured shall, without delay, notify the insurer of any change in the matters to be disclosed in connection with such increase of risk; and

(2)   if the policyholder or the insured has failed to give such notification as mentioned in the preceding item within delay by wilful misconduct or gross negligence.

C.   Cancellation Due to Material Event (Ins. Law Article 57)

523. An insurer may cancel a life insurance contract (which shall be limited to a death insurance contract in the case of item (1)) in any of the following events:

(1)   if a policyholder or a beneficiary has caused or has intended to cause death of an insured intentionally in an attempt to make an insurer pay insurance benefits;

(2)   if a beneficiary has committed or has intended to commit a fraud in connection with the claim for insurance benefits under the said life insurance contract; and

(3)   any other material events than those mentioned in the preceding two items in which the insurer's trust in any of the policyholder, the insured or beneficiary is undermined or which makes the continuance of the said life insurance contract difficult.

D.   Cancellation by Policyholder (Ins. Law Article 54)

524. A policyholder may at any time cancel a life insurance contract.

X.   Exclusions

525. An insurer under a death insurance contract shall not be liable to pay any insurance benefit in any of the following cases; provided, however, that in the case of item 3 below, such immunity shall not apply to the liability to a beneficiary other than a beneficiary who has caused death to an insured intentionally:

(1) in the case where an insured has committed a suicide;
(2) in the case where a policyholder has caused death to an insured intentionally (except for the case mentioned in the preceding item);
(3) in the case where a beneficiary has caused death to an insured intentionally (except for the case mentioned in the preceding two items); and
(4) in the case where an insured has died in the war or any other disturbance. (Ins. Law Article 51).

XI. Distribution (Solicitor)

526. Life insurance distribution agents (solicitors) are normally, 'sales staff of life insurer', 'independent agents' or 'brokers' and they must be registered with the Prime Minister (IBL Article 276).

Life insurance solicitors are legally only 'intermediary' or 'act for company' to conclude insurance contracts (IBL Article 275) but practically it is not a right of the solicitor to act for the insurer to conclude a contract.

As to the company's sales staff, many insurance companies hired large numbers of middle-aged female personnel, partly to help widows after World War II; however, in recent years, younger and highly educated people have been hired.

Independent agents are placed primarily by medium size insurers, and industry leaders have also started to move forward to place independent agents though the number is relatively small.

In insurers started after the war, more male sales staff or independent property and casualty insurance agents are being used.

In order for brokers to sell life insurance, they must file an application (as defined by IBL Article 287, Endorsement Regulation of IBL, Article 213) and obtain the approval of the Prime Minister (Addendum of IBL, Article 119).

§3. TAX SYSTEM

I. Tax on Life Insurance

A. Life Insurance Premium Deduction

527. If the beneficiary is self, spouse or other relatives, a certain amount computed based on the premium paid annually will be deducted from income (income tax: maximum JPY 40,000; residence tax: maximum JPY 28,000).

B.   Individual Annuity Premium Deduction

528. If the beneficiary is the premium payer or spouse and the premium is paid for more than ten years before the start of the annuity payment a certain amount computed based on the premium paid annually shall be deducted from income (Income Tax: maximum JPY 40,000; residence tax: maximum JPY 28,000).

C.   Tax on Death Benefit

529.

(1) If the policyholder is the insured (policyholder = insured ≠ beneficiary): the death beneficiary is subject to inheritance tax and if the beneficiary is heir as spouse or child, a certain amount computed on the basis of the benefit is deducted from benefit as non-taxable amount.[124]
(2) If the policyholder is beneficiary (policyholder = beneficiary ≠ insured): death benefit is occasional income and charged income tax and residence tax.
(3) If all of the policyholder, insured and beneficiary are different (policyholder ≠ insured ≠ beneficiary): death benefit is regarded as donation and charged gift tax.[125]

D.   Tax on Maturity Benefit

530.

(1) If the beneficiary is policyholder (policyholder = beneficiary): maturity benefit is regarded as occasional income and charged income tax and resident tax.
(2) If the beneficiary is other than policyholder (policyholder ≠ beneficiary): maturity benefit is regarded as donation from policyholder and charged gift tax.

E.   Beneficiary and Inheritance

531. The right to claim benefit of the beneficiary is obtained as the effect of the insurance contract and so death benefit received is not regarded as the insured's inherited property. Even if the beneficiary is designated as 'an heir' instead of by a specific name, it is regarded as the beneficiary's own property and not inherited property according to precedent. Accordingly, it is charged as gift tax.

Death benefit is regarded as inherited property only if the beneficiary is not designated at all.

---

124.   If the beneficiary is other than the heir, the benefit is regarded as the bequest a subject to inheritance tax. Also it is not entitled to tax exempt benefit.
125.   Occasional income is income not derived from continuous acts of business and not reward for labour.

§4. OTHERS

I. Group Term Insurance

532. This insurance consists of two parts: one is the base part (comprehensive welfare group term insurance), which makes the bereaved family of employees the beneficiary, and the other is a human value rider which makes the employer the beneficiary.

The human value rider is intended to cover expenses to replace the dead employee and to train the replacement. The amount for the rider cannot exceed that of the base part and the claim for the rider must have the acknowledgement of the bereaved family.

II. Group Pension Insurance

533. Group pension insurance is to provide the facility to manage and administer funds when the employer establishes a pension scheme for employees. (Trust banks and investment advisory firms also provide this as a part of financial services.)

Group pension insurance is divided into a tax-qualified pension scheme (retirement pension), which fulfils the requirements for tax benefit under corporate tax laws, and a welfare pension fund insurance based on welfare pension fund insurance laws (for details of these, refer to separate pensions). In the former scheme, policyholder = employer, insured and beneficiary = employee and in the latter scheme, the employer establishes a welfare pension fund to manage the pension scheme and the fund becomes the policyholder and beneficiary, whereas the insured are employees. The fund uses the benefit received as resources to pay pensions to employees.

These take the form of pension insurance; however, these functions are really entrusting the management (investment) of the pension fund to the insurance company.

An insurance company can offer two types, one being managed in a general account together with other products and the other set up as a separate account.

In the past, these have been defined as 'benefit' type pensions and in these years, due to low investment yield and also due to the difficulty to maintain retirement pension schemes, negative split problem of insurance business, all of which have led to the introduction of a defined condition type pension scheme in 2001.

III. Personal Pension Policy

534. Life insurance companies also sell 'Personal Pension Policy' which is thought to complement public pension scheme.

Pension policies, sold by private insurance companies, are roughly classified into two types of products; that is, fixed annuity[126] (annuity certain which may pay benefits for a certain period without regard to the death or alive of the insured) and variable annuity (individual pension policy that the amount of pension benefit, death

---

126. There are two kinds of policy, that is, fixed term policy and whole life policy.

benefit or cancellation refund premium may be varied according to the actual result from investigation of the insurance premiums). These days, a bank is actively selling variable annuity policy to its customers.

IV   Medical Insurance

535. Medical insurance may be classified in two types of product such as term insurance type one and whole of life insurance type one.

Medical insurance, basically, covers expenses when an insured being hospitalized with a disease or injury. Nowadays, however, medical insurance is extending its coverage to a lump sum when an insured being hospitalized with a disease or injury, surgical operation expenses, non-hospitalized medical expenses and a lump sum when an insured being discharged from a hospital.

Some products limit their coverage to specific diseases (e.g., cancer or brain disease, etc.) or some diseases characteristic to women (e.g., breast cancer or uterine cancer, etc.).

As the life of people has been prolonged and elderly people increased, the interest of consumers moved to medical insurance from death insurance. Therefore, development of the medical insurance to cover the medical expenses burden including surgical operation costs mainly on a cancer, a cerebrovascular disease and heart disease, and hospital charges is flourishingly performed. The marketable products switch over from death insurance to medical insurance, too.

Since, these medical insurances are belonged to the so-called third field insurance (those insurances prescribed in IBL Article 3, paragraph 4, item 1 and 2) non-life insurance companies may underwrite a medical insurance, too.

Chapter 6.   Pension Insurance

§1.   STATUTORY REGULATION

536. Regarding Japanese pension laws, there are the National Pension Act (NPA) (Law No. 141, 1959) and so-called Employees' Pension Acts such as the Welfare Pension Ins. Law (Law No. 115, 1954), the Government Official Benefit Association Act (Law No. 128, 1958), the Local Government Official Benefit Association Act (Law No. 152, 1962), the Private School Employee Benefit Association Act, and Agriculture, Forestry and Fishery Corporation Employee Benefit Association Act.

The National Pension Plan, as the fundamental pension system, covers all residents (without regard to nationality) from the ages of 20 to 59 and moreover there are some supplementary pension systems such as welfare pension insurance, corporate pensions (welfare pension fund and tax- qualified pension), the National Pension Fund, etc.

These pension mechanisms are as shown below:

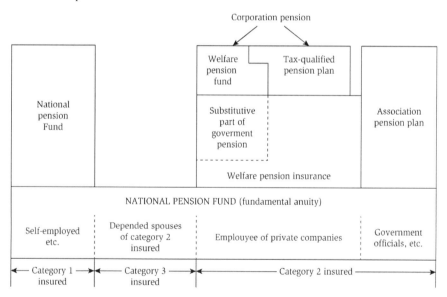

§2. National Pension Plan

537. The National Pension Plan was started in 1959 as a pension system for self-employed persons, etc., but in April 1986 it was revised to become a compulsory fundamental pension plan for all residents from the ages of 20 to 59 (the insured).

I.   Kinds of Benefit

A.   Old Age Basic Benefit

538. The age at which the insured will receive the annuity in full of the old age basic pension benefit is 65 years (NPA Article 26). And the age to receive the old age basic pension benefit can be deferred to 70 years (NPA Article 28) or advanced to 60 years (NPA Supplementary Provision Article 9(2)(2)) with a certain increase or reduction in annuity.

B.   Permanent Disability Basic Benefit

539. Permanent disability basic benefit is paid if the insured sustains serious permanent disability (first class disability is permanent total loss of function of both upper limbs and second class disability is permanent total loss of function of one upper limb) in consequence of bodily injury or disease which was primarily checked with a doctor during the term being assured. The annuity is a flat-rate amount without regard to the length of the term of being insured, but with regard to the class of disability.

C.   Bereaved Basic Benefit

540. In case of death of the *insured* or the person who is receiving the old age basic benefit, his dependent wife with child (under 18 years old in general) or his child (under 18 years old in general) can receive the bereaved basic pension.

D.   Duty of Payment of Premium

541. The insured has an obligation to pay the premium. The master of the household has joint responsibility to pay the premium with the insured belonging to the master's household. And the spouse has also joint responsibility with the other spouse (the insured) to pay the premium (NPA Article 88).

E.   Preoccupation Right of Premium

542. The order of preoccupation right of the premium is next to national taxes and local taxes (NPA Article 98).

§3.   WELFARE PENSION INSURANCE

543. The subject of this insurance business is the government (Ministry of Welfare and Labour: Social Insurance Agency) (Welfare Pension Ins. Law Article 2). This insurance (earnings-related type pension) compulsorily applies to companies that employ more than five employees and such employees under the age of 65 years become insured (WPI Law Articles 6, 7).

I.   Kinds of Benefit

A.   *Old Age Welfare Benefit*

544. In the past, special old age welfare benefit was composed of flat-rate part and earnings-related part starting to be issued to the insured aged 60 years and after the insured became 65 years old. Only the earnings-related part of old age welfare benefit is issued and the benefit equal to the flat-rate part of old age welfare benefit is issued under the National Pension Plan (old age basic benefit).

After revision, in 1994, of the Welfare Pension Insurance Law, the insured's age for beginning to receive the flat-rate part of Special Old Age Welfare Benefit was deferred to be issued up to 65 years of age according to the insured's date of birth. This deferment shall be done by year from 2001 to 2013 (male: female – from 2006 to 2018) and ultimately only the earnings-related part, as new old age welfare benefit, will started to be issued to the insured from age of 60 years and the insured can receive the old age benefit of the National Pension Plan after 65 years old and, furthermore, after 2013 (male: female – from 2018), the earnings-related part will be deferred to be issued up to 65 years of age year by year.

B.   *Permanent Disability Welfare Benefit*

545. Permanent disability benefit will be paid in addition to the benefit of the National Pension Plan if the insured sustains serious permanent disabilities (first class disability permanent total loss of function of both upper limbs, second class disability permanent total loss of function of one upper limb and third class disability total loss of function of two joints among three major joints of one upper limb) in consequence of bodily injury or disease which is primarily checked with a doctor during the term being assured.

And, moreover, if the insured sustains such permanent disabilities as remarkable disturbance in the functioning of one of three major joints of one upper limb, etc., a disability lump sum shall be paid.

C.   *Bereaved Welfare Benefit*

546. In general, three-fourths of old age welfare benefit that the deceased insured may receive shall be paid to the bereaved family.

D.   Duty of Payment of Premium

547. The insured and the employer have to bear respectively half of premium and the employer has an obligation to pay premium in full (WPI Law Article 82).

E.   Preoccupation Right of Premium

548. The order of preoccupation right of the premium is next to national taxes and local taxes (WPI Law Article 88).

F.   Current Trends

549. Recently, the necessity of reforming the public pension system has become imminent, considering the recent increase of the ageing population and fewer children as well as changes in economic trends and the balance between the burden and benefits, and revisions for level of premium, level of benefit, proportion of premium borne by the government, etc.

§4.   NATIONAL PENSION FUND

550. The 'category 1 insured (self-employed persons, etc.)' of the National Pension Plan were to receive only old age basic benefit, while employees of private enterprises or government (or local government) officials that are insured with welfare pension insurance (compulsory) and the Welfare Pension Fund (formed optionally) can receive not only old age basic benefit but also employees' pension plan benefit as supplementary benefit. So in April 1991 the National Pension Fund was founded for category 1 insured of the National Pension Plan as the supplementary pension. Persons aged from 20 years to 59 years can affiliate to the fund.

551. The National Pension Fund is the legal person that is admitted by the Minister of Welfare and Labour and managed by council elected from persons insured (Articles 122, 123).

552. There are two types in the National Pension Fund (NPA Article 115(2)):

(1) Regional-type national pension fund: this type of fund is organized with persons (category 1 insured of national pension) residing in the same prefecture and established by prefecture (NPA Article 118(2)). More than 1,000 participants per fund are required as minimum affiliates (NPA Article 119(4)). As of March 1999, forty-seven funds have been organized.

(2) Professional-type national pension fund: this type of fund is organized with persons (category 1 insured of national pension) engaging in a same business or service and established one by one business (or service) in the whole country (NPA Article 118(22)). More than 3,000 participants per fund are required as minimum affiliates (NPA Article 119(5)). As of March 2001, twenty-five funds have been organized.

553. The participant is able to make plural contracts with the fund. The first contract must be a perpetual annuity (issuing benefit from age of 65 years), which is selected, at his/her choice, from either 'A type (with the guarantee to pay benefit up to age of 80 years and also issuing bonus benefit if the Fund is able to get more interest than that expected as basic rate of interest)', 'B type (without guarantee but issuing bonus benefit if the Fund is able to get more interest than that expected as basic rate of interest)'.

From the second contract on, the participant has to select, in consideration of the maximum premium (JPY 68,000 per month), among five types such as perpetual annuity 'A type', perpetual annuity 'B type', annuity with definite period 'I type (with the guarantee to pay benefit from age of 65 years to 80 years)', annuity with definite period 'II type (with the guarantee to pay benefit from age of 65 years to 75 years)' and annuity with definite period 'III type (with the guarantee to pay benefit from age of 60 years to 75 years)'. The amount of annuity with definite period must be less than the amount of perpetual annuity (including that of the first contract).

554. Investment of assets must be entrusted to trust companies, life insurance companies, the Confederation of Farmers' Cooperatives, the Confederation of Fisheries' Cooperatives or investment counsel (NPA Article 128(3)). The Confederation of National Pension Funds, the legal person admitted by the Minister of Welfare and Labour, manages such funds as belong to persons leaving the National Pension Funds halfway or persons having been members of dissolved National Pension Funds.

§5. CORPORATE PENSIONS

555. In Japan, there was a retirement lump sum system before the World War II and after the War this retirement gratuity system prevailed among companies through the labour movement. Companies, taking account of their cash flow, changed their retirement lump sum system to a retirement pension system or retirement pension system together with a lump sum system.

There are two types of tax-favoured corporate pensions in Japan today: employees' pension funds and tax-qualified pension plans.

I.   Tax-Qualified Pension System

556. Under the 1962 taxation reform, corporations' contribution premium to their pension systems that had certain conditions was excluded from taxation.

Thirteen conditions are stipulated in Government Ordinance Article 159 of the Corporation Tax Law (Law No. 34, 31 March 1965) and the main conditions are the following:

(1) The aim of the system must be only for the retirement pension.
(2) The corporation has to make trust contracts, life insurance contracts life benefit contracts with trust companies, life insurance companies or the Confederation of Farmers' Cooperatives for their retirement pensions.

(3)   The amount of benefit has not to be decreased in general, etc.

557. A corporation with more than 100 employees can make a trust contract for a retirement pension with trust banks while a corporation with more than only fifteen employees can make a life insurance contract for a retirement pension with life insurance companies. The corporation is able to choice either a perpetual annuity or an annuity with a definite period. It is said that the adequate proportion of premium borne by employees is less than 50%.

II.   Welfare Pension Fund

558. A company or a group of companies can establish a welfare pension fund. A welfare pension fund, a legal person admitted by the Minister of Welfare and Labour, takes the place of the government in providing the substitutive proportion (earnings-related part of old age benefit) of the welfare pension and each fund must provide supplementary benefits, as a corporate pension, on the top of that. Supplementary benefits must be more than 10% of those of the substitutive proportion. In general, these funds provide perpetual annuities and the age of the first pension award is 65.

559. There are three kinds of forms for organizing welfare pension funds: the single organization formed by a single company (minimum number of insured is 500), union organizations formed by a company and its subsidiaries (minimum number of insured is 800), and associated organizations (minimum number of insured is 3,000).

560. Today, a welfare pension fund has to entrust management (including investment) of liability reserves only to trust banks or life insurance companies. Through revisions to the Corporation Tax Law in 1990, 1998 and 1999, a fund is able to manage its liability reserves in-house.

561. Pension fund assets of persons who leave funds halfway or belong to a dissolved fund are managed under the Confederation of Welfare Pension Funds.

§6.   THE CURRENT TREND OF CORPORATE PENSIONS

562. The Defined Contribution Pension Act (Law No. 88) came into force on 1 April 2001 and the Defined Benefit Corporate Pension Act (Law No. 50, in force from 1 April 2002) was also issued 15 June 2001. These Acts are expected to provide management and labour with choice for their corporate pension system, to reduce corporations' share of the expenses.

563. A welfare pension fund can provide only a perpetual pension in general which is composed of the substitutive proportion of the welfare pension and corporate pension; but corporations are now in difficulty in maintaining their retirement pension schemes with growth in expenses due to a low investment yield.

564. The Defined Benefit Corporate Pension Act is able to make a welfare pension fund to return the substitutive proportion of the welfare pension to the government.

Therefore, a welfare pension fund can be changed to a defined benefit corporate pension (fund-type corporate pension or agreed-type corporation pension) with the only function of corporate pension, which is to provide a perpetual pension or a pension with more than five years' annuity payment period.

565. A tax-qualified pension system has its defects. The Defined Benefit Corporate Pension Act disestablishes tax-qualified pension system with ten years' grace period (until 31 March 2012) because of this defect in the function of its finances as having no reserve basis and not having clear stipulations about liability for the trustee of the investment of reserves.

And a new defined benefit corporate pension (fund-type corporation pension or agreement-type corporate pension) which provides a perpetual pension or pension with more than five years' annuity payment period is provided by the Defined Benefit Corporate Pension Act.[127]

566. As for corporate pensions, there have only been defined benefit-type pensions in Japan.

However, due to the low investment yield today, the negative split problem and also due to the coming into force of the Defined Contribution Pension Act, companies are showing a tendency to switch part of their defined benefit-type pension system to the defined contribution-type pension system.

127. Fund-type corporate pension: 'Fund', person admitted by the Minister of Welfare and Labour, manages the pension system. The fund, in general, entrusts its investments to monetary facilities (trust company, life insurance company, confederation of farmers' cooperative, confederation of fisheries' cooperative or investment counsel), the fund, however, can partially do it in-house like the Welfare Pension fund does.
Three hundred or more insured, as a minimum number of insured, are required to found the fund.
Agreement-type corporate pension: This system is organized and managed by a corporation. The corporation has to entrust its investments to monetary facilities (trust company, life insurance company, confederation of farmers' cooperative, confederation of fisheries' cooperative or investment counsel) agreed between labour and management.
In-house investment is not allowed. There is no minimum number of insured in this system.

Part VI. Private Insurance and Social Security

Chapter 1.   Social Security in Japan

567. Social security is one method to realize public politics and it has the same schemes as in private insurance, collecting premiums from affiliates and paying benefits to the insured. The relationship between social security and private insurance may be said to be complementary. However, there are some differences between social security schemes and private insurance schemes such as: (1) the insurance premiums for social security may not be proportionate to the risks; (2) a part of the premium of social security may be borne by the government; and (3) participation in certain social security schemes is compulsory.

Social security may supply certain compensation to people facing financial difficulties for some reason (suffering from illness, being in need of nursing care, being unemployed, etc.), or underwriting risks without any limitations, that are difficult for a private insurance company to underwrite such as earthquake risk, insecurity risks not coming up to the law of large numbers (country risks), and private insurance schemes may provide supplementary coverage for social security (e.g., workmen's compensation, pensions, medical expenses, etc.).

568. Japanese social security can be divided into three categories: social insurance as basic security, and industrial promotion insurances (one for economic policies and the other social security).

§1.   Social Insurance

569. Social insurance systems in Japan can be classified into the following:

(1) medical insurance:

  (a) health insurance system based on the Health Insurance Law and other similar laws;
  (b) public nursing care insurance system based on the Nursing Care Insurance Law.

(2) a pension system based on the National Pension Law, the Welfare Pension Insurance Law and other similar laws;

(3) a workmen's compensation system based on the Labour Standards Law (1947, Law No. 49) and the Workmen's Compensation Insurance Law (1947, Law No. 50);

(4) an employment insurance system based on the Employment Insurance Law (1974, Law No. 116).[128]

I.   Health Insurance

570. Health insurance covers disease, bodily injury and death (except those suffered through work-related activities) or childbirth suffered by the named insured and his/her dependent relatives (Health Ins. Law Article 1).

This insurance mainly pays in kind but some kinds of benefit (allowance for delivery, expenses for burial, etc.) are paid in cash. The insurer is the government or the Health Insurance Union.[129]

II.   Nursing Care Insurance

571. A local government (city, town, village, etc.) as the insurer indemnifies residents over 40 years old (the insured; people aged from 40 years to under 65 years called category 2 insured, 65 years and over called category 1 insured) against when the insured is recognized as needing nursing care (e.g., the insured cannot walk, eat, go to the lavatory, bathe or dress by himself/herself) or a condition needing support with fear of being in need of nursing care condition due to bodily injury, disease or injury caused in the brain (e.g., senile dementia and Alzheimer's dementia).

However, category 2 insured can be indemnified against only when the insured is recognized in such a condition as caused by his/her advance in years.

Benefit of this insurance is in kind such as nursing care, rehabilitation, hospitalization to a sanatorium, etc.[130]

III. Pension System

572. The government manages this system as an insurer. Not only old age benefit, permanent disability benefit, bereaved benefit, etc., but also death lump sums may be supplied.[131]

---

128. Before 1974: unemployment insurance.
129. Compare Part V, Ch. 3.
130. Compare Part V, Ch. 3; §2 Nursing Care Expenses Insurance.
131. Compare Part V, Ch. 6, Pension Insurance.

IV.   Workmen's Compensation Insurance

573. When an employee sustains any injury or suffers from disease (including death or permanent disability therefrom) due to his/her occupational duty (including commuting), benefits may be supplied from the government (the insurer).

V.   Employment Insurance

574. Employment insurance, provided according to Employment Ins. Law (Law No. 119, 28 December 1974), is provided by the government (EIL Article 2(1)).

Employment insurance may not only grant necessary benefits (unemployment benefits, placement promotion benefits, etc.) if workers lose jobs trying to expand employment chances but also take part in three employment projects: the employment stabilization project, the efficiency development project and the employment welfare project, for the development and improvement of workers' abilities (EIL Article 3).

The main purpose of unemployment benefits is to grant benefits and to stabilize employment-seekers' livelihood for a certain employment-seeking term, if an insured (worker) has lost a job because of bankruptcy of an undertaking, retirement, personal reasons, etc., and is unable to get a job regardless of his/her intention and abilities to work. Benefits eligibility, in general, shall be conditional on the person having been an insured for six months or more and more over six months or more in which the number of days on having become the basis for payment of wage is fourteen days or more per month. The number of days of the granting and amount of money of granting are decided in consideration of the period of having been an insured, the daily amount of wage (averaged daily amount of wage of previous six months to the day of job loss) and whether the insured is a person for whom it is difficult to get a placement (e.g., physically handicapped person) or not. The number of days of granting is decided in the period from 90 days to 180 days, and the amount of money granted is ordinarily 50%–60% of the average daily wage.

Placement promotion benefits are granted in following events:

(1)   where a benefit eligible person (a person lost job) has been placed in stable job earlier;
(2)   where a benefit eligible person difficult to place in job, such as a physically handicapped person, has been placed in a permanent job;
(3)   where a benefit eligible person changes residence or dwelling place to take up the job introduced by the public employment security office or for undertaking public vocational training, etc.;
(4)   where a benefit eligible person is performing job-seeking activities over the areas of wide scope caused by the introduction of the public employment security office.

Employment insurance grants, as benefits of the three employment projects, many kinds of subsidy, bounty, etc., for the purpose of contributing to employment stabilization, prevention of unemployment, improvement of employment structure and expansion of employment chances, development and elevation of workers' abilities or otherwise increase of workers' welfare.

§2. Industrial Promotion Insurance

575. In this field, the government may act in two roles. The government, as an insurer, underwrites risks directly or receives reinsurance, as a reinsurer, to back up the original insurers (local government, associations, etc.).

576. As to insurances that the government underwrites directly, there are:

- trade insurance[132] based on the Trade Insurance Law (1950, Law No. 67);
- forest insurance based on the Forest Insurance Law (1937, Law No. 25);
- credit insurance for medium and small companies based on the Law of Credit Insurance for the Medium and Small Companies (1950, Law No. 264).

As to reinsurance, there are:

- farm-owners' insurance that is transacted, being based on Agricultural Disaster Indemnity Law (1947, Law No. 185), by a farm-owners' benefit society or local government (commune);
- fishermen's mutual insurance which is transacted, being based on the Fishery Disaster Indemnity Law (1964, Law No. 158), by a fishermen's benefit society;
- fishing vessel mutual insurance that is transacted, being based on the Fishing Vessel Damage, etc. Indemnity Law (1952, Law No. 28), by the Fishing Vessel Mutual Insurance Association.

§3. Other Social Security

I. Deposit Insurance System

577. The Deposit Insurance Corporation of Japan (DICJ), founded by the government, the BOJ and private financial institutions, has been established based on the Deposit Ins. Law (Law No. 34, 1971).

It is an operating agency:

to protect depositors, among others, by reimbursing insured depositors and purchasing deposits and other claims as necessary when a financial institution has suspended repayments of deposits, etc., and moreover, concerning the resolution of failures of financial institutions, to establish a system of arrangements for appropriate financial assistance in mergers and other transactions involving failed financial institutions, public management by financial administrators, transfer of the business

---

132. According to the revision of the Trade Ins. Law (March 2005), a certain part of this insurance business may be underwritten by a private insurance company.

of failed financial institutions, and measures for management of financial crises, etc., thereby contributing to the maintenance of the credit system (DIL Article 1).

578. The DICJ collects premiums from affiliated financial institutions (branch offices of foreign banks are excluded from this system) for the operation of the deposit insurance system.

Until 31 March 2002, all kinds of deposit had been covered in full, however, since April 2002 only liquid deposits are fully covered as a special measure. The maximum amount of deposits protected by the insurance is JPY 10 million in principal plus its interest.

Liquid deposit was divided into two categories of liquid deposit without interest and liquid deposit with interest on April 2005, the former should be covered in full and the later one should be covered only up to JPY 10 million.[133]

II.   Postal Life Insurance System

579. Postal life insurance, together with postal services, postal savings services, etc., had been taken in charge of the Ministry of Postal Services but in accordance with the central government reform, the Ministry of Postal Services was reformed, in January 2001, together with the Ministry of Public Management and the Home Affairs Agency to the Ministry of Public Management, Home Affairs and Posts and Telecommunications (MPHPT) and Postal Service Agency, and in April 2003 the Postal Service Agency became the Public Company (Japan Post) that still controlled the business of postal life insurance together with postal service and postal saving services.

On 1 October 2007, based on the Japan Post Law, operations formerly conducted by Japan Post were transferred to Japan Post Corporation (holding company, all of the shares are held by the government) and four other private business corporation such as a mail delivery company (Japan Post Service Co., Ltd), an over-the-counter service network firm (Japan Post Network Co., Ltd), a postal savings company (Japan Post Bank) and an insurance services company (Japan Post Co., Ltd). On 1 October 2012, Japan Post Service incorporated with Japan Post Network and became Japan Post Holdings Co., Ltd.

580. On November 4, 2015 Japan Post Insurance Co., Ltd, the government possessed 100% of stock, has exhibited 11% of the shares and has been listed in the First Section of the Tokyo Stock Exchange.

---

133. The DICJ can establish, according to the Deposit Ins. Law (Art. 92), bridge banks, as subsidiaries. This system, at the beginning, was introduced as temporally measures (until March 2001), however, this system has been changed to permanent measures through the revision of the Deposit Insurance Law, and which assume the business of failed financial institutions in order to provisionally maintain and continue when no private institutions can be found to acquire the assets and assume the liabilities of failed financial institutions in short order. The life of the bridge bank is limited in two years after the business of failed financial institutions are transferred. The limited life can be extended by a further year.

Postal life insurance contract had been protected by the government, however, after privatization of Japan Post Insurance, postal life insurance contract shall be protected under PPOS.

From historical viewpoint, the government (the Ministry of Land, Infrastructure and Transport) had managed the Postal Life Insurance System,[134] founded in 1916, based on the Postal Life Ins. Law (Law No. 68, 16 May 1946).

In the early twentieth century, private life insurance companies were selling their products mainly to wealthier people. So the postal life insurance system was founded with the aim of popularizing low-value life insurance, with a budget premium, to ordinary people.[135]

581. After World War II, private life insurance companies have intended to sell small amount of life insurance, and they have competed with the government. Postal life insurance, however, has been growing of insured amount so far up to JPY 202,072.7 billion for life insurance and JPY 2,453.2 billion for annuity (as of the end of 2001 fiscal year). However, after privatization of postal life insurance at October 2007, insurance contracts in force had been transferred to Management Organization for Postal Savings and Postal Life Insurance (established basing upon the Act of Management Organization for Postal Savings and Postal Life Insurance (Law No. 101, 2005)). So that, insured amounts of Japan Post Insurance are JPY 6,516 billion for life insurance and JPY 633.5 billion for annuity (as of the end of 2012 fiscal year).

582. Under the postal life insurance system, the maximum total insurance coverage for life insurance, annuities and riders are limited (generally, the maximum insurance coverage is set up to JPY 10 million for life insurance per policyholder and JPY 0.9 million/year for annuity per insured person).

Information for risk selection is a statement on health condition made by the insured and an interview report by the staff of post office. A medical report on the insured is not requested. Each post office may transact life insurance contracts, receiving premium and paying insurance money or annuities.

III. Housing Loan Insurance

583. The Government Housing Loan Corporation (special public corporation), founded in 1950 basing on the Housing Loan Corporation Act (Law No. 156, 6 May 1950), had underwritten, according to the Housing Loan Ins. Law (Law No. 63, 11 July 1955), housing loan insurance (a kind of credit insurance).

---

134. To Postal Life Insurance, only the Postal Life Ins. Law applied and the Com. Code did not apply. Therefore, as to the dispute on payment of insurance money, no civil suit could be brought to court about the judgment of the Postal Life Insurance Jury (Postal Life Ins. Law Art. 88 (1)) and the right of claim for death benefit or annuity could not be seized (Postal Life Ins. Law Art. 81).

135. Postal life insurance underwrites small amount insurance (ordinarily the maximum amount of life insurance is JPY 10 million, the maximum benefit of pension insurance is JPY 90,000 per year and underwrites it without medical examination. Post offices allocated over the country (approximately 24,200 post offices) are able to conclude insurance contracts, receive insurance premiums and pay benefits.

In April 2007, Japan Housing Finance Agency (incorporated administrative agency) was founded, basing on the Incorporated Administrative Agency Japan Housing Finance Agency Act (Law No. 82, 2005), as the successor of the Government Housing Loan Corporation (GHLC).

Japan Housing Finance Agency (JHF) takes over the rights and the obligations of GHLC, and implements the securitization business, to support for stable supply of long-term fixed-rate loans, as its main mission (main business of GHLC was direct housing loans).

JHF operates independently with fee income from securitization, not depending on borrowing and subsidies from the government.

IV. Others

584. The Government Compensation Plan in CALI – see Part IV Automobile Insurance.

585. Reinsurance in earthquake insurance for dwelling houses – see Part III, Property and Liability Insurance, Chapter 9, Catastrophe Insurance.

A. *Housing Warranty Against Defects*

586. The Act for Protection of Housing Quality Assurance (Law No. 81, 1999) has required a seller of a newly built dwelling house ten-year defect warranty liability regarding to such principal parts of the house as foundation, pillar, beam, roof, outer wall, etc. To secure the execution of defect liability,[136]the Act for Execution of Defect Liability (Law No. 66, 2007) that requires a seller of a newly built dwelling house to secure means – deposit money or insurance policy underwritten by the judicial person for defect warranty liability insurance designated by the Minister of Land, Infrastructure, Transport and Tourism – was enforced on October 2009.

B. *Medical Compensation System Regarding Obstetrics*

587. This system was founded, on 1 January 2009, as a system capable of both causal analysis/recurrence prevention of cerebral palsy and compensation for children born with severe cerebral palsy in spite of the normal pregnancy and delivery.

The Japan Council for Quality Health Care Foundation,[137] the administrative organization of the said system, conducts joint procedure of a delivery organization, insurance contract, collecting insurance premium, examining an event and payment of benefits, etc.

---

136. The person who acquires a newly built home insured may directly claim the necessary money to repair defects from the concerned judicial person if the seller could not repair defects because of bankruptcy, etc.
137. Established on Jul. 1995, Contributories of the fundamental property; Ministry of Health, Labour and Welfare, Japan Medical Association, Japan Hospital Association, National Federation of Health Insurance Societies, etc.

The insurance contract itself may be concluded between the Japan Council for Quality Health Care Foundation and private non-life insurance companies (six companies).

Part VII. Insurance Intermediaries

Chapter 1.   Law Establishment and Supervision

§1.   PREFACE

588. The IBL stipulates that 'insurance solicitation shall mean acting as an agent or an intermediary in connection with the execution of insurance contracts' (IBL Article 2, item 22) and that 'the parties specified in the following as those allowed to engage in the insurance solicitation activities shall engage in such activities' (IBL Article 275).

That is:

(1)   a registered life insurance solicitor who can act as agent or as intermediary with respect to the execution of insurance contracts for and on behalf of the insurance company concerned;

(2)   an officer (excluding an officer having representative power and a statutory auditor) or an employee of a non-life insurance company or a registered agent of non-life insurance or an officer (excluding an officer having a representative power and a statutory auditor) or employee of such an agent – acting as agent or as intermediary with respect to the execution of insurance contracts for and on behalf of the insurance company concerned;

(3)   a registered insurance broker or an officer (excluding an officer having representative power and a statutory auditor) or employee of such broker – acting as intermediary with respect to the execution of insurance contracts (restricted to those specified by the Cabinet Ordinance insofar as insurance contracts where a foreign insurer (with no branch office within Japan) other than a foreign insurance company are concerned) other than those performed by a life insurance solicitor or a non-life

insurance solicitor with respect to the execution of insurance contracts for and on behalf of the insurance company concerned.[138]

589. At the time the IBL was revised, broker had to be approved by the Prime Minister in case when dealing with life insurance. A broker, however, is able to handle life insurance by the IBL revision of 2014 and also minimum amount of the security deposit at the time of business-opening of broker from JPY 40 million to JPY 20 million.

590. An insurance broker is not allowed to run a non-life insurance agent or a life insurance solicitor (IBL Article 289).

By the amendment of IBL in May 2000, a bank, etc., may sell insurance products, after 1 April 2001, as a life insurance solicitor, non-life insurance agent or an insurance broker. At the beginning, a bank, etc., may sell only such products relating to housing loans as long-term fire insurance, long-term income indemnity insurance with repayment for a debt supporting endorsement and credit life insurance (only credit life insurance produced by the subsidiary insurance company or sister insurance company of the bank, etc.) and overseas travel personal insurance. After 1 October 2002, personal pension insurance (fixed annuity type and variable annuity type and annuity-type personal accident insurance, etc.), were added to products which a bank may sell, and the restriction on credit life insurance was also abolished. From December 2005, single premium whole of life insurance, term life insurance, short-term endowment insurance and personal liability insurance, have been added. And after December 2007, such restrictions on life insurance were totally abolished, so banks, etc., may sell all insurance products.

§2. Registration

591. A life insurance solicitor, non-life insurance agent and insurance broker, among those parties who are allowed to engage in the insurance solicitation activities,

---

138. An insurance broker can conduct such insurance solicitation activities with a non-admitted foreign insurance company (with no branch office within Japan) for reinsurance contracts; insurance contracts which cover vessels having Japanese nationality used for international marine transportation and the cargos on the way of international transportation by such vessels and the liabilities arising therefrom, or any of them; insurance contracts which cover aircraft having Japanese nationality used for commercial airline business and the cargos on the way of international transportation by such aircraft and the liabilities arising therefrom, or any of them; and such other insurance contracts as prescribed by the IBL Enforcement Regulation (IBL Art. 275(1), item 3, Cabinet Ordinance Arts 19, 38-2, IBLER Art. 281-4). The Regulation stipulates such insurance contracts as the following: insurance contracts which cover launches into cosmic space, transported cargo relating to such launches (including satellites), and means of transportation of such cargo and the liabilities arising from such activities; insurance contracts which cover vessels used for international marine transportation or aircraft used for commercial airline business and the international cargo transported by such vessels or aircraft and the liabilities arising therefrom, or any of them (excluding those listed in Art. 19(2), (3) of the Ordinance); and insurance contracts which cover international cargo (excluding those listed in Art. 19(2), (3) of the Ordinance and the immediately preceding item).

must secure registration from FSA (in practice, the Finance Bureau of the area where the parties have their main office has the competence).[139]

592. If an applicant for registration comes under any of the following items, the application will be rejected (IBL Article 279):

(1) a person who was given a sentence of imprisonment (including a penalty corresponding thereto under foreign law) and three years have not elapsed since the date on which he/she served out his/her sentence or was released from such penalty;

(2) a party whose registration has been cancelled under the IBL and three years have not elapsed since the date of the cancellation;

(3) a party that acted in an extremely improper way with respect to insurance solicitation within a period of three years prior to the date of application;

(4) a person who is incompetent or quasi-incompetent or a person who is treated similarly under foreign law, etc.

593. The former Law Concerning the Control of Insurance Solicitation of 1948, replacing by the IBL of 1995, restricted life insurance solicitors not to engage in insurance solicitation activities for any other life insurance company.

Under the IBL of 1995, a life insurance solicitor has to be a qualified solicitor in principle, but in cases where there is no fear of the protection of policyholders, etc., taking into account the solicitor's ability to perform business relating to such insurance solicitation or other conditions, a life insurance solicitor is able to have two or more insurance companies (IBL Article 282).[140]

---

139. To engage in insurance solicitation activities, officers or employees of non-life insurance agents and of brokers must be notified to the Finance Bureau.

140. Cases where restrictions relating to life insurance solicitors do not apply (Cabinet Ordinance Art. 40):

(1) where there is any person among the life insurance solicitor and its employees (or, if such life insurance solicitor is a corporation (including an unincorporated association or foundation which has designated a person or persons to act as its representative or administrator), then the officers (including representatives or administrators of the association or foundation) and employees thereof) who has such qualification as prescribed by the Secretary of FSA as a person who is able to acquire the necessary knowledge, etc., or perform proper business administration for the purpose of accurate and fair conduct of businesses relating to solicitation for insurance for and on behalf of two or more insurance companies concerned; or

(2) where the life insurance solicitor is affiliated with two or more insurance companies concerned by designating a party which is prescribed by the Secretary of FSA as a life insurance company (including a foreign life insurance, etc.) which has a close relationship with the life insurance solicitor as its insurance company concerned, and where the life insurance is deemed to be in the situation prescribed by the Secretary of FSA as the situation where such life insurance solicitor is capable of accurate and fair conduct of the businesses relating to solicitation for insurance for and on behalf of such two or more insurance companies concerned.

594. As for the insurance solicitation, only direct trust from an insurance company to an insurance solicitor was admitted, but along with the progress of grouping of insurance companies, insurance companies, assuming prior approval of the Prime Minister, become able to entrust their insurance solicitation for utilizing the sales infrastructure of other insurance companies to other insurance companies in the group and the insurance companies entrusted may re-entrust insurance solicitation to their insurance solicitors (IBL Article 275 Item 3-5).

Chapter 2.   Insurance Solicitation

§1.   Acquisition of Expert Knowledge

595. Since insurance intermediaries need to have expert knowledge on insurance systems, each life insurance company and non-life insurance company trains persons who want to be insurance intermediaries, and an insurance company registers (or notifies) successful candidates to the FSA.

After such registration (or notification), an insurance company provides to insurance intermediaries several qualification tests on expert knowledge of the insurance system.

Each life insurance association and broker association has its own unified examination, and each non-life insurance company provides its examination accordingly.

596. By the amendment of IBL (May 2014, enforcement May 2016) the basic rules of the insurance solicitation have been changed:

(a)   previous IBL, for the insurance solicitation, prohibited only inappropriate behaviour such as to make a false description, revised IBL, however, regulates insurance solicitation corresponding with each stage (from the grasp of the needs of customer to the conclusion of the insurance contract). The main things are those how the solicitor understands the customer needs, together with leaving them to record. Further, insurance solicitor is regulated to provide the information necessary for the customer to determine the suitability of insurance.

(b)   from the fact that it has been an increase in the number of NORIAI agent (omnibus agent) solicitors are become to have responsibility to maintain mandatory system in accordance with the solicitation of insurance, in addition to the traditional regulation such as insurance company assumed oversight responsibility for the solicitation acts of the solicitor belonged to itself.

§2.   Prohibition Against Acts Relating to Execution of Insurance Contracts or Insurance Solicitation

597. The IBL prohibits insurance intermediaries from the following acts relating to the execution of insurance contracts or insurance solicitation (IBL Article 300(1)):

(1)   making false statements to a policyholder or an insured, or not informing such persons of important matters regarding the contractual terms of the insurance contract;
ecommending a policyholder or an insured to make false statements regarding important matters to the insurance company;

(2) preventing a policyholder or an insured from informing the insurance company of important facts, or recommending a policyholder or an insured not to inform such important facts;

(3) causing a policyholder or an insured, without disclosing disadvantageous facts, to terminate the current insurance contract and apply for new insurance contract, or to apply for a new insurance contract and terminate the existing insurance contract;

(4) making a commitment to a policyholder or an insured for a discount in or about rebates on an insurance premium or any other special benefits, or offering such benefits (except the case that such benefits have been authorized by FSA);

(5) giving or indicating to a policyholder, an insured or any unspecified persons comparative information on contents of insurance contract which may mislead him/her;

(6) giving a conclusive judgment, or giving or indicating information such as mislead those persons into believing that such information is reliable, to a policyholder, an insured or any unspecified persons with regard to uncertain matters;[141]

(7) any act causing a policyholder or an insured to apply for an insurance contract or terminate the existing insurance contract by threatening him/her or abusing the status in business, etc. (Enforcement Regulation Article 234, item 2);

(8) any act informing or indicating to a policyholder, an insured or any unspecified persons anything misleading on the matters concerning the insurance contract, etc., on which may materially affect his/her judgment (IBLER Article 234, item 4), and so on.

598. A person who falls within any of the items mentioned above (1)–(3), is liable to imprisonment with labour for a term not exceeding one year or to a fine not exceeding JPY 1 million, or to both (IBL Article 317–2(4)). There is no provision regarding to a person who falls within items of others; the FSA, however, may suspend such a person's registration or order him/her to improve his/her activities, or suspend all or some of his/her activities for a certain period (IBL Articles 306, 307). These intermediaries may be indicted under civil law.

599. A non-life insurance agent and an insurance broker shall not make it its primary business purpose to carry out insurance solicitation activities for insurance contracts in which its employer is the policyholder or the insured (called self-contracts) (IBL Article 295(1)).

For the purpose of applying the provision of the preceding paragraph, a non-life insurance agent or insurance broker shall be deemed to have made it its primary business purpose to carry out insurance solicitation activities for self-contracts, when the total amount of insurance premiums for the self-contracts solicited by the non-life insurance agent or insurance broker exceeds 50% of the total amount of insurance premiums for all contracts solicited by the non-life insurance agent or insurance broker (IBL Article 295(2)).

---

141. Uncertain matters may mean the claims payable, refunds, or any other benefits or premiums, that the amount is subject to fluctuation according to the performance results of asset management or any other cause.

§3. LIABILITY OF CONNECTING INSURANCE COMPANY AND SECURITY
MONEY OF INSURANCE BROKER

600. The connecting insurance company is liable for damages caused to policyholders by its life insurance solicitors or non-life insurance agents in connection with their insurance solicitation and this does not prevent the connecting insurance company from exercising its right to claim compensation against such persons (IBL Article 283).

This provision is considered to be one of particular rules of responsibility of employer (Civ. Code Article 715).

There are some privileged cases such as when the insurance company concerned has exercised reasonable care with respect to the election of such intermediaries and exerted due efforts to prevent the damage caused to policyholders in connection with insurance solicitation activities conducted by such insurance intermediaries (IBL Article 283); it is, however, deemed to be quite difficult to carry the company's point because of the current tendency to favour consumers.

601. The right of the policyholder to demand compensation for damage lapses by prescription if not exercised within three years from the time the policyholder became aware of the damage and the insurance company concerned; the same shall apply if twenty years have elapsed from the time when the unlawful act of such insurance intermediaries was committed (IBL Article 283, Civ. Code Article 724).

602. The insurance broker, independent from the insurance company, has to personally compensate damage caused to policyholders in connection with its insurance solicitation activities. Therefore, the insurance broker must deposit money as security with the deposit office (IBL Article 291) and the policyholder is entitled to have priority rights over any other creditors with respect to the security money (IBL Article 291(6)).

603. The amount of security money shall be JPY 40 million, at the date of commencement of broker business; however, after the date of expiration of three months following the end of the first fiscal year of the insurance broker, the amount of security money will be the amount equal to the total of commission, fees and any other consideration received by the insurance broker in connection with its brokerage service for execution of insurance contracts during the prior three years up to the date immediately preceding the date of commencement of such fiscal year (or JPY 40 million if such total amount does not reach JPY 40 million, or JPY 800 million if the total amount exceeds JPY 800 million).

Government bonds and other securities, prescribed by the Regulation, may substitute for the security money (the amount of such securities can be reduced by a certain proportion). If the insurance broker has entered into an 'insurance broker's liability insurance' contract, and has obtained the approval of the Prime Minister, therefore, the insurance broker is not required to deposit security money except for the first JPY 40 million.

§4. REMUNERATION

604. Insurance intermediaries may receive their remuneration at the time of concluding an insurance contract, extending the duration of the policy, renewing the insurance contract or collecting the surcharge.

Non-life insurance companies should have provided the maximum level of remuneration (the commission rate should be decided based on the agent's volume of premium, number of policies, level of expert knowledge and accuracy of service, etc.) to its agents in the 'statements of the methods of operation' which should be submitted to the Prime Minister to seek authorization for insurance business; therefore, the agent commission rates were substantially same rates among non-life insurance companies.

After April 2001, non-life insurance companies, through deregulation, may decide their agent commission rate at their own discretion with new additional elements such as loss ratio of insurance contracts handled by the agent, supporting capability for policyholders claiming after an event, use of a computer, a sense of belonging, etc.

As to the remuneration of life insurance solicitors, life insurance companies have at their own discretion decided the remuneration of solicitors, mainly counting numbers and sum insured of new business and business in force handled by each solicitor. It is because most life insurance solicitors are employees of the life insurance company concerned that there has been no serious competition in remuneration among life insurance companies.

§5. COLLECTION OF PREMIUMS

605. A non-life insurance agent has the right to represent the insurance company concerned and therefore he/she is entitled to make an insurance contract and to collect the premiums on behalf of the insurance company. A life insurance solicitor is also admitted to have the rights to represent insurance company concerned under the IBL; however, life insurance companies permit their solicitors to do solicitation only. Therefore, life insurance solicitors have no right to collect insurance premiums on behalf of the insurance company. Insurance brokers are not entitled to make insurance contracts and to collect the premium on behalf of the insurance company either.

606. As to the methods of collecting premiums, normally intermediaries collect premiums on behalf of the insurer or transfer money to the insurer and in these days, the insurer more and more directly collects premiums through credit transfer. Credit transfer has no effect on the level of remuneration of intermediaries; however, in the non-life insurance field such credit transfer fees are generally borne by the agent while the insurer generally bears them in the life insurance field.

Part VIII. Reinsurance, Co-insurance, Pooling

Chapter 1. Introduction

§1. REGULATION FOR REINSURANCE, CO-INSURANCE, POOLING

607. Reinsurance, co-insurance and pooling are common mechanisms among Japanese insurers as in other countries to spread risks to other insurers; the Insurance Law, however, has no provision for these systems.

The IBL provides some items for these systems from the viewpoint of the Law Relating to the Prohibition of Private Monopoly and the Methods of Preserving Fair Trade, because these systems, especially the co-insurance and pooling systems, inevitably involve concerted acts of insurers.

In the 'statements of the methods of operation' which should be submitted to Prime Minister to apply for authorization for each line of insurance, the insurer must describe provisions for 'reinsurance' according to the regulation of the IBL (Enforcement Regulation Article 8) but the insurer describe only whether the insurer has the intention of doing reinsurance business or not, and how much of the sum insured the insurer may retain.

608. The IBL stipulates 'concerted acts' performed between non-life insurance companies in its items from Article 101 to Article 105.

The following concerted acts for underwriting activities are excluded from the application of the Law Relating to the Prohibition of Private Monopoly and the Methods of Preserving Fair Trade if carried on with approval of Prime Minister and agreement of Fair Trade Commission (IBL Article 101(1), item 1):

(1) concerted acts with regard to the business of writing insurance on aircraft (including rockets), on cargoes carried by the aircraft, on third-party liability arising from aircraft accidents and/or on bodily injury sustained by passengers by air;
(2) concerted acts with regard to the business of writing insurance on nuclear installations and/or on third-party liability arising from accidents involving nuclear installations;
(3) concerted acts with regard to the business of writing compulsory automobile liability insurance (provided for in the ALSL) business;

(4) concerted acts with regard to the business of writing earthquake insurance (defined in the Earthquake Insurance Law).

609. As to insurances other than those specified above, concerted acts relating to contracts of reinsurance or contracts of insurance, between non-life insurance companies may be admitted with regard to (IBL Article 101(1), item 2):

(1) determination of insurance policy conditions (excluding those regarding premium rates) and of methods of settling claims;
(2) determination of the methods of parties to reinsurance and of the volume of the transaction of reinsurance;
(3) fixing of reinsurance premium rates and reinsurance commission.

Chapter 2.   Co-insurance

610. The Ins. Law prescribes, in its Article 20, the case that two or more insurers underwrite the same insurance object:

(1) Even in the case where damage that should be covered by a non-life insurance contract is to be covered by other non-life insurance contract, the insurer shall be liable to pay insurance benefits with respect to the entire of the amount of damage to be covered.
(2) In the event that the total amount of the insurance benefits to be paid by each insurer of two or more non-life insurance contracts exceeds the amount of damage to be covered (if the amounts of damage to be covered calculated pursuant to the respective non-life insurance contract vary, the highest one) and if one of the insurers has paid insurance benefits beyond its share (the amount obtained by multiplying the amount of damage to be covered by the proportion of the amount of insurance benefits to be paid by each insurer assuming that there is no other non-life insurance contract to the total insurance benefits) and has thereby procured a discharge for common benefit, such insurer shall be entitled to reimbursement only for the portion that exceeds its own share from other insurers in proportion to their respective shares.

611. In insurance practice, two methods may be presumed for insurers underwriting the same insurance object. The one is co-insurance, where two or more insurers underwrite the same policy and the other is double insurance, where two or more insurers underwrite the same insurance object in separate insurance policies, but the Ins. Law has no provisions to distinguish between co-insurance and double insurance.

Although double insurance and co-insurance are used in both direct insurance and reinsurance, the following paragraph only deals with co-insurance in direct insurances.

612. The co-insurance system is normally used for huge risks over the capacity of one insurer; however, in the Japanese insurance market, if enterprises become the applicant for insurance contracts (group life insurance, group pension insurance as to life insurance), enterprises have the tendency to appoint a leader insurance company and contract insurance with plural insurers.

Since co-insurance is a concerted act among insurers, an insurance company must specify in its statement of methods of operation that the insurance company may delegate its activities and affairs connected with insurance business to other insurance companies and must acquire the approval of the FSA and the Fair Trade Commission – for a non-life insurance company, subject matter delegated to the other company and the standard supplementary clause used for co-insurance must be stipulated in the statement of the methods of operation and for a life insurance company, subject matter delegated to other companies and the contents of the co-insurance agreement which may be contracted among the leader company, other companies and policyholder. The liability of each co-insurer is not joint but separate corresponding to each proportion or amount underwritten.

613. The leader insurance company appointed by the policyholder may perform or deal with the following activities and affairs on behalf of other co-insurers:

(1) receiving an insurance application form and issuing policy, etc.;
(2) receiving, storing and/or returning insurance premiums;
(3) approving of alternation or cancellation of insurance conditions;
(4) receiving or approving the information note submitted according to the insured's duty to disclose material facts and the insured's duty to give notice of alternation of risks during the policy period;
(5) receiving of claims notes, etc.;
(6) paying of claims.

614. Any notification or declaration of a policyholder's intention made to the leader insurance company is assumed to be made to all the co-insurance companies, and those of a leader insurance company's intention carried out to the policyholder are also assumed to be carried out by all the co-insurance companies.

Chapter 3.   Pooling System

615. Underwriting pools are used both in direct insurance and reinsurance. Ordinarily, underwriting pools are used, in the hard reinsurance market, for specific huge risks that cannot but be jointly underwritten by many insurers.

The original insurer (direct insurer) cedes, according to the manner provided by the pool, to the pool the insurance contract underwritten in full or with a balance deducted. The pool retrocedes, according to the rules predetermined, risks reinsured in full to members or retains a part of them for retrocession to members and cedes the excess part (a part after retention) to other non-members (including foreign insurers).

In the Japanese insurance market, there used to be many underwriting pools such as those of cargo, hull, machinery (including election insurance), aviation, earthquake (for dwelling risks), oil pollution, compulsory automobile insurance (CALI), nuclear energy (direct insurance pool), but today only the earthquake insurance pool, aviation insurance pool and nuclear energy insurance pool remain.[142]

616. All earthquake risks (for dwelling risks) written by domestic and foreign direct insurers in Japan are wholly reinsured with Japan Earthquake Reinsurance Co. Ltd. (JER). The JER portfolio retrocedes, after retention, to the direct insurers (including the Toa F&M Reinsurance Co. Ltd) and to the government (ELC bases).

617. Direct insurers cede risks to the aviation insurance pool after original retention to the pool. The pool retrocedes after retention (for retrocession to members) to non-member insurers (including foreign insurers).

618. The Japan Atomic Energy Insurance Pool (established by all Japanese non-life insurance companies and some foreign insurance companies doing business in Japan) underwrites directly risks and cedes risks to foreign insurers after original retention for recession to member insurers.[143]

---

142. CALI: see Part IV, Automobile Insurance.
143. Other insurance pools: other insurance pools had been abolished since insurers in Japan had increased their capacity enough to underwrite such risks, and in fear of influence or restriction to insurance premium rates of direct insurers which, as a result, might be against the Anti-monopoly Law.

Chapter 4.   Reinsurance

§1.   General

619. Reinsurance business ranks as a non-life insurance business (a kind of liability insurance) in Japan, so the IBL provides that reinsurance relating to insurances licensed for a life insurance company can be underwritten by the life insurance company although reinsurance ranks as non-life insurance (IBL Article 3(4), item 3).

Reinsurance and personal accident insurance, etc., (so-called third field insurances) may be underwritten by both life insurance companies and non-life insurance companies. The IBL, however, provides that no person shall be authorized for both life insurance and non-life insurance businesses (Article (3)), so that reinsurance businesses between life insurance companies and non-life insurance companies are prohibited, and only a reinsurance company can underwrite reinsurance businesses of both life insurance and non-life insurance.

620. A reinsurance agreement (equivalent to the general conditions of an insurance policy), as used among insurance companies, may be used without authorization of the Prime Minister while the general conditions of an insurance policy have to be authorized by the Prime Minister.

Reinsurance business, in Japan, also has many business customs such as 'utmost good faith', and 'existing custom', which differ from any provisions of laws or ordinances considered to have juristic effects between parties concerned if there is no expression of their intention not to conform to such customs and if such customs violate obligatory laws or ordinances (Civ. Code Article 92).

621. A reinsurance treaty, the document expressing intention between parties concerned, effectively restrains such parties in respect of each other's intention provided the contents of the treaty are not in violation of statute law and/or case laws, not contrary to public policy or good morals, not deviating from scope of activities of an insurance company provided by the IBL.

622. The IBL generally prohibits foreign insurers without a branch office in Japan from effecting insurance contracts with persons having an address or place of abode in Japan or on property situated there (including a vessel or aircraft of Japanese nationality); this does not, however, apply to reinsurance contracts (IBL Article 186, Cabinet Order Article 19).

Therefore, direct insurance companies, principally non-life insurance companies, do reinsurance business in the global market.

623. In the non-life insurance field, two domestic reinsurance companies and also three foreign reinsurance companies have been licensed in Japan (as of May 2010).

§2.   RELATION BETWEEN REINSURANCE COMPANY AND THE ORIGINAL
      INSURED

624. The direct insurance contract and the reinsurance contract are legally separate from one another and as a result, effects in one contract do not have an effect on another contract.

For instance, a direct insurer may not refuse the insured in a direct insurance contract (original insured) to pay claims payable because of non-payment of the reinsurer and the original insured may not claim directly to the reinsurer.

The original insured, however, is able to seize or subrogate the right of reinsurance claim if the direct insurer fails to pay claims payable (Civ. Code Article 423).

§3.   REINSURANCE AND UNDERWRITING RESERVES

625. With regard to any insurance contracts that may have been reinsured, an insurance company may refrain, in general, from crediting an amount to the underwriting reserves corresponding to the portion of reinsurance (IBL Article 116(3), IBLER Article 71). But, it is said that this article is under examination after the events of 11 September 2001 in New York.

Part IX. Taxation of Insurance

Chapter 1.   Insurance Company

626. National taxes and local taxes may be imposed on insurance companies. The insurance companies may also cover the consumption tax (national tax, 5% of income) laid on an insurance agent's commission.

In Japan, there is no so-called insurance premium tax system; corporate enterprise tax (and local taxes) imposed on insurance companies, however, is calculated on their volume of insurance premiums.

The tax authorities have a right to inspect insurance company's books to check the proper payment of taxes due at any time (cf. Part I The Insurance Company Chapter 7. Taxation of the Company).

277– 627

Chapter 2.   Taxation Allowance for Insurance Premiums

§1. INDIVIDUAL POLICYHOLDER

627. Insurance premiums, if the policyholder is an individual, may be deducted from taxable incomes up to certain volume to reduce income tax and inhabitant tax:

(1) Qualifying non-life insurance contract: Dwelling house earthquake insurance contract for building possessed by the policyholder and his/her spouse or relatives under the same livelihood, for household goods (except precious metals, precious stones, jewellery, etc., and works of art which are worth over JPY 300,000 per piece or pair). A taxation allowance for dwelling house earthquake insurance premiums is made for:

(a) national tax

Premiums Paid for One Year	Amount Deductible from Taxable Incomes
Under JPY 50,000	Amount of premiums paid
Over JPY 50,000	JPY 50,000

(b) local tax; up to JPY 25,000.

(2) Life insurance contracts:

(a) life insurance contracts (except pension insurance contracts) in which the beneficiary is the same as the policyholder, his/her spouse, children or relatives;
(b) individual pension insurance contracts, with tax-qualified individual pension insurance endorsement, provided:

(1) the beneficiary is either a person who has to pay premium or his/her spouse and moreover the same as the insured;
(2) the payment of premiums shall be periodically done through ten years more before the commencement of payment of annuity (single premium pension insurance contract is excluded from this taxation allowance system);
(3) the payment of annuity shall be paid periodically for more than ten years or for life after the day the beneficiary reaches to be 60 years old and moreover after such days as provided in the policy.

(d) nursing and medical expenses insurance contracts in which the beneficiary is the same as the policyholder, his/her spouse or relatives, provided, those

20

contracts shall secure medical expenses incidentally borne for bodily injury or disease.

Taxation allowance for life insurance premiums:

(1) life insurance contract – up to JPY 40,000 for national tax and JPY 28,000 for local tax;
(2) pension insurance contract and nursing & medical expense insurance contract – same as above (each).
(3) for combination of life insurance contract, pension insurance contract and nursing & medical expense insurance contract – up to JPY 120,000 for all (national tax) & up to JPY 70,000 (local tax).

§2. Corporate Policyholder

628. If the policyholder is a corporation, the total amount of insurance premiums which are paid on behalf of the corporation itself may generally be reduced by such taxable incomes as form the base of calculation of national tax and local tax.

Selected Bibliography

§1. The Following Are the Leading Books on Japanese Insurance Law. They Are All Written in Japanese

Egashira, K. *Commercial Transaction Law* (6th ed., Kobundo 2010).
Ishii, T. &Ohtori, T. *Maritime Commercial Law and Insurance Law* (Keisoshobo 1976).
Ishida, M. *Insurance Law* (rev. ed., Seirinshoin 1997).
Ishida, M. *Insurance Business Law* (rev. ed., The Non-life Insurance Institute of Japan 2007).
Kato, H. *Introduction to Social Insurance Law* (Tokyo 2000).
Nishijima, U. *Insurance Law* (3d ed., Yuyusha 1998).
Omori, T. *Insurance Law* (rev. ed., Yuhikaku 1986).
Sakaguchi, M. *Insurance Law* (Bunshindo 1991).
Suzuki, T. *Commercial Law: Insurance Law, Maritime Law* (2d ed., Kobundo 1993).
Yamashita, T. *Insurance Law* (Yuhikaku 2005).

§2. The Following Are the Books on Japanese Laws and Japanese Insurance Contracts Written in English

The Non-life Insurance Institute of Japan, *The Insurance Business Law of Japan* (1999).
The Hoken Mainichi Shinbunsha, *The Insurance Business Law and Related Governmental and Ministerial Ordinances* (Anderson-Mori trans., 1997).
The Commercial Code of Japan (EHS Law Bulletin Series 2003).
The Civil Code of Japan (EHS Law Bulletin Series 2003).
The Law for Special Exception to the Commercial Code concerning Audit, etc. of Kabushiki-Kaisha (EHS Law Bulletin Series 2003).
The Law Relating to Prohibition of Private Monopoly and Methods of Preserving Fair Trade (EHS Law Bulletin Series 1992).
The Employment Insurance Law (EHS Law Bulletin Series 2002).
The Non-life Insurance Institute of Japan, *Marine and Inland Transit Insurance in Japan* (4th ed., 1991).
The Non-life Insurance Institute of Japan, *Miscellaneous Casualty Insurance in Japan* (4th ed., 1993).
The Non-life Insurance Institute of Japan, *Fire Insurance Business in Japan* (1997).
The Non-life Insurance Institute of Japan, *Miscellaneous Casualty Insurance Business in Japan: Commercial Lines*, Tokyo: 2000.

Selected Bibliography

Index

Index